PIONEERS IN EDUCATION:
ESSAYS IN HONOR OF PAULO FREIRE

MICHAEL F. SHAUGHNESSY,
ELIZABETH GALLIGAN
AND
ROMELIA HURTADO DE VIVAS
EDITORS

Nova Science Publishers, Inc.
New York

LIBRARY OF CONGRESS CATALOGING-IN-PUBLICATION DATA

Pioneers in education : essays in honor of Paulo Freire / Michael F. Shaughnessy, Elizabeth Galligan and Romelia Hurtado de Vivas (editors).
  p. cm.
ISBN-13: 978-1-60021-479-0 (hardcover)
ISBN-10: 1-60021-479-7 (hardcover)
1. Freire, Paulo, 1921-1997. 2. Popular education. I. Freire, Paulo, 1921-1997. II. Shaughnessy, Michael F. III. Galligan, Elizabeth. IV. Hurtado de Vivas, Romelia.
LB1025.2.P52 2008
370.11'5--dc22
        2007040806

Published by Nova Science Publishers, Inc. ✦ New York

Books are to be returned on or before
the last date below.

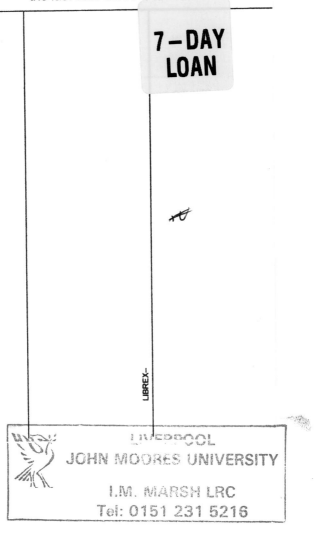

**7 – DAY
LOAN**

LIBREX–

PIONEERS IN EDUCATION: ESSAYS IN HONOR OF PAULO FREIRE

CONTENTS

In: Pioneers in Education: Essays in Honor of Paulo Freire   ISBN: 978-1-60021-479-0
Editors: M.Shaughnessy, E.Galligan et al., pp 1-5   ©2008 Nova Science Publishers, Inc.

INTRODUCTION

Michael W. Apple

INTRODUCTION TO ESSAYS IN HONOR OF PAULO FREIRE

I am writing this brief introduction just after I have returned from some lectures and political work in Brazil. Part of the time I was there was spent at PUC-SP (the Pontifical University of Sao Paulo)—Paulo Freire's "home" for so many years. I mention this at the outset because if there were ever any doubts about the continuing power of Freire's vision and influence, being in Sao Paulo, and especially at PUC-SP, make such doubts less than fully accurate to say the least.

I met with students and faculty members from all over Brazil. Not only was the geographical range impressive, but the areas in education and other fields that were the sites of their struggles were equally impressive. They dealt with many things: the development of critical educational policy and practice in social movements among the oppressed in communities of color; literacy programs in favelas and in rural areas; curricular and pedagogical interruptions in such things as language education, history, mathematics, and "special education;" the specificities of gender inside and outside of schools, and many others.

A number of them took the Freirian tradition into "risky" places as well. For example, in a nation where the military dictatorship had murderous power for many years, graduate students/activists were intervening in ways that were strongly influenced by Freire into the long established manner in which military police were educated. Altering the authoritarian traditions that provided so much of the identity of military police became the goal. Critical democracy and critical citizenship, being at one with and defending the people, became the norms which guided the pedagogical process. What is happening at PUC-SP is but one instance. The formation of the "Citizen School" and participatory budgeting in Porto Alegre (Apple, et al. 2003; Apple and Buras, 2006), the Escola Cabana reforms in Belem, and the critical political and educational efforts of the landless movement, all signify the creative and successful uses of Freirian-inspired work in Brazil (see also Boal, 1985).

I could mention may other examples well beyond the borders of Brazil. But my basic point is that, even though there have been and are criticisms of some aspects of the Freirian traditions^i both in Brazil and elsewhere, his work continues to inspire generations of committed educators who wish to not only "speak truth to power" but also to actively intervene in the processes that create such differential power in the first place. Thus, the essays in this book and the experiences they detail could have been multiplied many times over.

The Tasks of the Critical Educator

Why are the critical traditions so important now, not only in Freire's Brazil but in many other nations and in what we might say is "the belly of the beast," the United States? As many of us are all too familiar with in the US, this is a time of unrelenting attacks on hard won gains, on social solidarity, and on anything that is public. Anything that is critical in cultural and educational work is seen as dangerous to the production of the possessive individualism that stands at the heart of both "our" economy and increasingly our daily lives. This shouldn't surprise us. As I have detailed elsewhere, there has been a good deal of creative ideological and pedagogic work done by the Right to change our common-sense (Apple, 2006).

By its very nature the entire schooling process--how it is paid for, what goals it seeks to attain and how these goals will be measured, who has power over it, what textbooks are approved, how pedagogy will go on, who has the right to ask and answer these questions, and so on--is political. The educational system will constantly be in the middle of crucial struggles over the meaning of democracy, over definitions of legitimate authority and culture, and over who should benefit the most from government policies and practices.

That this is not of simply academic interest is made more than a little visible in the current attempts in many nations to radically transform education policy and practice. These proposals involve conscious attempts to: institute neo-liberal "reforms" in education (such as attempts at marketization through voucher and privatization plans); neo-conservative reforms (such as national or state-wide curriculum and national or state-wide testing, a "return" to a "common culture," and the English only movement in the United States), all of which have been shown to be extremely damaging (Valenzuela, 2005); and policies based on "new managerialism" with its focus on strict accountability and constant assessment. When the efforts of authoritarian populist religious conservatives to install *their* particular vision of religiosity into state institutions are also added to this mix, this places education at the very core of an entire range of political and cultural conflicts. Symbolic violence and economic violence are here linked in powerful ways in what I have elsewhere called "conservative modernization" (Apple, 2006).

Subaltern groups have been neither passive nor silent in the face of these attacks in education and the rest of society of course (Apple and Buras, 2006). But we are facing an uphill situation and wishful thinking will not make all this go away.

---

^{i} The plural is crucial here. Within the critical education communities, there have been various ways in which the work of Freire has been taken up, transformed, and mobilized. Some of the criticisms that have arisen in response to Freire's writings and the assumptions that underlie his work have been respectful, genuine, and provide cautionary insights, although at time they may have been overstated. However, some of the criticisms of "the" Freirian traditions are more than a little essentializing, as if these traditions were static and reified. This is a mistake made all too often and, as well, treats Freire himself in such a way that assumes that he never changed. For some of this debate, see Au and Apple (in press).

One of the responses to this situation historically within critical educational communities has been to mobilize Gramsci's famous dictum of "Pessimism of the intellect, optimism of the will." It is a powerful rhetorical device, one that can be used to give strength in difficult times. But too often it has remained on simply a rhetorical level. Paulo Freire went beyond rhetoric. Among the most powerful resources that Freire gave us were both hope and a clear sense of what could in fact be done. This dual sense lies at the heart of the chapters in this book.

As we reflect on the continuing legacy of Paulo Freire, on the resources that he gave us, and on his effects on the lives of the authors in this volume and so many others throughout the world, it may be helpful to think about what the role of critical educators is in societies riven by massive inequalities. In my mind, in general, there are five tasks in which critically engaged scholarship/activism in education must engage.

1. It must "bear witness to negativity." That is, one of its primary functions is to illuminate the ways in which educational policy and practice are connected to the relations of exploitation and domination in the larger society.
2. In engaging in such critical analyses, it also must point to contradictions and to spaces of possible action. Thus, its aim is to critically examine current realities with a conceptual/political framework that emphasizes the spaces in which counter-hegemonic actions can be or are now going on.
3. At times, this also requires a redefinition of what counts as "research." Here I mean acting as "secretaries" to those groups of people and social movements who are now engaged in challenging existing relations of unequal power or in what elsewhere I have called "non-reformist reforms" (Apple, 1995).
4. In the process, critical work has the task of keeping traditions of radical work alive. In the face of organized attacks on the "collective memories" of difference and struggle, attacks that make it increasingly difficult to retain academic and social legitimacy for multiple critical approaches that have proven so valuable in countering dominant narratives and relations, it is absolutely crucial that these traditions be kept alive, renewed, and when necessary criticized for their conceptual, empirical, historical, and political silences or limitations. This includes not only keeping theoretical, empirical, historical, political, and practical traditions alive—and very importantly as I just noted, extending and (supportively) criticizing them. But it also involves keeping alive the dreams, utopian visions, and "non-reformist reforms" that are so much a part of them (see, e.g., Jacoby, 2005; Teitelbaum, 1993).
5. Such work must also assist in the building of counter-hegemonic communities, supporting social movements and mobilizations, engaging with them and learning from them so that we all can go forward. Thus, all of the work of critical education is *dependent on* having real connections—not simply rhetorical ones—to these social movements and mobilizations. And it is dependent on our willingness to take risks and to not be defensive when those with whom we are working are critical of our efforts.

I am certain that those of you who are reading this book could add more to this list. But I note them here because not only do they establish some of the challenges that we face, but they also help us see what it is that Paulo Freire accomplished. While I am not a "Freiriano" and have deep grounding in the indigenous tradition of radical education in the United States (see Teitelbaum, 1993; Apple, 2000), I know of very few critical educators in the history of these long and vital struggles who embodied these challenges—who lived them every day—as well as Freire. I gained this respect from spending time with him in "academic" and political settings and from being with him when he was Secretary of Education in Sao Paulo. In Brazil and in the United States, I publicly engaged with him on issues of crucial importance, on some of which we had disagreements (Apple, 1999). But I also learned an immense amount from him not only about how to think the political and the educational together. In our public appearances together and in our many private conversations, I also learned how to model, to live out, the norms surrounding critical dialogue. His actions sometimes went further than his theory. But he was always fully present and continued to learn—and to teach.

As someone who is proud to say that he was a friend and comrade, it seems to me that the best way to show our respect for him is to continue the struggles to which he was committed, to extend them to new terrains, to learn from him the ability to take criticism well, and to be radical and humble at the same time. This won't be easy.

But in a world in which identifiable groups of people are facing economic, political, and cultural forces of destruction and immiseration (see. e.g., Davis, 2006) and where critical educational work has never been more important, committing ourselves to an ongoing politics of active interruption of dominance and exploitation is itself evidence of our personal answer to that age-old question: "Whose side are you on?"

We are not starting anew here. As the chapters included here demonstrate, critical traditions are alive and well. When connected to the ongoing labors of critical educators in schools and communities throughout the United States (see, e.g., Apple and Beane, 2007) and elsewhere, Gramsci's reminder of optimism of the will may turn out to be less rhetorical than the Right assumes. And Friere's legacy will give new life and hope to future generations of committed activist educators.

REFERENCES

Apple, Michael W. (1995) *Education and Power*, 2nd edition. New York: Routledge.

Apple, Michael W. (1999) *Power, Meaning, and Identity*. New York: Peter Lang.

Apple, Michael W. (2000) *Official Knowledge: Democratic Education in a Conservative Age*, 2nd edition. New York: Routledge.

Apple, Michael W., et al. (2003) *The State and the Politics of Knowledge*. New York: Routledge.

Apple, Michael W. (2006) *Educating the "Right" Way: Markets, Standards, God, and Inequality*, 2nd edition. New York: Routledge.

Apple, Michael W. and Buras, Kristen L. (Eds.) (2006) *The Subaltern Speak: Curriculum, Power, and Educational Struggles*. New York: Routledge.

Apple, Michael W. and Beane, James A. (Eds.) (2007) *Democratic Schools*, 2nd edition. Portsmouth, NH: Heinemann.

Au, Wayne and Apple, Michael W. (in press) "Freire, Critical Education, and the Environmental Crisis," *Educational Policy*.

Boal, Augusto (1985) *Theater of the Oppressed*. New York: Theater Communications Group.

Davis, Mike (2006) *Planet of Slums*. New York: Verso.

Jacoby, Russell (2005) *Picture Imperfect: Utopian Thought for an Anti-Utopian Age*. New York: Columbia University Press.

Teitelbaum, Kenneth (1993) *Schooling for Good Rebels: Socialist Education for Children in the United States, 1900-1920*. New York: Teachers College Press.

Valenzuela, Angela (Ed.) (2005) *Leaving Children Behind: How "Texas Style" Accountability Fails Latino Youth*. Albany: State University of New York Press.

In: Pioneers in Education: Essays in Honor of Paulo Freire   ISBN: 978-1-60021-479-0
Editors: M.Shaughnessy, E.Galligan et al., pp 7-23   ©2008 Nova Science Publishers, Inc.

Chapter 1

THE ROLE OF FREIRE'S "BANKING" ANALOGY IN THE EDUCATIONAL IMAGINARY

Megan Laverty

The concern of this paper is to analyze the operation of the "banking" analogy in Freire's writings and recent educational debates. It begins with an explanation of the analogy proceeded by an examination of how it both advances Freire's argument but also works against it. As a significantly influential image, the "banking" analogy provides a clue, I argue, to the distinctiveness of the educational imaginary. Turning Freirian scholarship upon itself, I consider whether the popular appeal of problem-posing education—concealed in its rhetoric of social justice and human liberation—is imaginary. I use the term "imaginary" to refer to the character of this appeal and not its unreality. Problem-posing education appeals to contemporary imagination, by way of its juxtaposition with the "banking" analogy, because it exploits the imagination's current captivation with economic experience and thinking—gratifying a capitalistic fantasy. In the contemporary imaginary possession of money and wealth is associated with the having of freedom and agency so that banking/traditional education is rejected as an exercise in wish fulfillment: Freire's redistribution of intellectual "capital" is desirable as a promise of agency and, the potential enlargement of that agency by way of entrepreneurial/dialogical activity.

My suggestion is that new and compelling images for dialogical education and authentic authority are needed if its pedagogical practice is going to be more than an unregulated "market place" of individuals and ideas. As an initial step in this direction, I suggest that our conception of *authentic authority*—how to recognize it and judiciously use it—can be enriched by elements of traditional education that have been eclipsed by the "banking" analogy. These include: the relational and temporal elements of traditional education each having ethical, aesthetic and intellectual dimensions; the attendance in traditional education to a deep striving for perfection and the profound satisfaction associated with perfecting an activity, craft or discipline; and finally, the significance of our admiration for other individuals and their role in our lives. My aim in drawing attention to these elements is not to advocate for traditional education or criticize Freire's advocacy of problem-posing education. It is to make the more minor point that the "banking" analogy's contributes to the popular and enduring success of Freire's educational philosophy *as it* constitutes that philosophy's very limitations.

Other commentators, in the spirit of respectful criticism and inquiry, also identify tensions in Freire's educational philosophy resulting from his failure to give up the terms that he criticizes. Specifically, they focus on the conflict between the ontological and epistemological foundations of Freire's thought with his historicist, pedagogical and political commitments. Clarence W. Joldersma argues that Freire's constructivist epistemology is in conflict with his ethical project of justice. He makes the case that whereas Freire retained the epistemological model of "the oppressors" and extended it to all human beings, what he really needed to do, was create an epistemological model of non-domination.[1] Frank Margonis and Ronald David Glass argue that the Freire's commitment to a humanist ontology and vocation is as oppressively prescriptive as the tradition which he seeks to overcome.[2] Glass writes "But Freire's assertion of an ontological privilege for humanization as the only possibility for an authentic existence reduces to just the sort of *a priori* historical claim he recognizes as fundamentalist, conservative and contradictory to the position he seeks."[3] Peter L. Berger, Frank Margonis and Kathleen Weiler all argue that Freire's approach to "consciousness raising" risks reifying the very divisions that it is attempting to overcome, as is evidenced in some of Freire's representations of "peasants" and "students". Margonis writes that "Freire's description of the oppressed privileges his vision of what people should be, not a sympathetic characterization of students' beliefs and practices."[4]

None of the commentators have addressed the imaginary tensions in Freire's work created by his use of the "banking" analogy. An analysis of the "banking" analogy challenges ready acceptance of it and its inherent, simultaneous, overestimation and underestimation of traditional education. The "banking" analogy overestimates both the power of the teacher, by way of dichotomized teacher-student relationship, and the power of knowledge discourses to be universalizing and unproblematic. The "banking" analogy underestimates the intrinsic value of traditional education; its deep emotional resonance and the profound satisfaction of perfecting a craft, discipline or oneself. My argument is that the "cost" of simultaneously overestimating and underestimating traditional education—as camouflaged by the "banking" analogy—is to our conception and practice of dialogical pedagogy and the of authentic authority therein.

[1] Joldersma, Clarence W., "The tension between justice and freedom in Paulo Freire's epistemology," Journal of Educational Thought (2001) Vol. 35, No. 2 :129-148.

[2] Glass, Ronald David, "On Paulo Freire's philosophy of praxis and the foundations of liberation education," Educational Researcher (2001) Vol. 30.No. 2: 15-25; Frank Margonis "Relational pedagogy without foundations: reconstructing the work of Paulo Freire," Philosophy of Education Society Yearbook 1999, Randall Curren (editor): 99-107.

[3] Glass, Ronald David: 20.

[4] Margonis, Frank: page number required.

FREIRE, BANKING AND THE EDUCATIONAL IMAGINARY

Freire has had an undeniable and impressive impact on educational reform in both developed and developing countries.[5] He is probably the most widely known educational theorist we have today. Speaking from within the academy, he has been enormously influential on teacher education. The number of professors, from fields as diverse as nursing, music education, and early childhood, who incorporate Freire's educational philosophy into both their writing and teaching, is overwhelming. This enthusiasm for Freire's writing is due, in part, to both the readiness with which his critique of traditional education is grasped and the suggestiveness of his dialogical, problem-posing alternative. The accessibility of Freire's critique of traditional education derives from the persuasiveness of his 'banking' analogy.

First introduced in the *Pedagogy of the Oppressed*, Freire's "banking" analogy has remained fairly constant throughout its various iterations. Traditional education and banking are identified as both involving the act of depositing: the teacher or "bank-clerk educator" actively deposits quantifiable measure of her intellectual capital into students' passively empty minds.[6] In the language of Stanley Aroniwitz, "the students are 'objects' into which teachers pour prescribed knowledge."[7]

The following description by Charles Bingham captures a typical reaction to the "banking" analogy upon learning about it for the first time. He writes:

> Freire's analysis is convincing, and it forces a pressing question: How can educators combat this banking authority? I would like to begin answering this question by referring to a familiar refrain, one that I hear almost every time I expose my students to this text by Freire. This refrain might seem familiar to those who remember reading Freire for the first time, or to those who use *Pedagogy of the Oppressed* in the classroom. The refrain is "Stop banking." Indeed, this is one way to read Freire, namely, that his text is primarily a warning against the banking system. Along with this refrain, I usually get the message that what Freire wants teachers to do is give up authority in the classroom. In order to give up the banking system, and to empower students accordingly, authority must be yielded.

As this quotation indicates, the "banking" analogy is found to be so immediately persuasive that it is readily embraced and popularized.

So persuasive is the "banking" analogy that its status as *an analogy* comes to be overlooked. Instead it is "interpreted more literally both by adherents and by critics," having become a euphemism for the transmission model of education (exemplified in lecturing and testing for the recall of information).[8]

Banking education is now popular shorthand for traditional education and a rallying symbol for proponents of problem-posing education. Literalist interpretations of the

---

[5] Weiler, Kathleen, "Myths of Paulo Freire," Educational Theory (1996), Vol. 46, No. 3; 353.

[6] Freire, Paulo, Pedagogy of the oppressed (London and New York: Continuum, 2000), 72. Referred to from now on as PO.

[7] Freire, Paulo, Pedagogy of Freedom: ethics, democracy and civic courage (New York: Rowman & Littlefield Publishers, Inc., 1998), 4.

[8] Scheffler, Israel, The Language of Education (Springfield, Illinois: Charles C. Thomas, 1960), 36.

"banking" analogy have contributed to a methodological construal of its difference from problem-posing education as seen in the following quotation from Pamela Jean Owens: "In the conventional banking method of teaching world religions, for example, classes consist primarily of lectures and, perhaps, videos or other forms of teacher-directed presentations."[9] Critical theorists such as Peter McLaren and Peter Roberts lament that although the persuasive force of the "banking" analogy contributes to Freire's influence it also obfuscates the sophistication of his arguments.

The influence of the "banking" analogy extends beyond its persuasive force to the level of enframement. It has been effective in structuring recent educational debates around the politics of teaching and learning. Today's focus is on the way in which different pedagogies either reinforce and perpetuate wider social, political and economic inequalities or serve to disrupt and overturn them. Mary Leach writes, that "the academy and the classroom are coming to be viewed even by the popular press as "contested terrains"—that is, as political and cultural sites that represent struggle over what constitutes "proper" knowledge by differently empowered social constituencies."[10] What is at issue is the role of education in transforming our shared, and different, social realities so as to make them more just, inclusive and equitable. Educators are thinking about ways to make pedagogical practices consistent with moral and political ideals. The language of education is political and economic as it is dominated by concepts of "social justice," "praxis," "conscientisation," and "liberation."

As one of, if not the most, influential images in education today, the "banking" analogy provides us with clues to the contemporary character of the educational imaginary. The educational imaginary refers to the collection of images that enable us to picture what educational concepts like "teaching", "studying" and "learning" are thought to mean. It grounds and frames our educational thinking as, in turn, the ellipses and lapses in educational thought, govern it. As with other scholars of the imaginary, I am using "image" in a broad sense to include similes, metaphors, analogies, thought experiments and stories. My interest here is not with the ways in which the different types of images distinguish themselves from another, but rather with what they all share, in virtue being *images*, particularly in their relationship to thought. Images, irrespective of what type, are taken from experience and, for that reason, reveal something about our embodied subjectivity precisely at the point of engaging it. Because the tendency of human thinking is to articulate normative commitments descriptively, it uses images as expressions of thought and evidence of the thought being true. For example, rather than claiming that "human beings should be reasonable" we claim that "human beings are naturally reasonable" and then find instances of human reasonableness as illustrating what it means to be reasonable and providing unspoken evidence for the verity of the claim.

It is in an effort to understand the operation of the "banking" analogy that I turn to works from recent philosophers of education, most notably, Thomas Green, Andrew Ortony and Israel Scheffler. I acknowledge that although these writers reveal a profound appreciation for the pedagogical value of images—what Michelle Le Doeuff refers to as sending the images

[9] Owen, Pamela, Jean, "Experience the other as the self" cultural diversity as liberating praxis", Teaching Theology and Religion (2005) Vol. 8, No. 4, 245.
[10] Leach, Mary, "Can we talk?," Harvard Educational Review (1992) 62: 257.

downstream—they do not present an analysis of the role of images in philosophical argument.[11]

Such an analysis is important in the case of the "banking" analogy because it is part of Freire's larger argument; to understand it is to understand the argument and the role of the analogy within it. What does the analogy conceal in the interests of the argument? And how does the analogy work against the argument? I turn to the writings of Michelle Le Doeuff and Marguerite La Caze for a strategy of how to read images in the context of philosophical texts.

THE EDUCATION IMAGINARY

A common convention in philosophy is to trivialize images as "mere" illustrations or as parts of the text that are to be passed over as entertainment. Because images are reflective of a philosopher's embodiment and, therefore, contingency, they are associated with the irrational—what Le Doeuff refers to as sending the images upstream. Philosophers of education typically have more respect for images in virtue of their ability to enlighten individuals in ways that explanations do not. It is well known in education that metaphors and analogies can capture the imaginations of students, engaging and animating their thinking. In the language of Andrew Ortony, they provide "a powerful means of moving from the known to the less well-known or unknown, and this, of course, is an important pedagogic function."[12]

Imagery, in all its forms, allows students to draw reasonable conclusions about the less familiar on the basis of relevant similarities with what is more familiar.

Images are continually used in teaching, either consciously or unconsciously and, philosophers of education analyze how images function in the interests of maximizing their "educational utility."[13] They focus on the ways in which images express ideas succinctly and vividly—ideas that might otherwise be characterized circuitously or not at all—and generate a deeply personal understanding of the subject matter by way of their affective resonance. Images organize reflection implicitly rather than explicitly, so as to invite the student to search for similarities (and differences) between the two contexts. It is in this sense that Freire's use of the "banking" analogy in *Pedagogy of the Oppressed* can be seen as enacting the liberatory practices that he is arguing for.

Images are important for teaching, but they are also an important means by which to reflect on teaching. The practice of teaching is so multi-faceted that it is extremely difficult to describe and the descriptions that we do have do not always provide us with an understanding of the teaching practice. It is for these reasons, that images for what it is to teach are central to and, critical for, discussions of education. They have an esteemed tradition within the educational literature. Some familiar comparisons include: teacher as artist, teacher as gardener, teacher as stranger, and teacher as social engineer. In all cases, the purpose of the comparison is to emphasize a particular dimension of teaching or, alternatively, to construe the overall practice of teaching in its light. It allows us to consider what about teaching comes

---

[11] La Caze, Marguerite, The Analytic Imaginary (Ithaca and London: Cornell University Press, 2002), 24-25.

[12] Ortony, Anthony, "Why metaphors are necessary and not just nice", Educational Theory, Vol. 25, No. 1 (Winter 1975), 51.

[13] Ortony, 51.

to be illuminated or highlighted, when viewed through a particular lens. For example, to talk about the teacher as artist is to see teaching in terms of its creative dimension; teachers need for independence and freedom so that they can make judgments of appropriateness;[14] and their vision and commitment to working with available "materials".

These analogies serve to unify the teaching experience. Their effect is to cover over and suppress the educational implications of disciplinary differences, age differences, cultural differences, socio-political differences, racial differences and geographical differences for example. In addressing all teachers, they distract attention from the significance of our differences as teachers of different disciplines and different student demographic. Although it may be a limitation of educational discourse that we use these images to talk about teaching, its corresponding strength is that it allows for the full expression of an educational vision. There is a normative quality to these images, for although they - artist, stranger, gardener or social engineer - aptly describe teaching, in a very broad sense, they are programmatically divergent. In other words, they reflect alternative conceptions of the teacher's task that animate the manner in which the teaching is conducted. The point here is that how an individual approaches, and intervenes in, the practice of teaching is dependent on his/her conception of it - whether as an "artist" or "gardener" for example. It follows then, that exemplary teaching (the way in which we solve problems within it) is fostered by a prescription for how best to think about it. Similarities between the two contexts - teaching and art or teaching and gardening - are highlighted to inspire teachers' thinking, in the interests of best teaching practice.

Within this context, Freire's use of the "banking" analogy is distinct for he uses it to diagnose/criticize traditional teaching practice and justify his alternative to it. The "banking" analogy is a constitutive part of a much larger argument; it is inextricable from the thought itself. Understanding the "'banking" analogy and its influence requires attending to the argument of the text and any difficulties for that argument concealed by the image. For an analysis of how images operate in philosophical arguments specifically, I turn to the work of Michele Le Doeuf and Marguerite La Caze.

Le Doeuff's assumes in her reading of philosophical texts that although concepts and images are distinct, "there is a continual feedback or dialectic" between them.[15] Hence, she reads philosophical texts for the manner in which "meaning conveyed by images works for, and against, the system that deploys them." Images work for the text because they "decree 'that's the way it is' without fear of counter-argument, since it is understood that a good reader will by-pass such 'illustrations'—a convention which enables the image to do its work all the more effectively." They work to distract critical attention away from the argument, excluding certain views and eliciting reader agreement by hiding assumptions that may be problematic. It follows, therefore, that the subsequent *analysis* of these images can work against the text because they are "the site where problematic assumptions can be discovered and explored."[16] Images also work against the text because their possibilities for meaning exceed those constrained by the text, hence they can convey different and even opposing ideas. They play, in the language of La Caze, "a more varied and contestable role than is avowed by the philosopher."

---

[14] Simpson, et all, vii.

[15] Le Caze, page 22.

[16] Le Caze 41.

Within a philosophical work, images simultaneously resolve and create different points of tension. I now turn to La Caze's operationalization of Le Doeuff's reading strategy. Le Caze explains that there are four stages in relating the image to the thought of the work, not all of which are always possible.[17] First, note how the image is derived: what causes it to appear in the argument? Second, identify its appearances. Third, trace the source of the image: who and how was it used in previous philosophical writings? And fourth, engage in a structural analysis. Stages One and Two identify the intended function of the image. Stages Two and Three identify transgressions of that intended function.

Le Caze assumes that images are constitutive of thought, identifying at least three levels of their operation. The first level, called 'expressibility', refers to the necessity of the image for expressing the particular thought. The second level, called 'enframement' refers to the image's role in providing a framework that gives substance to the thought being expressed. And the third level, called 'persuasiveness' refers to the image's ability to make the thought convincing. In the next section of the paper, I engage in Stage's One and Two of the methodology outlined above and demonstrate how Freire's 'banking' analogy operates on all three levels of expressibility, enframement and persuasion.

FREIRE'S BANKING ANALOGY

In *Pedagogy of the Oppressed*, Freire presents an argument by analogy. He bases his analogy on a similarity between the activities of teaching and banking for in both cases something, whether it is money, as in the case of banking, or information, as in the case of education, is transmitted from the person who has it, to the person who does not have it. Both banking and teaching involve non-reciprocal transmission as described by Freire in the following quotation:

> Education thus becomes an act of depositing, in which the students are the depositories and the teacher is the depositor. Instead of communicating, the teacher issues communiqués and makes deposits which the students patiently receive, memorize, and repeat. This is the "banking" concept of education, in which the scope of action allowed to the students extends only as far as receiving, filing, and storing the deposits (Freire, p. 72).

As this quotation indicates, Freire is describing the activity of teaching as being a lot like the activity of banking: there is a depositor and *intended* depositories; there is the act of depositing or issuing communiqués; and students, the depositories, who *receive, file and store* these communiqués. This quotation also reveals that Freire is inferring other, somewhat more attenuated, similarities on the basis of the "banking" analogy.

In banking, we directly infer an individual's intention *to deposit* from the activity of *depositing* itself. It is unreasonable to consider that the depositor might have an objective other than that of depositing money. The comparison of teaching with banking implies that the teacher's intention is also to deposit information in the student. She is the "bank-clerk educator" (Freire, p.72). Hence Freire elaborates the banking analogy by characterizing the

---

[17] Le Caze, page 26.

"stages in the action of the educator" (Freire, p. 80) as expressing his overall intention. In the first stage of action, the teacher "cognizes a cognizable object while preparing his/her lessons in their study; during the second, he or she expounds to his/her student about that object" (Freire, p.80). The analogy effectively conflates the activity of teaching with its intention, implying that the objective of traditional education is to deposit already cognizable pieces of information in the students' minds.

The teacher's intention to "deposit" information into the minds of his or her students is reflected in his/her self-conception. The teacher conceives of themselves as engaged in gift-giving: he or she is giving a gift that will promote the well-being of those who receive it (Freire, p.155). This gift is knowledge, or alternatively, a totalized view of the world. The teacher's task is to "fill the student by making deposits of information which he or she considers constitute true knowledge" (Freire, p.75). This gift is made possible by the teacher's disciplinary expertise and precludes student perspectives.

Even though students are in the world, spontaneously and reflectively engaging with it, they are without the disciplinary and pedagogical expertise of the teacher and so are in need of what he or she has to offer.

Freire writes that knowledge is a gift bestowed by "those who consider themselves knowledgeable upon those whom they consider to know nothing" (Freire, p. 72). Two things follow. First, because students are not recognized as having knowledge, the effect of banking education is to regulate and control the way in which the world "enters into" their consciousness. Second, teachers are not encouraged to perceive the contradictions in their totalized viewpoint (Freire, p. 75).

Implicit in the institution of banking is the presumption that banks are there to receive the monetary deposits from their patrons. The money remains the property of the patrons and, other than recording the transaction and "storing" the money, the bank remains disengaged and passive; the subjectivity of the "bank" is neither acknowledged nor elicited. The comparison of banking with traditional education implies that students, as the intended recipients of these deposits, have no choice but to passively receive them. "The students are not called upon to know, but to memorize the contents narrated by the teacher" (Freire, p.80). Students are not free to be self-determining with respect to their education, because the possibilities for engagement are predetermined by educational convention and, the intentions of those more powerful to uphold convention: the information remains the "property of the teacher" (Freire, p.80).

Freire concludes, on the basis of the similarities between banking and traditional education, that the effect of traditional education is to objectify students. He writes that "the anti-dialogical, dominating *I* transforms the dominated, conquered *thou* into a mere *it*" (PO, p.167) Traditional education turns students "into "containers," into "receptacles" to be "filled" by the teacher" (Freire, p.72). The teacher is the "Subject of the learning process" not the students (Freire, p.73). The teacher teaches as students are taught; she thinks as the students are thought about; he or she disciplines as the students are disciplined; he or she is the authority and students are obedient to that authority; he or she chooses as the students adapt and comply (Freire,p.73).

The teacher is the "depositor, prescriber, domesticator"(Freire, p.75). Students are objectified as "empty". Without the information that they receive from the teacher, they are nothing. Traditional teaching projects onto students the very ignorance that they are in the process of trying to overcome.[18] So, rather than education being conceived of as a response to the needs of young people, it projects onto them a conception of neediness and inadequacy in order to justify it's oppression of those young people, no matter how well intentioned.

Traditional education is a form of conquest and violence that makes it anti-dialogical and non-communicative (PO, p.109). Freire writes that the humanist discourse, in essence, masks a desire to "turn women and men into automatons" (PO, p.74). Traditional education is an act of violence because it prevents others from engaging in intentional and meaningful inquiry that is natural to, and necessary for, human existence (PO, p.85). Its aim is to conquer the students by means of control and projection.

> The conqueror imposes his objectives on the vanquished and makes of them his possession. He imposes his own contours on the vanquished, who internalize this shape and become ambiguous being "housing" another. From the first, the act of conquest, which reduces persons to the status of things, is necrophilic (Freire, p.138).

As an anti-dialogical and non-communicative pedagogy, traditional education is devoid of love and trust. "Conversely, such trust is obviously absent in the anti-dialogics of the banking method of education" (Freire, p.91) Traditional education represents a pathology of love: "sadism in the dominator and masochism in the dominated."(Freire, p. 89)

Freire uses the "banking" analogy to support the argument that traditional education both supports oppression and is in itself oppressive. The first and less contentious claim is that education serves oppression. "Within the structure of domination they [schools] function largely as agencies which prepare the invaders of the future" (PO, p.154). Traditional education is motivated by the "ideological intent" to indoctrinate individuals "to adapt to the world of oppression" (PO, p.78). [19] The second, more contentious claim, is that education, conceived of on the model of banking, is itself oppressive—a pedagogy of oppression— because it is dehumanizing and thereby making it impossible therefore "to use banking educational methods in the pursuit of liberation, for they would only negate the very pursuit"(PO, p. 78).

Freire argues that we are justified in rejecting traditional education because it supports and, is itself constitutive of oppression. He writes that "those truly committed to liberation must reject the banking concept in its entirety" and "abandon the educational goal of deposit-making" (PO, p.54). It is important, however, that this necessary rejection of traditional education *not* be seen as a rejection of humanism.[20] Instead, Freire is going to re-describe the humanist vision as essentially dialogical.

> The dialogical *I*, however, knows that it is precisely the *thou* ("not-I") which has called for his or her own existence. He also knows that the *thou* which calls forth his own existence in turn constitutes an I which has in his I its thou. The *I* and the *thou* thus

---

[18] Freire writes of student that "they call themselves ignorant and say the 'professor' is the one who has knowledge and to whom they should listen.....Almost never do they realize that the, too, 'know things', they have learned in their relations with the world and with other women and men" (PO, 63).

[19] "The educated individual is the adapted person, because she or he is better fit for the world. Translated into practice, this concept is well suited to the purposes of oppressors, whose tranquility rests on how well people fit the world the oppressors have created, and how little they question it (PO, 75)

[20] Weiler, Kathleen, "Myths of Paulo Freire,"; 361.

become, in dialectic of these relationships, two *thous* which become two *I's* (Freire,p. 167).

Learning, he argues, is integral to our "ontological vocation to be more fully human," (PO,p. 74). It is defined as those occasions when people come together in an action of mutual trust, love, humility and cooperation, to inquire together in an effort "to *name* the world" (PO, p.177). "Subjects meet in cooperation in order to transform the world" (PO, p.167). Dialogue is an "existential necessity" because it is "in speaking their word that people, by naming the world transform it" and in so doing "achieve significance as human beings" (PO, p.88). It is a process of self-organization in which the teacher and students "experience true authority and freedom, which they then seek to establish in society by transforming the reality which mediates them" (PO, pp.178-9).

For many of the "banking" analogy speaks to our own educational experience *as students*. It taps into our feelings of powerlessness as students and of our having to compete for scarce resources and "earn" the requisite intellectual wealth; it speaks to a felt lack of concern for our own individual perspectives on the part of our teachers; and it evokes feelings of fear (fear of being left behind, fear of being without, fear of not being self-sufficient, and fear of losing). As Ronald C. Arnett writes, "Each of us has experienced moments in which we felt embarrassed and lost face due to our lack of understanding of a given environment. The "expert" can make us feel stupid for not knowing what is alien to us."[21] The economic imagery of the banking" analogy plays on the assumed connection between educational success and financial security, exploiting deep financial insecurities associated with educational failure. [22] An appeal of problem-posing education in that it assures of intellectual or cultural capital as it assures us, by association, of future economic capital - it enables us to feel self-righteous in the process assuaging our deepest anxieties.

I am suggesting that an appeal of problem-posing education is its gratification of a capitalistic fantasy. It appeals to our desire to secure economic capital (read as intellectual capital) and the desire "to make it big" it by way of our involvement in entrepreneurial activity (read as dialogue). The rap singer, Fifty Cent, is one enactment of this capitalistic fantasy, for although a gangster and a criminal, he is also worth sixty million dollars. The persuasiveness of the "banking" analogy contributes to the force of Freire's overall argument. To accept that traditional education and banking are alike makes it extremely difficult to defend traditional education, as the necrophiliac objectification, dehumanization and conquest of their students. Who, for example, is going to say, "I conceive of my students as empty receptacles!" It follows that any defense of traditional education is going to require a critical analysis of Freire's "banking" analogy and the creation of a new, alternative images that do not exploit our economic anxieties - simultaneously initiating and reflecting changes in the educational imagery.

Freire acknowledges that the "banking" analogy directly corresponds to Sartre's "digestive" or "nutritive" analogy for education, whereby the "knowledge is "fed" by the

[21] Arnett, Ronald C., "Paulo Freire's revolutionary pedagogy: form a story-centered to a narrative-centered communication ethic", Qualitative Inquiry (2002) Vol. 8, No. 4: 494.

[22] It is not accidental to Freire's use of the "banking" analogy that he experienced abject poverty as a child: his family lost its middle class status during the depression of the 1930's; he was malnourished as a child; and he was a witness to the different living standards of countries during his years in exile.

teacher to the students to "fill them out""(PO, p.76). That Freire did not use the "nutritive" analogy is significant. Implicit in the "nutritive" analogy is the suggestion that what one is being "fed" by the teacher is of intrinsic value, for teacher and student, namely, it promotes health.[23] It assumes both that we can know what is in our students' best interests (what will promote individual health) and that teaching is a generous gesture, done for the benefit of others and not ourselves.

The "nutritional" analogy nicely assimilates, and by assimilating elevates, teaching to the medical model. It represents the teacher as an individual with something to offer those who have a very specific need of it. As with medicine, the teacher knows what is in the student's best interests and administers to their needs in the spirit of humanitarian generosity. Although the "nutritional" analogy is as old as Plato's, *Gorgias*, it frequently does not ask the important pedagogical question about whether the *manner* in which a patient/ student is "fed" might be of positive or negative consequence. An effect of the "nutritional" analogy is to focus attention on the, *what*, of teaching to the exclusion of the, *how,* of teaching. Freire is asking about the *how* of teaching. He foregrounds the pedagogical question by substituting the "banking" analogy for the "nutritional" analogy so as to question some of its assumptions. The "banking" analogy ambiguates the value of what is being transacted between teacher and student and its ultimate purpose. The suggestion that what is being "deposited" in the student is equivalent to "money" or "intellectual capital" is an important move in the argument for three reasons. First, the value of money is extrinsic, as opposed to, intrinsic: it has value only in terms of its buying power (it is a means to an end). Second, when money is given, as opposed to being exchanged—as in the case of charity and philanthropy—it validates the giver rather than the receiver. Third, the value of money is culturally specified: some cultures do not have money and some cultures have money, but distribute it evenly, so that it lacks the kind of sovereign value that it has in a capitalist society.

By using the "banking" as opposed to "nutritional" analogy for education, Freire puts the suggestion in place that the value of what is learnt in school is arbitrary, extrinsic and serves to reify the social and intellectual position of teachers, rather than to facilitate the transition of students into society. It serves to project ignorance and inadequacy on to young people, conceiving of them as "objects of assistance" (PO, p.83), and by so doing serves to solidify adult or expert authority. Of course, Freire will argue for these claims in *Pedagogy of the Oppressed* and later works, but the important point is that they are assumed, and therefore, suggested by his use of the "banking" analogy. He is already, by way of the "banking" analogy, undermining or challenging the unquestioned paternalism that pervades educational discourse and practice.

RE-IMAGINING EDUCATION

In this section of the paper, I consider assumptions implicit in the "banking" analogy, the articulation of which creates problems, or at least tensions, for Freire's argument. My intention in bringing these potentially disanalogous tensions to the surface is not to mount a defense of traditional education; rather it is to enrich and deepen our understanding of the

---

[23] Plato made much of this analogy in distinguishing true teachers from panderers.

problem-posing approach to education. For while it is possible for teachers to feel righteous about their rejection of traditional education and adoption of problem-solving education, in the interests of liberation and our ontological vocation, the actual practice of this libratory approach is vulnerable, given the economic character of the educational imaginary, to being a free-market of individuals and ideas. Freire's introduction of the "banking" analogy serves to highlight the teacher as the exclusive owner of intellectual capital and justify his redistribution of this intellectual capital to the students by way of his problem-solving alternative. He is defending a free unregulated market economy of ideas, exploiting the capitalist domination of the educational imaginary.

Freire perceived the difficulty early on in *Pedagogy of the Oppressed* and, in an effort to circumvent it, gave a detailed account of what a dialogue should *not* be like.

> And since dialogue is the encounter in which the united reflection and action of the dialogues are addressed to the world is to be transformed and humanized, this dialogue cannot be reduced to the act of one person's "depositing" ideas in another, nor can it become a simple exchange of ideas to be "consumed" by the discussants. Nor yet is it a hostile, polemical argument between those who are committed neither to the naming of the world, nor to the search for truth, but rather to the imposition of their own truth. Because dialogue is an encounter among women and men who name the world, it must not be a situation where some name on behalf of others. It is an act of creation; it must not serve as a crafty instrument for the domination of one person by another. The domination implicit in dialogue is that of the world by the dialogues; it is conquest of the world for the liberation of human kind (Freire,pp. 88-89).

If it is true that images provides us with the pictures for what our thoughts are to mean, then the difficult with emancipatory dialogue is that we lack the necessary images by which to envision its possibilities. We do not know what such a dialogue looks like, except that it is egalitarian (we are all I's and all thou's) and unregulated (authority is emergent) - the educational imaginary risks remaining economic unless we can usurp its sovereignty with other alternatives.

Freire is right to point out that traditional education involves the transmission of a disciplinary framework or outlook by way of discrete pieces of content or information. However, the "banking" analogy represents this transmission as endlessly reiterated, irrespective of what has gone before and what projections there are for the future—transmission occurs outside temporal history. It is the atemporality of the "banking" analogy that threatens the legitimacy of the teacher's presumed of authority and the possibility of emergent student authority; it has the effect of dichotomizing and, as a result, simplifying the teacher-student relationship. The categories, "student' and "teacher," become reified into binary oppositions associated with such other dualisms as active and passive, subjects and objects, knowledgeable and ignorant, oppressor an oppressed. The "banking" analogy in effect reduces the complexity of the teacher-student relationship in traditional education, legitimating only one of the many emotional responses evoked by it: inspiration, admiration, attachment, fear, frustration, intimidation, excitement, for example.

The atemporality of the "banking" analogy masks the role of meaning in traditional education, perpetuating the myth that knowledge and its transmission is at the center of the pedagogical relationship. An acknowledgement of ourselves as, educating and being educated, in time, allows for an appreciation of the Murdochian point that we learn concepts in depth and what a concept means at one point in our lives can be entirely different from what it means at another point.[24] The significance of this point for education, is that it allows for the suggestion that what differentiates the teacher from the student, in the context of traditional education, is not the ownership of knowledge but a deepened understanding of science, history or art, for example. His or her role is to perform a simultaneous connection and gap between his or her own thinking and that of the students, as a way of envisioning for students future possibilities for their own understanding. The teacher demonstrates to the students what they are not, so as to reveal what they can become. This way of understanding traditional education requires an acknowledgement of the inherent temporality of teaching and the role this gives to meaning.

The acknowledgement that teaching occurs *in* time and, moreover, *takes* time, complicates and destabilizes the polarities of "teacher" and "student", making them more difficult to maintain. To conceive of teaching as temporally constituted is to be reminded of it as historically, contextually and relationally sensitive.[25] It is true that at the beginning of any teaching relationship a teacher does not know his/her students, he/she has certain objectives for his/her teaching that are not necessarily inclusive of their perspectives, and she presumes to have the institutional authority in the relationship. The "banking" analogy highlights the *advent* of the teaching relationship. However, teaching is not static. It is premised on the assumption that an interaction takes place between teacher and student that produces a transformation in the student and modifies the original relationship: the teacher does come to have knowledge of his/her students and makes adjustments to his/her objectives accordingly; students come to recognize and appreciate *the reasons for* the teacher's authority as their understanding continues to deepen; and some students in the class emerge as having more authority than others (differentiations are made between different kinds of authority—intellectual, disciplinary, and strategic for example).

These last two points are worth emphasizing for two reasons. First, even though the advantage of problem-solving education is that allows for emergent authority—it allows student to choose what they accept as authoritative or truthful—the teacher-students and student teachers are not always at the point of embarking on a dialogue. The dialogue is sustained over a course of hours, days, weeks and months, allowing for certain patterns of authority to emerge. Emergent authority, in this dialogical context, is oftentimes the result of how others can "teach" us, not in terms of what they know, but in terms of how this knowledge informs their understanding, behavior and lives. Second, unless students develop reliable criteria for what is acceptable as authoritative or truthful, they are vulnerable to remaining with what is familiar, known and ultimately safe. They may be subject to intimidation, peer pressure, and their desire to be accepted by their classmates; and they are susceptible to clever arguments and powerful rhetoric. As possible victims of covert forms of manipulation the students would seem to be no less oppressed than before. The question of what is going to constitute authentic authority in this context is very real and pressing for anyone who practices dialogical pedagogy in their classroom.

---

[24] Murdoch, Iris, The Sovereignty of Good (New York and London: Routledge, 1970) ; 26

[25] Paul Taylor argues, in his criticism of Freire, that the way in which we, as individuals actually give meaning to our experiences, and assume subjective agency, occurs somewhere within the inter-arching continua that falls between these polarities. See Kathleen Weiler's article, "Myths of Paulo Freire"; 363.

Analysis of the "banking" analogy raises at least three further questions: does transmission entail or require the passivity of students?; Is transmission *all* that traditional education involves?; and is transmission the intended function of traditional education. Dealing with the questions in this order, the banking analogy implies that students are necessarily passive in the transmission process; it assumes that they have no choice as to what they internalize. The cognitive passivity of traditional education is contrasted with the cognitive activity of problem-solving education. Students are presumed to be passive because they are listening and not talking, they are receiving information about the world rather than discovering the world for themselves, they are memorizing the information rather than applying and experimenting with it; and they don't own knowledge because they are not responsible for cognizing it.

The "banking" analogy reinforces the distinction between method and content, as it simultaneously tries to overcome it. The analogy helps reinforce the view that when, in education, there is a focus on conveying content, the student is passive and dependent, and when there is a focus on method the student is active and independent, or at least, mutually dependent on their peers. The point about the problem-posing approach then is that it replaces passivity with activity and dependency with independency. But there is at least a question about whether if, when there is focus on content, there is necessarily no focus on method, so that the student is passive and dependent. If we think about text based courses and the explanations of texts that those teachers provide: the student is not unreflectively or passively receiving the interpretation, but actively trying to work out how the teacher got from the text, which the student is familiar with, and the interpretation that she is citing or explaining. Similarly with philosophical teaching: the students are working extremely hard to make sense of what the teacher is saying, in light of what she or he has read or thought he or she read.

An appeal of the "banking" analogy that contributes to our readiness to reject traditional education is that it assumes that teachers are more powerful than they in fact are. It encourages teachers to imagine themselves as having already overcome some of the anxieties associated with teaching: feeling vulnerable; feeling that one's failures will be conspicuous; feeling tested and challenged by the students. Teaching anxieties are not mere phantoms but arise from their direct experience of student subjective agency. Every teacher knows that the intention to teach x, for example, does not always translate into having successfully taught x. Students are far more cognitively and pedagogically active than the "banking" analogy implies. Students makes decisions all the time as to what they accept or reject; accepting new ideas requires effort and students do not always succeed; students test new ideas against old ones and against their experiences; students are teaching one another all the time. If teaching were like banking, teachers would not need to measure the effectiveness of their teaching because their success would be assured.

In banking, means and end are essentially the same: the end is to successfully deposit the money and the means is the successful depositing of that money. The "banking" analogy encourages the intuition that teaching operates in a similar manner: the transmission of information from teacher to student is the means *and end* of traditional education. But how sound is this intuition? Is transmission the end of traditional education or are there others? Is there perhaps an infinite regress of ends? For example, do we teach children to spell words for the sake of spelling words, or do we teach them to spell so that they can read and write? Do we teach children to read and write for the sake of reading and writing, or do we teach them to read and write so that they can participate and in a human community? The "banking" analogy focuses on the mechanism of teaching to the exclusion of the dreams, visions, and hopes that animate it.

I have already indicated that a possible end of traditional education is the revelation of, and invitation to participate in, a certain kind of relationship with a discipline or inquiry. The teacher professes his or her self as an instantiation of this relationship, performing the results and, ongoing processes, of his/her own educational transformation. He or she is thinking about their relationship to their expertise in the enactment of it as she illustrates how intellectual servitude to a discipline—and the commitment to "teaching" it—is capable of being intellectually and personally transformational, as evidenced in their speaking, living and teaching. The teacher still has doubts, but, the point is, that these have been constructively transformed. If this is an end of traditional education then the teacher wants the child to be able to appreciate and not just receive information, to create meaning and not just consume it. The assumption of teaching is that inquiry, whether it is historical, philosophical, artistic, scientific, enriches our lives.

If this is an end of traditional education, then feelings discredited by the "banking" analogy resurface as legitimate. It is appropriate for a student to feel inspired by a teacher and for a teacher to feel friendship for a student. It is appropriate for a teacher and student to feels as though they are members of a scholarly community albeit differently placed. It is appropriate for the student to seek vindication from a teacher and a teacher to feel sometimes that roles have been reversed.

CONCLUSION

I conclude with some very brief comments on the relevance of these insights for dialogical pedagogy. My analysis of the "banking" analogy is not a call for a return to traditional education - whatever in reality that turns out to be - but is instead a move forward in the advancement of dialogical pedagogy for the following reasons. First, it explains both the popularization of Freire's educational philosophy and common misunderstandings of it. Second, it problematizes the discursive assumption that we know what traditional education and problem-posing education are; the analysis invites us to re-examine traditional education for aspects eclipsed by the "banking" analogy and to give serious consideration to the nature of authentic dialogical authority. Third, the aspects of traditional education eclipsed by the "banking" analogy provide us resources for conceiving the character of authentic dialogical authority: it involves an exemplary unification of thinking, saying and doing; it involves the personal transformation resulting from any serious engagement; and it involves the individual expression of subjectivity in the very acknowledgement of another's. It is by way of these insights that the distinction between traditional education and problem-posing education, dichotomized and reified by the "banking" analogy, begins to dissolve and make way for new and alternative resolutions of the educational terrain.

REFERENCES

Altman, Matthew C. "What's the use of philosophy? Democratic citizenship and the direction ofhigher education," *Educational Theory* (2004) *Vol. 54, No. 2,* 143-155.

Arnett, Ronald C. Paulo Freire's revolutionary pedagogy: from a story-centered to a narrative centered communication ethic," *Qualitative Inquiry* (2002) *Vol. 8, No. 4,* 489-510.

Berger, Peter L., "The false consciousness of "consciousness raising", *Worldview* (1975): 33-38.

Bingham, Charles, "On Paulo Freire's debt to psychoanalysis: authority on the side of freedom," *Studies in Philosophy and Education* (202) *21,* 447-464.

La Caze, Marguerite, *The Analytic Imaginary* (Ithaca and London: Cornell University Press, 2002).

Deutscher, Max (ed), *Michele Le Doeuff: operative philosophy and imaginary practice* (Amherst, New York: Humanity Books, 2000).

Freire, Paulo, *Pedagogy of the Oppressed* (London and New York: Continuum, 2000). *Pedagogy of Freedom: Ethics, democracy, and civic courage* (New York: Rowman & Littlefield Publishers, Inc. 1998).

Freud, Anna, "The role of the teacher", *Harvard Educational Review (1952),* 22.

Giroux, Henry A. "Paulo Freire's approach to radical educational reform: a critical review of *Pedagogy in process: the letters to Guinea-Bissau* by Paulo Freire", *Curriculum Inquiry (1979) Vol. 19, No. 3,* 257-272.

Glass, Ronald David, "On Paulo Freire's philosophy of praxis and the foundations of liberation education," *Educational Researcher (2001) Vol 30, No. 2,* 15-25.

Haynes, Felicity, "Metaphor as interactive", *Educational Theory (1975), Vol. 25. No. 3,* 272-277.

Joldersma, Clarence W., "The tension between justice and freedom in Paulo Freire's epistemology," *Journal of Educational Thought (2001) Vol. 35. No. 2,* 129-148.

Kim, Hye-Kyung, "Critical thinking, learning and Confucius: a positive assessment," *Journal of Philosophy of Education (2003) Vol. 37, No. 1,* 71-87.

Lakoff, George and Mark Johnson, *Metaphors we live by* (Chicago: The University of Chicago Press, 1980).

Lambert, Lake, "Active learning for the kingdom of God," *Teaching Theology and Religion (2000) Vol 3. No.2,* 71-80.

Leach, Mary, "Can we talk?," *Harvard Educational Review (1992) 62,* 257-63.

Margonis, Frank, "Relational pedagogy without foundations: reconstructing the work of Paulo Freire," *Philosophy of Education Society Yearbook 1999,* Randall Curren (ed), Urbana: 99-107.

Ortony, Andrew, "Why metaphors are necessary and not just nice," *Educational Theory, Vol. 25, No. 1 (Winter 1975),* 45-53.

Owens, Pamela Jean, "experiencing the other as the self: cultural diversity as liberating praxis," *Teaching Theology and Religion (2005) Vol. 8, No. 4,* 245-252.

Reed, Ronald F. and Tony W. Johnson *Philosophical Documents in Education* (New York: Longmans, 1996).

Roberts, Peter, "Structure, direction and rigour in liberating education," *Oxford Review of Education (1996) Vol. 22, No. 3,* 295-???.

Scheffler, Israel, *The Language of Education* (Springfield, Illinois: Charles C. Thomas, 1960).

Simpson, Douglas J., Michael J.B. Jackson and Judy C. Aycock, *John Dewey and the art of teaching: toward reflective and imaginative practice* (Thousand Oaks: Sage Publications, 2005).

Weiler, Kathleen, "Myths of Paulo Freire," *Educational Theory (1996), Vol. 46. No. 3,* 353-371.

In: Pioneers in Education: Essays in Honor of Paulo Freire   ISBN: 978-1-60021-479-0
Editors: M.Shaughnessy, E.Galligan et al., pp 25-40   ©2008 Nova Science Publishers, Inc.

Chapter 2

FREIREAN "JUST IRE," HEALTH, AND "POEM-MAKING": A LETTER FROM WEST TEXAS

Virginia J. Mahan[*]
South Plains College, USA

ABSTRACT

In exposing the dynamics in which dominant group forces in the United States have oppressed subordinate groups, I routinely express Freirean "just rage" (Freire, 2004, p. 103). Although some psychologists consider anger to be a form of psychopathology, Freire viewed such ire as an apposite indignation. Regardless of its legitimacy, the emotional expression of anger is associated with physiological changes, most notably the sympathetic nervous system's "fight or flight" response, suppression of the immune response, and, over the course of time, an increased chance of developing cardiac problems (e.g., see "Anger Kills," 1998; Barker, 2003; Smith, 2005). This chapter illustrates poem-making (Fox, 2004) as a valuable tool for managing the adverse mental and physiological consequences associated with Freire's (2004) process of denunciation-annunciation and the expression of just ire.

"You're a poet and don't even know it" is a hackneyed idiom frequently bandied about in jest, particularly by children. Conversely, as a preliminary caution to readers, my caveat is: "I know it; I'm *not* a poet." However, that realization has not dissuaded me from "poem-making" (Fox, 1997), that is, writing verse as an antidote to the adverse mental and physiological effects of, as Paulo Freire phrased it, "just ire" (2004, p. 59), legitimate, appropriate anger when encountering the –isms: ageism, classism, heterosexism, racism, sexism, and fatalism (i.e., "injustice being a fatality against which nothing can be done" [Freire, 2004, p. 23]). For me, the poems embodied in this chapter developed as a form of catharsis. Indeed, they functioned as (a) a conduit for emotional release, (b) a way to diminish

---

[*] gmahan@spc.cc.tx.us, gmahan@southplainscollege.edu

the negative physiological consequences associated with anger, however valid and appropriate it may be, (c) a path to spiritual healing, and (d) a type of cultural resistance (Moane, 1999) in which writing is used as a form of opposition to dehumanization, discrimination, human suffering, inequality, and social injustice (Fox, 2003). To be sure, poem-making may serve as a vehicle for "denouncing how we are living and announcing how we could live " (Freire, 2004, p. 105), as well as a form of emotion-focused coping in which coping efforts are aimed at mitigating and managing the negative emotional impact of a stressful situation, in this case, oppositional and belligerent students. This style of coping is particularly helpful when the stressor is one that the individual is able to exercise no or only slight control over such as the bigoted attitudes of unreceptive, resistant, insensitive, and intolerant dominant group (DG) students (Lazarus & Folkman, 1984). Emotion-focused coping instead focuses on aspects of the situation that *do* remain under the individual's control, that is, the emotional impact of the stressor on him or her.

BACKGROUND

Benevolent Colonizers

Seven years ago, in preparation for teaching multicultural psychology classes, I came across a book written by Geraldine Moane, a lecturer in the Department of Psychology at University College Dublin in Ireland, entitled *Gender and Colonialism: A Psychological Analysis of Oppression and Liberation* (1999). Although Moane's manuscript evolved from her Irish experience and specifically addressed gender, only one aspect of minority studies, I nonetheless found her paradigm applicable to all American minority groups and began to use it as a template for my lectures. Moane's text proved influential in shaping my multicultural perspective and reflections vis-à-vis American Minority Studies classes, as well as in constructing my interactions with students. Indeed, it was Moane who introduced me to the term *benevolent colonizer*, first coined by Albert Memmi (1957/1967) to refer to members of the dominant group who are critical of their own group's oppression and who consequently find themselves marginalized by members of both the dominant and the subordinate group (SG). Indeed, Stanley Aronowitz has observed, "Even in ostensibly democratic societies, those who would bring dialogic and critical practices into classrooms risk marginalization" (2001, p. 15).

On the one hand, the DG tends to view benevolent colonizers as snakes in the grass, renegades who decry White privilege. On the other hand, SG members are apt to look at instructors who denounce-announce with suspicion. Along these lines, Sue and Sue (1990) suggested that many SG members experience cultural paranoia, also known as the paranorm. Given that cultural paranoia is a highly functional survival mechanism that protects against further psychological and physical harm stemming from oppression, it is not surprising that SG members are skeptical of the motives of benevolent colonizers. What is more, the racism and bigotry inherent in the hegemony divest benevolent colonizers of any sense of assimilation into the subordinate group, even if they are radical insurgents. According to Memmi (1957/1967), the benevolent colonizer consequently carries on in "solitude, bewilderment and ineffectiveness" (p. 43).

Other authors have commented on the same phenomenon. For example, Noel Ignatiev (2004, p. 605) of *Race Traitor* magazine routinely employs the term "race traitor" or "a traitor to the white race" to signify "someone who is nominally classified as white, but who defies the rules of whiteness so flagrantly as to jeopardize his or her ability to draw upon privileges of the white skin." Undeniably, as Macedo observed, "To willfully destroy one's class and color supremacy" is "a very difficult task" (2001, p.xxx). Indeed, Macedo decried those White liberal educators "who proselytize about empowering minorities while refusing to divest from their class-and-whiteness privilege—a privilege that is often left unexamined and unproblematized and that is often accepted as a divine right" (2001, p.xxx).

In teaching American Minorities Studies courses, I have been dealt many a bad hand of oppositional DG students who made it clear that they wanted me to withdraw from the game; because I was somehow cheating them out of the trump card of White privilege to which they are entitled. The reality of historical and continuing injustice leaves many DG students uncomfortable. Indeed, many WASP male students, as well as some of their aficionadas, will symbolically fling their king of clubs at me in disgust (i.e., emblematic of good ol' boys club with its inherent White, male, and heterosexual privilege), sending the accusatory message that I am a race traitor. Whereas I refuse to fold, I do at times feel alone, perplexed, and ineffectual.

Hence, glimpsing my own blurred image of a benevolent colonizer and my unsightly blemishes of class-and-whiteness privilege reflected in Memmi's descriptive looking glass, as well as recognizing my own struggles as an outsider neither fully accepted by members of the DG or SG, I experimented with poem-making as follows:

A benevolent colonizer—that's what I am;
Outspokenly opposed to all hegemony,
I traverse an uncharitable no man's land;
Minorities, mistaking me for the enemy,
Exhibit non-acceptance and mistrust;
White people, considering me a traitor,
Show condemnation and disgust;
Regarded by both groups as a betrayer,
I stumble into a pit, feeling impotent;
Between a rock and a hard place,
Alone, isolated, few understand my intent
To battle the absurdities and injustices of race,
To pledge allegiance to the flag of this land
Knowing there *is* liberty and justice for *all*;
So, against inequity I take my stand,
Albeit repeatedly pinned to the wall
By Whites who charge me with sedition,
Condemning me with scornful disgust;
By minorities who view me with suspicion,
Considerable skepticism, and mistrust.
Yes, a benevolent colonizer—that's what I am;
I navigate the harsh reality of no man's land.

In addition to giving vent to just ire, poem-making served to bolster my resolve to continue denouncing the "transgressions against human values" (Freire, 2004, p. 105) perpetrated by United States in general and Texas in particular and, in a prophetic manner, announcing how noble our nation and state *could be* if the injustices are rectified. This important task cannot be renounced, even in light of the inevitable opposition and rejection.

MULTICULTURAL EDUCATION AND JUST IRE

Not The Fabulous Four: Food, Festivals, Famous Figures, and Fictitious Accounts

Drawing upon Freire's statement regarding literacy education, I believe that a minority studies course can "only make sense on a human level if it comes also with a sort of historical-political-social psychoanalysis" (2004, p. 66). Yet, a multicultural philosophy, psychology, education, or humanities course on classicism, heterosexism, racism, and sexism "is often mistaken for some other kind of course, a misconception that tends to leave students frustrated and angry when they realize their mistake" (Heldke & O'Connor, 2004, p. xi). Without a doubt, many students expect me to preserve the status quo and reproduce the dominant group ideology and its historical contributions "à la banking system" (Freire, 2001, p. 40). Any conflicting perspectives deeply disturb their established, comfortable view of the world. However, in quite the opposite mode, I am determined to strip off my foul, filthy academic robe of concierge in "reproducing the values of the dominant social order" (Macedo, 2001, p.xxvi). Using a Freirean approach, I have chosen to don the fresh garb of intervention "in the world to rectify it, not to maintain it more or less as it is" (Freire, 2004, p. 39), covering topics that are considered "in bad taste," "pure demagogy," and "almost subversive" according to many student "defenders of democracy" (Freire, 2001, p. 36). In fact, one of the first assigned readings is William Bigelow's (1998) "Discovering Columbus: Rereading the Past" in which American hero Christopher Columbus, "discoverer" of the New World, is presented as a villain who perpetrated violence upon and economically exploited America's indigenous people by (a) demanding that they bring him gold and spun cotton, (b) chopping off their hands when they failed to deliver the specified quota, and (c) transporting Indians to Spain for the purpose of enslavement. Further upsetting their cognitive apple carts during the initial class lecture, I employ *Lies My Teacher Told Me* (Loewen, 2001) to expose the full reality of Helen Keller's adult life and to highlight the "censorship of certain bodies of knowledge" (Macedo, 2001, p. xix) and how dissent is all too frequently silenced (Loewen, 2001). Although the U.S. public shares a collective memory of Helen Keller as a blind and deaf child who in due course overcame major obstacles to become a college graduate, lecturer, and writer, few are aware that Keller became a suffragette, socialist, founding member of the National Association for Advancement of Colored People (NAACP), and contributor to the American Civil Liberties Union (ACLU) (Hubbard, 2002; Loewen, 1995). When students encounter this information, their knee-jerk reaction is: "How preposterous! What a bald-faced lie, or my teachers would have already exposed me to it." What is more, using the book *You Are Being Lied To* (Kick, 2001), I offer an alternative to the customary, standard accounts of "the slain civil rights leader," the Reverend Dr. Martin Luther King, Jr., in which the last three years of his life are entirely expunged, "as if flushed down a memory hole" (Cohen & Solomon, 2001, p. 63). Indeed, King's 1967 speech, *Beyond Vietnam*, in which King accused the United States of being "the greatest purveyor of violence in the world today" and which *Time* called "demagogic slander that sounded like a script for Radio Hanoi" (Cohen & Solomon, 2001, p. 63), is a perfect vehicle to introduce the machinery behind the control and erasure of culture (Moane, 1999) and symbolic annihilation (Gross, 1991, p. 21). The aforementioned mechanisms entail the non-inclusion or non-representation of subordinate group members and their contributions, as well as keeping invisible those perspectives that differ from dominant forces in power.

To be sure, students frequently view such freshly minted perspectives as counterfeit bills being deposited in their educational bank accounts. As opposed to acknowledging that *de facto* censorship permeates the media in general and the textbook publishing industry in particular and rather than listening to "the muteness of those who have been silenced" (Freire, 2001, p.86), many students prefer to believe sanitized and bowdlerized versions of history. Hence, students may respond with protests of indignation as if catching the teacher in an illicit heist, and they may vigorously defend their mental vaults where they have previously banked forged accounts.

In short, when students discover that the focus of my American Minorities Studies class is not the fabulous four—food, festivals, famous figures, and fictitious representations—but involves instead a comprehensive study of oppressive forces that have crushed and continue to limit subordinate groups, they raise an assortment of psychological defenses, including anger, denial, frustration, projection, and rationalization. To be sure, the "unmasking" and "interrogation" of the dominant ideology (Freire, 2001, p.91) can be a discomfiting process for many students. Moreover, "the target of their frustration is often their instructor" (Heldke & O'Connor, 2004, p. xi)—in this case, me!!! Unfortunately, these students have not yet grasped the old adage, "Kill the message, not the messenger."

In any event, three to four hours of each of my workdays are devoted to exposing students to the dominant forces throughout U.S. history that have animalized, dehumanized, erased, excluded, exploited, humiliated, murdered, and raped American minority groups and their environments. Thus, a large part of my time is spent in the expression of "just rage in the light of profound injustices which express, in terrifying levels, the human capacity for transgression" (Freire, 2004, p. 103). As a consequence, I have undeniably experienced both the best and the worst of pedagogical times.

Several years ago, I was teaching two different multicultural classes at two distinct institutions in conservative West Texas: one for undergraduate liberal arts majors and the other for graduate students in the field of education. On the one hand, the vast majority of these students were exceptionally open, receptive, perceptive, and insightful vis-à-vis minority issues, and thus interaction with them was an uplifting experience for me. Moreover, these students shared understandings and phenomenological accounts that guided me in a positive direction and continue to inspire me (see Freire's "There is No Teaching Without Learning" [2001, pp. 29-48]). On the other hand, I encountered several students who were intolerant, unreceptive, defensive, disrespectful, belligerent, and vindictive beyond anything that I had previously encountered or even presumed possible. Their expectations for my class, as well as their perceptions of what constituted a multicultural course, were apparently at great odds with mine. As these students seemed to be impervious to any reality or phenomenology beyond their own class-and-whiteness privilege, I ended each day feeling that my instructional goals had been totally stymied. Indeed, at the conclusion of each day when I had finished mentally jousting with these oppositional students and stripped off my protective scholarly armor, I felt more and more spiritually wounded and mentally drained. Moreover, catecholamines from my just ire were undoubtedly surging throughout my system, conspiring to clog up my arteries and, at some point in the future, prematurely snuff out this purveyor of divergent perspectives ("Anger Kills," 1998). In short, my goal of denunciation-annunciation was progressively thwarted at every step, and my body seemed to be revved up in a persistent "fight or flight" response ("Anger Kills," 1998).

After one particularly harrowing afternoon skirmish with the quintessence of an antagonistic, White male oppressor, two empathetic students, apparently experiencing similar frustration, lingered after class to thank me for my resolute doggedness in battling Eurocentric knowledge and to shore up my noticeably dampened morale. As a salve to my fresh wounds, they recounted the anecdote below as a reminder that such enmity is to be expected when teaching multicultural courses. In addition, the creation of this poem accorded me an emotional cleansing.

Power and Control

This summer, my students related the story
Of the multicultural professor before me,
A Black man whom they esteemed and adored
For candidly battling the "—isms" he so abhorred.

One day the prof's lecture was disrupted
By a woman who brusquely interrupted:
"My great granddaddy had a plantation
A hundred fifty years ago in this great nation,
And he owned *you people* as his slaves.
I wish we could go back to those good old days."
The prof closed his eyes, bowed his head.
The minutes went by and nothing was said.
The class couldn't tell if it was prayer or meditation,
Nor in retrospect judge the duration.
Stunned into silence, the students waited
While the lingering rancor abated
And the air of abject ignorance cleared
As the aura of pure aplomb appeared.

At last, the prof raised his head, composed and collected,
And, with complete disregard for the student's invective,
Directly resumed his lecture full throttle.
This prof now serves as my role model.
In multicultural courses we teach
That WASP males are in charge; we preach
That Whites possess most of the power.
Well, in this case, during that class hour,

The Black prof was in control, showing total dominion
Over his loathsome student's odious opinion.

Stumbling Blocks: Dreams and Counter-Dreams

The aforementioned incident well illustrates two of Freire's tenets. First, Freire (2004) maintained that there is no present that is not the stage for confrontations between forces opposed to advancement and those that struggle for it. In this sense, the strong marks of our colonial, slavery-ridden past are contradictorily present in our current reality and intent on posing obstacles to advancement toward modernity. Those are the marks of a past that, while incapable of enduring much longer, insist on prolonging their presence to the detriment of change. (pp. 32-33)

During encounters with oppositional and antagonistic students, it is helpful to bear in mind that such student stumbling blocks are merely temporary. Indeed, Freire reminded us that "dreams also have their counter-dreams" (2004, p. 32), and thus our visions of a more just world will "not take place easily, without obstacles" (2004, p. 32).

Regrettably, the realization of our dreams will entail struggle, including "advances, reversals, and at times, lengthy marches" (Freire, 2004, p. 32).

Teaching is Learning; Learning is Teaching

Second, it was Freire's contention that "there is no teaching without learning" (2001, p. 29). Indeed, at times it seems as if I have gained considerably more from students than I have taught them. In this case, as the days passed, the students' narrative continued to intrigue me and offer an avenue for recurring "critical reflection" (Freire, 2001, p. 30). Several weeks passed before I penned the above lyrics, written to pay homage to an unknown colleague who exemplified the paragon of self-control, the nonpareil for dealing with adversaries of multiculturalism, and who modeled one way of dealing with oppositional students: meditation and/or prayer. Poem-making works for me.

The Nero Complex: Fiddling While Racism Burns

Memmi (1957/1967) noted the "Nero Complex": members of the dominant group who are obsessed with denying the magnitude of their own group's oppression and who rationalize their legitimacy through relentless illustrations of the DG's virtues and the minority group's defects. To be sure, they steadfastly cling to their belief in the excellence of the system and tenaciously justify their privileged position. In class discussions of racism, this denial of hegemony and an ongoing system of domination-subordination emerges in a variety of forms, inevitably pushing my "just ire" button. For example, students may assert that racism is a thing of the past, as if it ended with the *Brown v. Board of Education* (1954) ruling or the passage of the Civil Rights Act of 1964 (i.e., PL 88-352). According to these students, we need therefore to just move on and forget about what has previously happened. After all, their reasoning goes, they weren't "even alive when all that happened and shouldn't have to pay for what others did" (Wise, 2003, p. 1). Equally annoying are those students who say, "Racism will always exist; nothing can be done," essentially the equivalent of "fatalism" (Freire, 2004, p. 23): "Reality is what it is. What can be done?" (Freire, 2004, p. 117).

As previously noted, in teaching multicultural courses, I routinely encounter defensive students who raise their shields of White orthodoxy while aiming barbs at both their instructor and at minorities. When DG students, sometimes for the first time in their lives, mentally collide with incontrovertible evidence of continuing inequity, the reality of such injustice may trigger cognitive discomfort and guilt, which may initially be too painful to handle. Accordingly, one of the typical defense mechanisms these students employ to deflect attention from the real issues is to announce: "*I* love America." Indeed, with the jingoistic climate after 9/11, this response commonly hovered in the classroom air. With this pronouncement, the implication is that anyone who censures unjust U.S. practices is somehow disloyal, or even, as I have been dubbed on occasion, a "terrorist."

In a similar vein, Wise (2003, p. 1) described the sick feeling he gets when, in a class discussion of racism, a student, cleaving to his or her Pollyanna view of the U.S. as a land of unimpeded equal opportunity, declares: "I believe in America. It's the best nation on Earth." What is more, Wise (2003) graphically portrayed the student's words as spewing out "weightless, yet thick, like the putrid froth one sees downriver from a paper mill" (p. 1). According to Wise, the assertion "*I* believe in America" is immaterial to the discussion of racism for several reasons. First, similar declarations were undoubtedly also voiced during the era of slavery, segregation, and lynching. Second, such statements employ a form of moral relativism akin to the familiar childhood diversionary stratagem. When confronted with breaking a windowpane with his or her ball, the child points out, "Well, Jamey broke *two* windows." Indeed, the fact that other countries show evidence of enormous degrees of injustice—considerably higher than in our own nation—does not absolve the U.S. of its own ongoing racial, ethnic, sexist, and heterosexist wrongdoings. Its misdeeds nonetheless continue to exist and therefore need urgently to be addressed.

Several years ago, after listening to still another variation of the "I believe in America" diversionary subterfuge and experiencing a rush of just ire, I felt the urge to poem-make in response to one student's stifling chain of prefabricated, sanctimonious platitudes, what Wise has referred to as "cheerleading for America" (2003, p. 3). The following is an example of cultural resistance:

> "*I* love America. This is a great nation,"
> Students will loudly proclaim
> In response to our disdain
> Of racist acts and the shame
> We benevolent colonizers feel toward U. S. hypocrisy.

> "*I* love America. I'm proud of this nation."
> I've heard this again and again
> As a means to berate and condemn
> Those whose beliefs differ from them
> Vis-à-vis injustice.

"*I* love America" is used
When a protester expresses dissension
To relieve strain and tension,
To deflect one's attention,
And veer away from the real issues.

"I love America" functions to
> derogate those with peace-oriented wisdom.
> justify the merit of an unfair system.
> extol the heinous, hierarchical hegemony.
> rationalize inhuman treatment of an enemy.
> excuse continuing savagery and violence.
> force dissenters into silence.
> dismiss ongoing odious oppression.
> suppress free speech and expression
> regarding the use of unjust power
> and induce protesters to retreat and cower.

Indeed, "*I* love America"
Is instinctively uttered,
Unthinkingly muttered,
Frequently sputtered
To mask the abuse of power.

I, too, love America, but . . .
> James Byrd
> Ruben "Hurricane" Carter
> Vincent Chin
> Amadou Diallo
> Mumia Abu Jamal
> Wen Ho Lee
> Abner Louima
> Leonard Peltier
> Ethel Rosenberg
> Ruben Salazar
> Matthew Shepard
> The Japanese Internment
> The Long Walk
> The McCarthy Era and Neo-McCarthyism
> The Scottsboro Boys
> The Trail of Tears
> Mary Turner
> The Tulia, Texas, travesty
> James Yousef Yee
> . . . and all the many unmentioned others who have suffered wrongs
> motivate me to continue to condemn unjust U.S. actions.

> We benevolent colonizers love America, too.
> Thus, we censure jingoistic factions,
> Object to international convention infractions,
> Protest injustice and discriminatory actions,
> So that we, too, may be proud of this nation.

Although many students and educators would condemn the political hue of the above poem, Freire (2004) maintained that it is impossible to separate politics from education. Therefore, a political act is pedagogical and, conversely, the pedagogical act is political. Accordingly, one task of educators is to unmask and interrogate the dominant ideology, not merely maintain the status quo (Freire, 2001). Indeed, stressing "the responsibility we have to take on the construction and betterment of democracy among us" (2004, p. 61), Freire called attention to teachers' obligation to include ethics in education and stressed the importance of "*ethicizing* the world" (2004, p. 7).

A LETTER TO PAULO FREIRE FROM WEST TEXAS

Paulo Freire, humbly seeking to emulate you and honoring your preference for writing your essays in the form of letters (2004), I would like to respond in kind . . .

Similar to you, I consider myself a Christian with more than a tinge of Marxist leanings. As you can expect, neither Marxism nor the liberal brand of Christianity that I embrace is highly regarded here in conservative West Texas, sometimes referred to as "the buckle of the Bible belt." Indeed, Lubbock, the city in which I teach and live, was recently rated as the second most conservative city in the nation (Voting Research, 2005).

Consequently, individuals with Freirean views tend to raise eyebrows. They are frequently looked upon with suspicion, labeled deviant, and pressured into silence. In one of your last essays, "Teaching is a Human Act" (Freire, 2001) you mentioned that one of the signs of the times that alarms you is "the insistence, in the name of democracy, freedom, and efficacy, on asphyxiating freedom itself and, by extension, creativity, and a taste for the adventure of the spirit" (p. 111). Yes, here in West Texas, divergent perspectives and dissent are typically discouraged and, at times, may even prompt allegations of disloyalty to the United States. Nothing, of course, could be farther from the truth. As a loyal U.S. citizen, my goal is to make this nation, a country that purports to be democratic and that pledges "liberty and justice for all," adhere to and honor its professed principles. Paulo, my promise to you is that I will never raise the white flag of fatalism or surrender to "crossing of arms before challenges" (2004, p. 38). Indeed, with the persistent racial injustice here in Texas and elsewhere in the U.S., in addition to the unsettling recent upsurge of racial turmoil in Australia and Europe, people are inclined to say: "Racism will always exist. Nothing can be done to change it." However, Paulo, you have reminded us that "reality, however, is what it is" *only* because "strong interests have the power to make it such" (Freire, 2004, p. 110). Rather than allowing the victims of oppressive economic, political, and social conditions to receive the blame, we must assemble an army of academics dedicated to examining the hegemony, to battling its inherent inequities, and to educating the public with regard to the dynamics behind this fresh wave of racial unrest.

No, Paulo, regardless of the pressure from conservative factions, I refuse to raise the white flag of determinism and surrender to an ideology of fatalism (Freire, 2001). On the one hand, I will continue to loudly denounce the spate of arsons, including the two in Greenville, Texas, of African American and interracial churches, which spiked again in 1996 and which gave rise to the fourth wave of church burnings in U.S. history (Peters, 1998). On the other hand, I will announce and applaud the Church Arson Prevention Act of 1996 (PL 104-155), "which makes it a federal crime to use force or the threat of force to interfere with a person's free exercise of religion" (p. 5), and its use in the recent arrest of a man who had sent an email threat to the El Paso Islamic Center warning that he would destroy the mosque if Iraq did not release imprisoned American hostages within three days (United States Department of Justice, 2004, pp. 4-5). I will continue to denounce racial profiling by Texas law-enforcement officers (Magers, 2005) who, according to one study that controlled for the driver's vehicle and road type, stopped and searched African American males two and a half times more often and Hispanic males four times more often than their White male counterparts (Steward & Berg, 2000). Alternatively, I will announce with pleasure the enactment of a 2001 law (S.B. No. 1074) that prohibits such practices by Texas police, calls for the monitoring of profiling, and requires agencies to submit an annual report. I will make known the dream that Texas will, as did New Jersey, Minnesota, Rhode Island, Hawaii, and California, eventually ban these discriminatory consent searches (Magers, 2005). Moreover, I will vigorously condemn the racially motivated and now-discredited 1999 drug bust in Tulia, Texas, in which 46 people, 39 of whom were Black, were arrested even though no drugs or money were uncovered during the arrests (Blakeslee, 2005; "No more Tulias?, 2005; "Settlement," 2004). Of particular note, some of victims spent four years in prison before their release and pardons by Governor Rick Perry in 2003. Likewise, I will decry the bogus drug bust of 15% of the young, male Black population in Hearne, Texas—arrests "made based on the uncorroborated word of an unreliable confidential informant who later recanted his testimony" ("In wake of," 2005, p. 1). However, I will also unreservedly announce the lawsuit settlements that ensued ("In the wake of," 2005; "Settlement," 2004; "Tulia residents," 2004). In other words, I will persist in the denunciation-annunciation process without renunciation of the task. However, in doing so, in expressing my just ire, I do not seem to easily transition back to a tranquil mental or physical state; I do not easily let go of this anger. Unfortunately for people like me, "some researchers now theorize that it's not just getting angry, but the physical stress of being angry for longer periods of time that takes its toll on cardiovascular health" (Smith, 2003, p. 3).

Anger is an unpleasant emotion state ranging in intensity from mild annoyance to full-blown rage and extreme wrath ("Controlling anger—before it controls you," 2005). Although, as you have pointed out, many persons regard anger as a form of psychopathology that must be kept in check via psychological treatment approaches, you consider it to be an appropriate response to "fatalistic docility," the "adaptation to situations that negate humanization" (Freire, 2004, p. 59), and to the view that change is impossible. Indeed, you even likened this righteous anger to Christ's wrath in the temple (Freire, 2001; "Anger," n.d.), described in John 2: 13-16, when Jesus drove the merchants and the moneychangers out of the holy place because they had made his Father's house of worship a marketplace. Legitimate anger, then, can be useful when it is employed as a tool for social change. Indeed, all great social movements in U.S. history, including the women's suffrage movement in the early 1900s, the anti-lynching movement of the 1930s and '40s, and the civil rights movement of the 1960s, were launched after someone experienced anger (Barker, 2003). Moreover, behavioral scientists agree that when anger is expressed in a constructive manner as did, for example, the Reverend Dr. Martin Luther King, Jr., it can be beneficial in correcting fundamental injustice ("Anger Kills," 1998; Barker, 2003). In a similar manner, Mahatma Gandhi, an advocate for non-violence, learned to convert the raw power of his anger into more creative and productive endeavors ("Anger Kills," 1998; Reder, 2005). Paulo, poem-making (see Fox, 1997, 2003, 2004) is my idiosyncratic means of channeling my anger into a healthier form of expression. Let me explain . . .

However justifiable my anger might be, regrettably, it is nonetheless associated with physiological arousal, including the release of adrenalin, noradrenalin, and cortisol, a stress hormone; an accelerated heart rate; quicker respiration; increases in blood pressure and hyperalertness, what amounts to an overactive sympathetic nervous system or the "fight or flight" response ("Anger Kills," 1998). What is more, research from the field of psychoneuroimmunology indicates that a suppressed immune system may be another end product of anger ("Anger Kills," 1998). Of significant concern to me is that accrued anger over time has been associated with coronary heart disease (CHD) as evidenced in an abnormal electrocardiograph, angina, or heart attack (Scholten, 2003). In essense, then, anger may affect both mental and physical health.

Paulo, as I never had the privilege of meeting you, I have no personal sense of your personality traits, other than at one time your weakness, your Achilles tendon, was smoking (Freire, 2004, p. 28). However, my own personality is best described as Type A behavior pattern, a hard-driven, workaholic, perfectionistic personality style which sometimes also entails a cynical mistrust of other people ("Anger Kills," 1998). Therefore, my expression of "just rage" inevitably triggers the aforementioned aroused sympathetic nervous system response. Buddha averred, "Holding on to anger is like grasping a hot coal with the intent of throwing it at someone else—you are the one getting burned" (cited in Scholten, 2003). Accordingly, to keep my anger from blazing, I employ poem-making (Fox, 2004) as a form of emotion-focused coping and as a catharsis to release my anger (Lazarus & Folkman, 1984).

Psychologists have underscored writing's healing effects, both mental and physical (e.g., Fox, 1997, 2004; Murray, 2002; Pennebaker, 1997). In addition to giving vent to emotions, enlightenment—interpreting and finding meaning from personal experiences—has proven beneficial, particularly since the writer may gain a greater understanding of the positive aspects of the stressful situation (Murray, 2002). Paulo, although plenty of research indicates that writing is therapeutic, I don't need these studies to tell me that writing mitigates the ill effects of my just ire. I subjectively feel more relaxed after poem-making.

One last thing, Paulo . . . although you have on one level left us, you will steadfastly remain with educators, like me, who are your disciples. You are beside me whenever I denounce the racial discrimination at the Lubbock City Cemetery (Pyle, 2004); the 40 hate groups in Texas ("U.S. Map," 2004); the brutal murder of James Byrd, Jr. in Jasper, Texas (Bragg, 1999); or legacy admissions, which give "preference" and "special treatment"—those things that opponents of affirmative action condemn—to children of alumni at Texas A & M and thus inequitably favor White applicants (Harmon, 2004; King, 2004). You live on every time that I announce a more just U.S., and you are present on every occasion that my vigor wanes and I am tempted to renounce the task of "*ethicizing* the world" (Freire, 2004, p. 7), bringing conscience into the knowledge process. You and your teachings will continue to survive. Indeed, my own conscience will continue to heed your guiding words and implement your "pedagogy of indignation" (Freire, 2004), because "not through resignation, but only through rebellion against injustice, can we affirm ourselves" (Freire, 2004, p.61). However, to guard against the adverse physiological and psychological effects of expressing my righteous anger over extended time and to maintain my optimal mental and physical health in order to better battle every form of bigotry, I will soldier on with poem-making. And, Paulo, I extend my apologies for the ham-fisted verse. I know it; I'm *not* a poet. However, this chapter sprang from "the fruit of the lived experience" (Freire, 2001, p. 36) of one White, female, liberal, rapidly aging Professor of American Minorities Studies who, after 15 years in West Texas, is still struggling with culture shock..

REFERENCES

Anger.(n.d.)Retrieved November 28, 2005 from http://www.enpsychlopedia.com/ psypsych/Anger

Anger Kills. (1998, May 1). The health report. Radio National. Retrieved December 20, 2005, from http://www.abc.net.au/rn/talks/8.30/helthrpt/stories/s10309.htm

Aronowitz, S. (2001). Introduction. In: P. Freire. *Pedagogy of freedom: Ethics, democracy, and civic courage* (pp.1-19). Lanham, MD: Rowman & Littlefield Publishers, Inc.

Barker, P. (2003). Anger. University of Colorado, Conflict Research Consortium. Retrieved November 28, 2005, from Beyond Intractability Web site: http://www. beyondintractability.org/m/anger.jsp

Bigelow, W. (1998). Discovering Columbus: Rereading the past. In: W. Bigelow & B. Petersen (Eds.), *Rethinking Columbus* (pp. 100-109). Milwaukee, WI: Rethinking Schools, Ltd.

Blakeslee, N. (2005). *Tulia: Race, cocaine, and corruption in a small Texas town*. New York: PublicAffairs.

Bragg, R. (1999, September 17). Jasper trial defendant says Byrd's throat was cut. *San Antonio Express-News*. Retrieved December 10, 2005, from http://www. texasnaacp.org/jasper.htm

Brown v. Board of Educ., 347 U.S. 483 (1954).

Church Arson Prevention Act of 1996, PL 104-155.

Civil Rights Act of 1964, PL 88-352.

Cohen, J., & Solomon, N. (2001). In: R. Kick (Ed.). *You are being lied to: The disinformation guide to media distortion, historical whitewashes and cultural myths* (p.63). New York: The Disinformation Company, Ltd.

Controlling anger—before it controls you. (2004). Retrieved November 28, 2005, from American Psychological Association Web site: http://apahelpcenter.org/ articles/article. php?id=29

Fox, J. (1997). *Poetic medicine: The healing art of poem-making*. New York, NY: Tarcher/G. P. Putnam's Sons.

Fox, J. (2003). Poems of witness: Living with heart in a conflicted world. Pre-/post-conference workshop conducted at the 23rd annual conference of the National Association for Poetry Therapy, Miami, FL. Retrieved January 31, 2004, from http://www.poetrytherapy.org/conference2003/popup.poemsofwitness.html

Fox, J. (2004). What is poetic medicine: The healing art of poem-making about?   Retrieved January 31, 2004, from http://www.poeticmedicine.com/classes/ poetic_medicine.html

Freire, P. (2001). *Pedagogy of freedom: Ethics, democracy, and civic courage.* Lanham, MD: Rowman & Littlefield Publishers, Inc.

Freire, P. (2004). *Pedagogy of indignation.* Boulder, CO: Paradigm Publishers.

Gross, L. (1991). Out of the mainstream: Sexual minorities in the mass media. In M. A. Wolf & A. P. Kielwasser (Eds.), *Gay people, sex, and the media* (pp. 19-46). New York: Haworth.

Harmon, D. (2004, February 8). Family ties: An unfair advantage? *The Christian Science Monitor.* Retrieved June 14, 2004, from http://www.csmonitor.com/ 2004/0206/p13s01-legn.htm

Heldke, L., & O'Connor, P. (2004). Preface. *Oppression, privilege, and resistance:Theoretical perspectives on racism, sexism, and heterosexism.* Boston: McGraw-Hill.

Hubbard, R. S. (2002, Fall). The truth about Helen Keller. Retrieved December 13, 2005, from the Rethinking Schools Online Web site: http://www. rethinkingschools. org/archive/ 17_01/Kell171.shtml

Ignatiev, N. (2004). Treason to Whiteness is loyalty to humanity. In: L. Heldke & P. O'Connor (Eds.), *Oppression, privilege, and resistance: Theoretical perspectives on racism, sexism, and heterosexism* (pp. 605-610). Boston: McGraw-Hill.

In the wake of ACLU civil rights lawsuit settlement, African Americans affected by Texas Drug Task Force scandal call for reconciliation at town meeting. (2005, June 2). American Civil Liberties Union. Retrieved December 10, 2005, from http://www.aclu.org/drugpolicy/racialjustice/10795prs20050602.html

Kick, R. (Ed.). (2001). *You are being lied to: The disinformation guide to media distortion, historical whitewashes and cultural myths.* New York: The Disinformation Company, Ltd.

King, M. (2004, January 16). Naked city: Texas A & M's racial legacy. *The Austin Chronicle.* Retrieved March 3, 2004, from http://www.austinchronicle.com/ issues/dispatch/nav/ print_or_email.php?URL

Lazarus, R. S., & Folkman, S. (1984). *Stress, appraisal, and coping.* New York: Springer.

Lin, K. (1999, May). When who you are is a gift to the world: An interview with poem-maker John Fox. *The New Times.* Retrieved January 31, 2004, from http://www.newtimes.org/issue/9905/99-05-fox.html

Loewen, J. W. (1995). *Lies my teacher told me: Everything your American history textbooks got wrong.* New York: Touchstone/Simon and Schuster.

Macedo, D. (2001). Foreword. In P. Freire, *Pedagogy of freedom: Ethics, democracy,and civic courage* (pp. xi-xxxii). Lanham, MD: Rowman & Littlefield Publishers, Inc.

Macedo, D. (2004). Foreword. In: P. Freire, *Pedagogy of indignation* (pp. ix-xxv). Boulder, CO: Paradigm Publishers.

Magers, P. (2005, February 24). Analysis: Texas monitors racial profiling. United Press International. Retrieved December 16, 2005, from http://www.washtimes.com/upi-breaking/20050224-061913-1229r.htm

Memmi, A. (1967). *The colonizer and the colonized.* Boston, MA: Beacon Press. (Original French edition, 1957.)

Moane, G. (1999). *Gender and colonialism: A psychological analysis of oppression and liberation.* New York: St. Martin's Press, Inc.

Murray, B. (2002). Writing to heal. *APA Monitor, 33*(6). Retrieved January 20, 2004, from American Psychological Association Web site: http://www.apa.org/monitor/jun02/writing.html

No more Tulias? (2005, October 9). *The Texas Observer.* Retrieved December 10, 2005, from http://www.texasobserver.org/showForPrint.asp?IssueDate=9%2F9%

Pennebaker, J. W. (1997). Writing about emotional experiences as a therapeutic process. *Psychological Science 8*(3), 162-166.

Peters, S. (1998). The press has lost interest, the nation has lost interest, the church arsonists have not. Retrieved December 10, 2005, from http://gbgm-umc.org/ advance/church-burnings/arson.html

Pyle, E. (2004). Oh, bury me not: In Lubbock, racism reaches beyond the grave. *The Texas Observer.* Retrieved October 12, 2005, from http://www.texasobserver.org/showForPrint.asp?IssueDate=12%2F17%@F2004&IssueFo. . .

Reder, A. (2005, August). Unmasking anger. Retrieved November 28, 2005, from *Yoga Journal* Web site: http://www.yogajournal.com/wisdom/805.cfm

Scholten, A. (2003). Hostility, anger, and heart disease. Retrieved October 26, 2005,from Columbia-St.Mary's Hospital Web site: http://healthychoice.epnet.com/getcontent.asp?siteid=csmary&docid=/healthy/mind/2003

Senate Bill No, 1074 (2001, May 24).

Settlement for Tulia's victims. (2004, March 11). *CBS News.* Retrieved December 10, 2005, from http://www.cbsnews.com/stories/2004/03/11/national/printable60522

Smith, D. (2003, March). Angry thoughts, at-risk hearts. *The APA Monitor, 34*(3). Retrieved November 20, 2005, from http://www.apa.org/ monitor/mar03/ angrythoughts.html

Steward, D., & Berg, M. D. (2000). A statistical examination of racial profiling: A preliminary statistical analysis of the search rates of minority and non-minority Texas motorists. Retrieved December 16, 2005, from http://www.txlulac.org/Downloads/racialprofilingreport.pdf/file_view

Sue, D. W., & Sue, D. (1990). *Counseling the culturally different: Theory and practice.* New York: John Wiley and Sons.

Tulia residents awarded $5M after discredited drug bust. (2004, March 11). *USA Today.* Retrieved December 10, 2005, from http://www.usatoday.com/news/nation/2004-03-11-tulia-texas_x.htm

United States Department of Justice, Civil Rights Division. (2004, May). USA Patriot Act leads to arrest in bias crime against El Paso mosque. *Religious Freedom in Focus*, 4. Retrieved December 16, 2005, from http://usdoj.gov/crt.religdisc/ newsletter/focus_4.htm

U.S. map of hate groups in 2004: Active U.S. hate groups: Texas. (2005). Retrieved November 9, 2005, from The Southern Poverty Law Center *Intelligence Project* Web site: http://www.tolerance.org/maps/hate/index.html

Voting Research. (2005, August 11). Study finds southern California cities among the most conservative in America. The Bay Area Center for Voting Research. Retrieved December 13, 2005, from http://www.votingresearch.org

Wise, T. (2003). White supremacy: No one is innocent. Retrieved January 23, 2004, from a web project of the Southern Poverty Law Center Web site: http://www.tolerance.org/news/article_tol.jsp?id=800

ABOUT THE AUTHOR

Virginia J. Mahan, Ed.D., is a Professor of Psychology and Humanities at South Plains College in Levelland, Texas. She has taught multicultural psychology, education, and humanities classes for the last eight years of her 15 years at SPC. Jonathan Kozol, Bell Hooks, Jane Elliott, and William Bigelow are just a few of her many role models.

In: Pioneers in Education: Essays in Honor of Paulo Freire   ISBN: 978-1-60021-479-0
Editors: M.Shaughnessy, E.Galligan et al., pp 41-66   ©2008 Nova Science Publishers, Inc.

Chapter 3

DIALOGUE ON TEACHING PRACTICE AND PRAXIS

Elizabeth A. Galligan and Diane Pinkey

FOREWORD

When we, the authors, asked ourselves about what format to employ in this piece honoring Paulo Freire, we realized there was no better model than the dialogic format used by Freire himself in the "talking books" he co-authored with Donaldo Macedo, Ira Shor, Myles Horton, and others. These books influenced each of us profoundly in our teaching of adult learners. As evolving practitioners of the Freirean approach, we write about our understanding and growth over time in our process of defining ourselves within a critical and transformative pedagogy, as those who are, in Freire's equation, learner/educators and educator/learners. We do not pretend to illuminate further intricacies of Freirean thought and analysis here. We speak as imperfect practitioners who are always in the process of becoming critical pedagogues. We have used the vehicle of dialogue to explore our paths in critical pedagogy with each other, and to facilitate the synergy between us that springs from focused attention and intense dialogue. We hope to open up a conversation with colleagues who also see themselves as change agents, committed to the pursuit of a more just and equitable world.

The authors followed a process based on a dialogic exchange that lasted almost six months. We interacted through our thoughts on paper, found favorite quotes from Freire and others, spoke with each other by phone, taped our conversations, examined them more than once, and continuously processed our reflections about our teaching practice. We have chosen to keep some of the conventions of conversation in this piece to reflect what we believe is an essential aspect of putting Freire's philosophy into practice - the habit of dialoguing with others in reflective ways, not only with fellow educator/learners and learner/educators but also with all of those with whom we share educational spaces. Freire awakened us to a different vision of the role of the teacher and the learner with a vision of education as a process of empowerment:

The role of the educator is not to "fill" the educatee with "knowledge," technical or otherwise. It is rather to attempt to move towards a new way of thinking in both educator and educatee, through the dialogical relationships between both. The flow is in both directions.

In fact, my actual crime was that I treated literacy as more than a mechanical problem, and linked it to conscientização*, which was "dangerous." It was that I viewed education as an effort to liberate men, not as yet another instrument to dominate them.

Paulo Freire resurrected the term "authentic" and suggested it as a yardstick by which every cultural worker, every learner/educator and every educator/learner could take a true measure of herself or himself. Do I walk my talk? Do I mean and practice what I think I mean and ought to practice? Do my actions and my words form a seamless continuum? Am I, as a teacher, authentic, or am I a sham, an imposter, a puppet who merely mouths words and speaks with a flannel tongue? When Paulo Freire, was working with UNESCO on literacy programs throughout the world, he was asked to oversee a program in Guinea-Bissau. He contested the idea of using the "language of the colonizers" in a program for the people even though it was his own Portuguese that was to be used. Freire believed this practice devalued the mother tongues of the people. Although Freire argued long and hard with the government, for practical and political reasons, and the greater good, he finally conceded. Nonetheless, Freire became a hero for bilingual educators, as an advocate who brought to the attention of the world the oppressive yoke of the imposed/forced acquisition of a foreign tongue and the subjugation of indigenous languages. That stance carries great meaning for us personally as former English as a Second Language teachers.

Freire never shied away from speaking *truth* to *power*. His actions were congruent with his words. He proposed that interior conviction and outward action be identical; he was one who "walked his talk" and exhorted others to do so. Freire had a fierce focus, an eye like a magnifying glass, when he looked at the causes of vast disparities between men and women based on race, class, gender, education, economic states, and the effects of historical-social-cultural factors. Paulo examined the verticality of the differential power structures which allocate different amounts of power to those within those structures. Freire instead conceived of the novel and hopeful notion that since institutional structures of power were man-made, they could be unmade. The conceptual framework Paulo envisioned was a move away from obstruction into *construction*, then to *deconstruction* which pulled apart the walls, floor boards, and ceilings and said, "Let's begin again," keeping in mind the dignity and worth of every person so that by his or her *reconstruction* of our world, that world ultimately will become a beautiful mansion.

Here the authors feel an emotional and philosophical connection with Paulo ~ his pedagogy of hope. We believe that Paulo Freire had the extraordinary effect that he did because he challenged us to confront our own "inauthenticities" and to realign ourselves with our vision. In that sense, Paulo Freire may be considered the chiropractor of human alignment; he straightened our spines; he helped the poor to walk upright rather than stooped; he raised our vision; he looked us straight in the eye, and he exhorted us to transform ourselves and, then, the world. In 1996 at the *Pedagogy of the Oppressed* Conference (POC)

*conscious critical awareness (Freire, 1969/1973/1994)

in Omaha, Nebraska, the year before he died, Paulo left us this gentle and hopeful observation: "I envision a world in which it is easier to laugh" (Galligan, 1996).

CONVERSATION/DIALOGUE ABOUT PRACTICE

EAG: Within the confines of hierarchical, fixed systems, it is not always easy to practice critical pedagogy. Many forces of the status quo are aligned against changes to any power structure. Our challenge is to oppose the sad reality that within the common structures of schooling, one's beliefs have been stuffed, suppressed, or submerged. One of my concerns for us as practitioners, then, is about congruence, walking our talk. In my notes from the *Pedagogy of the Oppressed Conference* held in 1996 in Omaha, Nebraska that you and I attended the year before Paulo died, I noted the response to a question from a man from Malta who asked, "How do I remain tactically an insider and strategically an outsider in trying to resist?"

That question plagues all of us, I think. I was a little nervous about what Freire's response might be. I don't have the exact words, but the gist of his reply was that it is possible to contest existing structures from within and that we need not be apologetic about being within those hierarchical structures if we are ourselves are listening, reflecting, and developing a "coalitional identity" (Galligan, 1996). Nonetheless, it's not always easy to practice pedagogy of liberation within the structures of higher education. For example, how can I, according to Freire's ideas for liberatory practice, write a syllabus before a class meets and hand it out on the first day when I don't know who is going to be in the room?

DP: I know that concern well. Last year, I taught a Foundations class for the teaching license program at the community college. It was one of those classic last minute hire situations, so I had no syllabus. I started the class with half of a very generalized syllabus because I wasn't sure what we would do in the class. It was interesting to see students' reaction to not coming on the first day with a syllabus. I observed that some students wanted that syllabus very much. One student was insistent that I give her a formalized agenda; she criticized me strongly in the class evaluation because I failed to present a completed syllabus. Yet several other students saw that I was allowing the curriculum to develop and acknowledged my choice. One student mentioned, "I just wanted to tell you how much I appreciated your following and not dominating the agenda. I can tell you worked deliberately and purposefully at modeling that not doing dominating the agenda. The belief of "flow that goes in both directions," of that learner/teacher knowledge exchange, takes hard work and courage to create. We must truly believe in fostering relationships of mutual respect as well as work hard at making them happen. Certainly Freire talks about our unique and powerful opportunity to create expanded relationships when he says, "We are the only beings capable of being both the objects and subjects of the relationships that we weave with others and with the history that we make and that makes and remakes us" (Freire, 1998).

EAG: Even when one is intellectually a critical educator, the traditional practices within education institutions such as lock-step coverage of assigned texts and material, devaluing of teachers, the "banking" mentality that is practiced, (the teacher deposits knowledge and the students withdraw it for tests) decision-making by others, and the limited opportunity of teachers in schools to select their materials all militate against the careful consideration, dialogue, and action that foster learning and change (praxis). At the university level, there are always syllabi to be prepared in advance of knowing the make-up of the class, a fixed duration in which to cover material, and differential power allotted to professor and student.

DP: I agree. In the higher education classroom where we both currently teach, we have no idea of the knowledge and experience students bring with them to the group. Nor can we determine what will develop as the students dialogue and learn together. This is always a consideration. Decisions about curriculum or course requirements are often made by the teacher or administrators in the department, not by the class participants. These restrictions and practices do militate against the idea of praxis. The reflection that needs time and space to bloom and ideally lead to action is often pruned in favor of covering course content. We unconsciously insist that the learning of the word as well as the learning of the world, occur in the classroom when it often takes place out in the world, away from the ivory tower. We place the classroom at the center of students' lives when it's not where they place it. Even those of us who think we are very "Freirean" because we have adopted the terminology come to view Freire's vision for education in the way he asked us not to, as a methodology. He warned of the possible outcome of that recipe approach. Freire reminded us of the following:

> Unfortunately, those who espouse the cause of liberation are themselves surrounded and influenced by the climate that generates the banking concept, and often do not perceive its true significance or its dehumanizing power...Authentic liberation - the process of humanization - is not another deposit to be made in men [or women, ed.]. Liberation is a praxis: the action and reflection of men upon their world in order to transform it...Those truly committed to liberation must reject the banking concept in it entirety, adopting instead a concept of men as conscious beings, and consciousness as consciousness intent upon the world (Freire, 1970,1993,1995).

EAG: In thinking about how knowledge is passed on, I remember a conversation between Freire and Ira Shor talking about knowledge. Shor says that knowledge in traditional education is "handed on as a corpse of information", "a dead body of knowledge, [when] that knowledge does not have "a living connection" [to the learners' reality]. He also observed that "learning is just a chore imposed on students by the droning voice of the official syllabus" (Shor and Freire, 1987). My favorite part is this: "Students are motivated out of the learning process when the course fully exists in the mind of the teacher, in the syllabus, reading list, and state requirements. *The learning has already happened someplace else* (Shor and Freire, 1987).

The truth of that last statement really resonates with me: I'm the one who is doing most of the learning if I fail to involve the students. When we are not allowing the students into the process, not listening nor co-creating the learning, we have fallen back into the old mold of, to use Freire's term, "banking education, in which, as he said, "we look upon content as something magical, ...something neutral that only need be deposited for its power to effect the desired change " (Freire, 1992, 1994). Freire in his view of pedagogy describes the production of knowledge rather as something that " involves action, critical reflection, uncertainty, curiosity, demanding inquiry, uneasiness - all these virtues go to the "cognitive subject," the one who learns"[emphasis added]. (Shor and Freire, 1987b). We need to remember this.

In one of his reflective essays on education, Freire strongly criticized Brazilian agricultural extension workers (and anyone who superimposes their knowledge on the people). Freire deconstructed the idea of "extension" in the sense of "I am extending this to you," a paternalistic attitude that implies power-over, and implies that all other power-over relationships oppose the importance of communication and dialogue. Freire said again and again that you have to listen to the people to hear the knowledge that is true folklore, or "country knowledge."

DP: Or "everyday knowledge."

EAG: Yes. When Freire connects the act of participation in the structures of society with a chance to analyze critically one's reality, the word and the world, (Freire and Macedo, 1987a,), we see how he places trust in the people's "everyday knowledge" and how he connects that knowledge to action in the world. The word that expresses this so well in Portuguese is "engajamento," engagement. To be engaged in action and to be engaged also in the sense of commitment and action, in participation that leads to the full flowering of the people.

> I was convinced that the Brazilian people could learn social and political responsibility only by *experiencing* that responsibility, through intervention in the destiny of their children's schools, in the destinies of their trade unions and places of employment through associations, clubs, and councils, and in the life of their neighborhoods, churches and rural communities by actively participating in associations, clubs, and charitable societies (Freire, p. 36). They could be helped to learn democracy through the *exercise* of democracy;...[it] can only be assimilated experientially....Nothing threatened the popular emergence more thán an educational practice which failed to offer opportunities for the analysis and debate of problems, or for genuine participation... {This was a }new stance toward their problems - that of intimacy with those problems, one oriented toward research an education of "I wonder" (Freire, 1994/1973).

DP: These issues of participation are concerns for us in trying to be authentic. I thought immediately of our nation's (the United States) quick call and response to invade Iraq. We invade a country in the guise of liberators, and there is no liberation or can be no liberation *because the struggle is not coming from the people*. I always wrestle with understanding and defining the place of the teacher in the classroom. It is a constant concern in any community work as well where we ask people to trust us in our roles as educators. My recent experience with the Santa Fe Living Wage campaign made me once again examine the development of the organizing effort at the grassroots. Freire notes that "Those who authentically commit themselves to the people must re-examine themselves constantly (Freire 1970,1993,1995).

EAG: You have had many experiences as an educator working on grassroots issues. How did the Living Wage Campaign fit into Freirean ideas?

DP: Because I believe in grassroots organizing, I was worried about the development of the campaign to raise the minimum wage as a top down initiative. First, the issue moved forward through the City Council to a roundtable of mayor-appointed delegates charged with developing an ordinance that both Labor and Business could live with. The campaign then developed primarily as a force of progressive activists in the community. In time, there was a building of a coalition with the local immigrant rights organization, Somos un Pueblo Unido, (We are a United People) as well as local churches, unions, and human rights organizations.

I think the Living Wage Network (as the campaign came to be named) is working to build more from the grassroots now that the ordinance is in place and the wage increase gets set to raise another $1 per hour. It seems odd in some ways to me that there wasn't a larger group of folks who called the issue their own, engaging in the struggle to increase the wage. But, maybe, now that the ordinance has put the wage increase in place, people will join the struggle to keep it in place and fight for the step increases in the wage that were written into the ordinance. We are now facing some opposition from a few city councilors.

I have a story that might support my hope that there can be many ways to see an organizing effort develop. Last year I started working with a College of Santa Fe student, Sara, who is making a documentary on the effects of the wage increase in Santa Fe. The film will add another view, outside of the City of Santa Fe's contracted research with the University of New Mexico that includes focus groups. The documentary intends to bring forth voices of people who were affected by the wage increase. Others, besides me, are concerned about the missing voices in the telling of the Living Wage story. These voices will remain anonymous or un-represented in the UNM focus group data; they are voices that will be silent in the shadow of more vocal and represented business owners and officials. The whole idea of anonymity in the focus groups is understood, i.e. as protection from bosses' retaliation, but remaining anonymous is problematic from an organizing perspective, right? After all, how can people develop solutions to their problems when they must remain invisible and ultimately, subjects of the research?

Back to the story... as a way to find unheard or unengaged voices, Sara and I decided to create a paper and pencil survey and use the survey to start a conversation/dialogue on the living wage ordinance and its impact in the community. I use the survey in my Developmental Writing classes; and it is working. Developing an interest, some students have studied the issue for their research projects; they have interviewed teen workers at the high school, small business owners, and immigrant workers. I was amazed at how many students knew so little about the ordinance except for media reports that the wage increase was forcing businesses to close and driving up the costs of goods, even gas!!! As part of the survey, students write about making ends meet in Santa Fe. I am amazed at what our community college students juggle and struggle with to work, to go to school, and to care for their families. I know I never faced their challenges when I was coming of age. After dialogue on the wage increase, just this week, one 18 year-old student made a statement at a press conference; she engaged in a brave action to speak publicly in support of the upcoming hourly wage increase. The survey is a good beginning for developing more grassroots interest from new viewpoints: the engagement of workers who are also students or students who are also workers. It offers a way for students to participate in the wage increase conversation.

EAG: Your efforts have helped introduce other voices that were left out of the conversation. You are uniting those voices with the ideas that came from the top down, and providing a place for different perspectives. It sounds very Freirean to me.

DP: Whether we are talking about Iraq or any grassroots human rights issue in which the "liberators" decide what's best for the people and fail to include the people who are directly influenced by the libratory actions, it makes no sense to me. Freire asks us to examine who we want to be when he states that "a real humanist can be identified more by his trust in the people, which engages him in their struggles, than by a thousand actions in their favor without that trust" (Freire1970,1993,1995). He cautions us to be mindful of the difference between being humanitarian and being humanist like when we *do for* rather than provide for a way for others to *do for themselves* in struggle. Those who authentically commit themselves to the people must reexamine themselves around this idea of being humanist. Teachers are constantly dealing with their own contradictions. As you mentioned, this reflection emerges when we start examining what's happened over the years and find ourselves being more authoritarian. We catch that tendency within ourselves and then step back from it and say, "Wait a second. What am I doing? This isn't who I want to be."

EAG: So, we put it in that process of continuing the reflective practice into looking at what we're doing. We're not expected to be perfect.

DP: You're right.

EAG: I like what you said about the distinction between being humanitarian, which is paternalistic and top down vs. being humanistic. It applies to our discussion on the function of democratic governance.

Our current situation in the United States really makes the question of "government by the people" new again, doesn't it? When people have no voice in their governance or naming their own reality, there is a dangerous alchemy that takes place: although we may be against the decisions at the top, they are made in our name. As time goes on, we are implicated in those positions and inadvertently we become aligned in some ways with those forces, whether it is the state, the institution, the government The process of co-opting the people's voices has the effect of changing those who are in favor of peace, for example, into seemingly supporting those who support war. We see this in our own country today. How do you think the wearing down of forces for change to more equitable conditions affects us in eroding the idealism and the vision that Paulo gave us?

DP: It is fitting to re-visit the meaning of idealism. I find refuge in Freire as I consider the challenges in our country today where idealism is seen as foolish. Naysayers (the dominant elite voices) view idealism as ridiculous; they clearly and adamantly express this view publicly. Look at talk radio! These dominant voices express pessimism in our dream of liberation; the negative voices shout us into silence. And we are seeing that articulation of negativity more and more; this is a debilitating turn. Who would have believed the deep impact of the reactionary upheaval that has occurred in the last 30 years... to think about where we are today with coming out of our experiences in the 60's and the 70's when our idealism was so high? Even young people will speak of political interest as "thinking like a hippie". It is such a distortion of the historical vestiges of social change when idealism is seen as some impossible dream. Young people face a hard road by lacking the belief in a dream of liberation. As teachers, we cannot drink the poison of pessimism. I embrace Freire's language of truth...of hope.

EAG: One of my favorite quotes from Paulo himself occurred during his address upon reception of his honorary doctorate from the University of Nebraska, in 1966. In that speech, Freire said "Hope is an ontological necessity."... It is intrinsic to our development as human beings." He even called the book in which he revisits and critiques his own life's journey, *Pedagogy of Hope* (1992/1994).

I believe that this hopefulness is the key for people who embrace the philosophy of liberatory pedagogy, and the reason we keep going back to it. The approach is founded so strongly on a positive view of human agency and human ability, a pedagogy that asserts the hopeful vision that since structures are made by humans, they can be unmade and then remade in a more just and humane way. This, to me, is really the essence of why Paulo Freire continues to inspire us. Within the struggle, one can become discouraged, but the hard times do not destroy the vision. But, as I think you said to me once, you have to count your small successes.

I have a story, too. In Clovis, New Mexico there is a teacher whose sixth grade students took action to change the name of the street their school is located on from Jefferson to "Cesar Chavez". These youngsters did their research, wrote letters to garner support, and found out how to go before the City Council and other entities. Some university faculty members even received personal hand-written letters from these kids asking for their support. Each letter was signed by an individual student. So, after some groundwork, the students went to the City Council with their request. Ultimately, the students were successful and the name of the street will be changed.

These students have had an experience of "fighting City Hall" and being successful. The youngsters themselves appeared on a local television station, explaining the work they had done, the surveys they created, and how they arrived at their proposal so they were able to share their success with a wider audience. This teacher used a very Freirean approach. She encouraged her students to pose the problem, reflect on the situation, decide what to do about it, show why the street should be renamed, and, with her guidance, they were inspired to participate in the structures of their reality as Paulo advocated. That, to me, is an excellent application of praxis. So, you need those small successes as we mentioned before.

DP: Hurrah for them! I want to talk about power and voice because I have changed my own use of language over time; I made a purposeful decision to get rid of this word "empowerment." It is time for mediated power to go, and it's time to return to using the word "power" - and using the word purposefully. Our power has been firmly and effectively taken away from us by creation of laws and policies that have been put in place in the last thirty years. This usurpation of power has resulted in a silencing of civic voices. The legal support for taking our power is a great disservice to the democracy and civic participation. What once was framed as the challenge of "fighting city hall" is now recognized in the somewhat frightening realization that the challenge is more like overthrowing the government. This impossible and undesirable task fosters apathy in participation and cynicism in government. For example, *The Patriot Act of 2001* is legislation that takes away our rights of participating in our democracy. Now it's become unlawful to dissent, to wear a political T-shirt, to take part in an anti-war rally. Imagine! We will be breaking the law as we engage with students, neighbors, and people in the community when we participate in the democracy through struggle or dissent.

EAG: Even small limitations of our freedoms can be disconcerting. Recently, I was putting out flyers on campus about a free movie to be held at the public library by a group of citizens concerned about civil rights and the right to dissent. The University secretary told me that "they" had changed the policy at the university about what you can put on a bulletin board and in mail boxes and what you can't. She said "I'll have to check on this". And I said, "Some of the people are members of this organization. May I put this in *their* mailboxes?" The answer was, "I don't think so". So, in a miniscule gesture of defiance, I put flyers only in mailboxes of the people I knew. All of a sudden, I felt that doors to free speech were slamming shut in the very hallways of my own institution.

We are so used to the erosion of freedom to contest limits on our actions in the educational institutions that many people don't even question it. Why is that? Universities used to be the core of academic freedom, the sites where you heard different viewpoints. Now we have all kinds of strictures on participatory democracy on whatever level. With Freire, the whole idea of education is tied to the notion of participatory democracy. Freire saw the people must participate in their own reality; their thoughts and ours must be valued; we all merit a hearing.

DP: Absolutely. Even children must be heard and encouraged to participate, like the children in Clovis did. Your reflection on a success story leads me to one I witnessed. It is a story about gaining voice in a family. I participated in this story as a GED teacher and as a friend. You and I know well these stories from our work in adult literacy classrooms. A supervisor at the Wastewater Treatment Plant at the City of Santa Fe did not have a high school diploma or GED. At that time, City Hall had changed all the job descriptions to require that credential. Since he was a supervisor, this worker was being pushed by the City training administrator to get his GED (General Education Diplomas) in accordance with the new requirement. The man had tried but couldn't pass the GED tests. On the day he told me his story about his struggle to learn to read and write, and how when his boss told him he must pass the tests or lose his job, he wept! I remember being so angry at the power of literacy to harm, what J. Elspeth Stuckey might call an example of "the violence of literacy" (Stuckey, 1991).

But the literacy story shines in a better light in the next generation when this supervisor's son *does* pass his GED tests after attending our workplace class in his work department at Parks and Recreation. His son then leads the drive to unionize public employees at the City which results in the development of the City AFSCME Union Local. Eventually, he becomes the Union's Local President. Last summer, at the one year celebration of the Santa Fe Living Wage ordinance, this former student and City Local Union President introduced me to his 13 year old son by saying, "This is the person that helped me get my high school diploma." I felt great pride at that moment to see the good of literacy work that finally emerged and created a voice of consequence coming forth from the Chavez family. I know for a fact that the diploma credential was nixed for a number of jobs at the City when the Union pushed for the change.

EAG: What a perfect example of how literacy was both a tool for "power over" and a tool for liberation!

DP: Both you and I come out of a background in Adult Basic Education (ABE) We were attracted to the field by the possibility to bring social justice into literacy work. We were drawn to the opportunity to work with adults who may have struggled in traditional schooling, who were "different" learners, who were giving their education a second chance, and we surely did embrace the lack of restrictions and constraints noteworthy of traditional schooling. We seized the freedom to experiment with what and how we could teach. Neither of us came out of a teacher education background; we both, in many ways, learned to teach by teaching. It's Myles Horton's belief that "we make the road by walking" (Horton & Freire, 1990). We fell in love with our students, and what they taught us about learning, as well as teaching, what they shared about their lives, as well as what they revealed about our own lives. We love them because they keep us human! Even given freedom outside hierarchical structures, we still have to re-learn to gain our freedom to participate in critical pedagogy. Each of us in the educational experience is acculturated to common structures, so we may, unreflectively, teach as we have been taught. We assume the pose of teaching that has been modeled throughout our schooling; our students assume the "learner pose" as well.

One change in my beliefs that colors everything I do is my acceptance of the slow pace of change. If we are serious about fostering critical consciousness, we must accept that our presence in the learning process may be long extinguished; students may arrive later rather than sooner in their awakening, their liberation. As teachers, we may never see the fruit of our labor. So we sow seeds, but there is hope.

I think of how the work I did on the Living Wage Campaign brought students into the conversation on the issue, but who knows where it will lead students in their own liberation? I see students "drop out" of school. The tendency is to blame them for not "making the grade." Yet, they may have to leave school for any number of reasons, even though they would prefer to stay. Sometimes, they need to earn money because they no longer have child care, or they need to care for a sick family member, or they want the chance to work in a job where they get other educational experiences. This morning I went to breakfast at a local restaurant and ran into Esther, an older student who withdrew from all of her classes this semester because her husband lost his job. She was picking up extra hours. She said, "I'm not giving up..." and then added wistfully, "Now I'll have to take all of that English class over again." So the college will count her as a "non-completer;" but I don't.

I'm certain she doesn't see herself as such, but what action will change the thinking of administration focused on their definition of success in college? Reflection on issues of concern in the classroom is one small moment in the liberation process, but moving forward to action is more elusive.

As you say, we can intellectually view ourselves as critical educators, but are we really what we say we are? This question keeps us engaging our understanding of our own authenticity. We started this conversation by using the metaphor of construction and building of a more human world - the construction of the mansion. That metaphor made me think of Martin Luther King Jr.'s framework of the "world house," and I imagined the dialogue between Freire and King. It seems fitting to bring these two voices together to shine light on the "good fight", wherever it may be waged. We are so hungry for inspiration in these regressive times, in this time of war, the war on terrorism. The language of the oppressor resonates in all corporate media and confounds our ability to "speak truth to power."

King envisioned a world house in which we would come to live together in peace by addressing problems of racism and economic exploitation, poverty and materialism, and war. We would have to construct this house. As educators, that construction does indeed come from de-constructing the "official word". As educators, this is our assignment, so we can reflect on how productively we fulfill this task. Tell your story of how Freire came into your life; it is a story many educators may not know. You experienced the political upheavals in Brazil in the 1960s that forced Freire to flee his own country.

EAG: My acquaintance with Paulo Freire and his pedagogy began in Brazil in 1962 when I went as a volunteer to work with an international organization. At the time, I was very conservative and conventional, and I was slow to change my views. I consider myself now very lucky to have been in Brazil from 1962-65 at a time of boiling political and social conflict. I was there before the military overthrew the government and after. That's an important part of my own life story.

Social action was the tenor of the times in Brazil in the 1960s. Faced with the "realidade brasileira," the Brazilian reality, and the dramatic problems of a developing third world country. Reformers' concerns included land reform, issues of the poor, illiteracy, education, and the dramatic inequalities between the wealthy and the poor. Brazilians at that time also had strong sense of nationalism and began to reject imperialism and outsiders' ideas. But the reactionaries opposed the notion of educating the poor; they opposed land reform; they despised activists of all stripes.

Ironically, there were groups of many stripes in Brazil at the time: Chinese Communists, Russian Marxists, Socialists, and the left wing of the Catholic Church, among others, but there were some common goals. As a result, in that charged atmosphere, we all marched together. I remember once our little band of women from different countries was marching in the streets of Sao Paulo under the banner of "O Frente Unida" – "the United Front". What united us was the belief that reform had to occur in order to create a more just and equitable society. We marched together even though the actual ideologies and strategies for change were dramatically different between groups. The movement for much needed social reform was disparaged by the right as" revolutionary,""comunista," socialista", "marxista", "leftist."

Those with vested interests, - the powerful, the rich, most politicians, and the conservative majority of the Catholic Church - reacted vociferously because they feared the loss of power. The right responded to increasing demands for social reform and social justice with tremendous fear and resistance to any reforms. Why did the powerful react so violently? They feared the voice of the people, people who could think for themselves; they did not want a literate and informed population.

By 1963, it was becoming clear that serious confrontation between the right and the left was looming. Nonetheless, members of our organization were encouraged to volunteer with the National Campaign for Literacy (alfabetizacao) with Paulo Freire as its director. Each of us enthusiastically filled out little enrollment cards as volunteers to work with this "revolutionary" literacy program although I didn't know much about the Freirean "approach" at the time. In fact, the first time I heard about "problem-posing" as a teaching methodology, I didn't get it. My initial reaction was that teachers were not supposed to be problem-posers; they were supposed to be *problem-solvers* because they had the answers. I thought the questioning process, this so-called critical pedagogy, would a useless and pointless waste of time. Luckily, others wiser than I, urged me to go to the Universidad de São Paulo in January, 1964, to hear Paulo Freire, the professor whose ideas were creating such a stir. There was standing-room only in the auditorium. The room was electric, the energy was strong, the enthusiasm palpable. As I recall, Paulo Freire, diminutive, dark-haired, forceful, and eloquent, spoke of the inadequacy of the traditional educational system and the role of literacy in the development of a real democracy. In Brazil at the time, many people were receptive to the idea that real change was possible. The country was on the move. Many were already engaged in the movement for social justice; I began to understand and analyze poverty, power, and social issues in ways I never had; it was exciting.

Unfortunately, I never had the opportunity to actually practice the Freirean approach or work with the literacy program in Brazil because on April 4, 1964, the military stepped in and took over the government in a bloodless coup d'etat. Civilian rule was suspended. The country was in the hands of what became a long-term military dictatorship. It was a very anxious time for all of us. From one day to the next after the coup, all major newspapers were shut down across the country. On the radio, the only thing one could hear was martial music; the news was completely controlled and limited to occasional communiques or instructions from the new "rulers." Communications between the states were cut off ; access to news or events in other states of Brazil was limited and controlled. During the reign of terror and torture that followed, both the military and the police were identical in their trampling of civil rights. They silenced their opposition, dismantled many of the reforms for social justice; shut down incipient community groups like the "circulos de cultura "[culture circles], arrested anyone suspected of anti-government activity, picked up people for questioning for no apparent reason and held them without any compunction; enforced limits on free speech, assembly, and forbid any criticism of the (new) government. People were arrested simply for having a copy of Mao Tse-Tung's *Little Red Book* on the bookshelf. Can you believe it?

After the coup, the new "rulers" implemented various modes of torture for those who were thought to have been subversives; this policy lasted for almost twenty years until the country returned to civilian rule. Shortly after the coup, someone from the government even came to inspect those little inscription cards in the files in our group's headquarters to discover the names of those who had signed up as literacy volunteers with Freire. I realized then the power of the state. All of us were suspected of actions against the government and were possibly at risk just because we wanted to be part of the Campaign for Literacy - and justice.

What did I learn by being in Brazil at this "elbow of time," a time when everything took a dramatically different turn? Because of the 1964 coup, I learned that fascism was fascism whether from the right or the left; I saw firsthand that the abuse of power by the state was awesome and ugly. I learned how much power the government could exert against its "enemies". From these experiences, I learned why Freire's work for the poor and for literacy was considered dangerous. I saw how Paulo become anathema in Brazil; at the time, I had not known that one could be summarily deprived of all civil rights, but that's what the new government did to Freire. The government suspended his civil rights ("cassarem su mandato"). Because of the lack of any civil rights, Freire was completely vulnerable and without protection of law. Freire had to leave the country like a criminal fugitive! He remained in exile from Brazil for many years. This experience taught me a sense of the importance of that "eternal vigilance" that Thomas Jefferson said was "the price of freedom". Freire's leadership and commitment to the literacy and freedom movement was a threat to the powerful. I finally realized what the Campaign for Literacy meant: literacy meant the power to resist oppressive limitations created by others; literacy offered the opportunity to take charge of one's own life, to become "knowing subjects."

Through my own eyes, I saw the importance of resistance and actions for freedom. My respect for Freire and the need for a critical pedagogy that questioned inequities evolved from watching that brave struggle in the context of Brazil. As I have said ever since: "Brazil humanized me." Perhaps now I would say that it politicized me.

Brazil changed my life and my politics in profound ways by understanding of class and oppression, race, power, and of myself. The implications for me now are to re-read Freire's works, return more deeply to those commitments, and live them out in profound and authentic ways, and not to worry so much about the cost to me or to my career. About twenty years later, I re-engaged with those experiences when I began to work on a doctorate. The first paper I wrote was about Paulo Freire; I called it "Curriculum Construction: P. Freire and Associates, Building Contractors." (Galligan, 1991,unpublished ms.)

Finally, I had a chance to explore the works of Freire and others who embraced his philosophy of education, such as Peter McLaren, Michael Apple, Nina Wallerstein, Antonia Darder, Patti Lather, bell hooks, Joel Spring and other intellectuals who espoused the pedagogy of transformation. Some of Freire's approach to teaching had come naturally to me in the intervening twenty-some odd years of teaching ESL to adults from various social strata and national origin. As one of my university mentors affirmed, "You have a teaching philosophy; you just don't know it has a name." Its name was critical pedagogy and its primary proponent was Paulo Freire. After other encounters with Freire on the page, I knew where I stood. I have considered myself a "Freirean" ever since. That's a very long answer as to how my thinking has evolved. Wow! How about you?

DP: I didn't have a 1960s experience with Freire. My introduction took place in the 1980s when I took part in the literacy campaign that swept through the U.S. at that time. Progressive educators in adult basic education were all discovering or rediscovering Freire at that time, I believe. Many teachers who were doing literacy work looked to Freire for a pedagogical grounding. It made sense since he had led the Brazilian literacy campaign. *Pedagogy of the Oppressed* (1970/1993/1995) was being read by a new audience of educators. I can't help but consider the irony that the public spokesperson for literacy was Barbara Bush while the private leader for many was Paulo Freire. During the 1980s, I joined with a group of educators in Rhode island who were getting together to talk about the politics of literacy and share ideas for practice in Adult Basic Ed, GED, and ESL classes in community and workplace settings. This was a very important time for me, for my development as a learner and teacher. It was authentic... that peer group studying and learning together: experimenting with Freirean ideas in the classroom and sharing success and failure. We were all creating and sharing materials to use as codes in problem posing.

In the Workplace Adult Education Program classes (ESL and GED), I was having students build the curriculum. We toured factories as a class; in one factory the immigrant union members got the union contract to use for class curriculum; most had never seen their union contract before taking these classes. The contract was also written in English, and many of the factory employees' first language was Cape Verde Creole and Portuguese. I got in a lot of trouble with the union too; they didn't want the workers to see what was going on in the contract pay scales. I think because the wage formulas were complicated, perhaps, hard to explain. At that time, building the curriculum offered a great deal of freedom. I count myself lucky, since Union-Management workplace education programs proceeded with little interference from bureaucracies of "banking" ideas of education. I felt that I could take risks and hire teachers to do the same because we were our own school. We were not scrutinized by the state governed program; we were always teaching off site from high schools where traditional GED and ESL classes usually took place.

Even in the 1990s when I was doing GED for the City of Santa Fe, we offered classes in Parks department garages or City fire stations; those classes were free of scrutiny from the "data collectors." Sorry if I digress, but I need to get in my dig at data collection as it has taken on such significance in the offering of Adult Basic Education today! Of course, I'm critical of the level of accountability required for the small pittance of money offered to help adults read, write, and learn English compared with the unexamined showering of billions of dollars on the Pentagon and the Defense Department endeavors. Back to the workplace...By working off-site, we also could create classrooms that didn't have to look like the dreaded environments so held in contempt by students who hated school. And yet, school for some would continue to be the "bane." I always used to ask students individually, "Did you have a class you liked, or a teacher you liked when you were in school?" One student's answer always haunts me, "I never had a class I liked; I never had a teacher I liked; I just didn't like school." Period! Punto! At the time, I couldn't bring myself to believe him; now I do. Now I've heard the story told many times over.

EAG: That's another part of art of the liberatory aspect of "education for freedom," the setting and the ability to experiment, to be able to push the envelope. Teaching from this perspective almost demands that you have a special kind of physical freedom, - that your conditions somehow support your efforts. I don't think those conditions occur very frequently in our own educational institutions in general.

DP: I agree. The question is whether or not we can create those conditions within the school, college walls. The 1980s literacy movement in the United States was a fertile time in some ways. Once again -I don't want to be nostalgic for the good ol' days - but the good old days provided opportunities to take risks in our classrooms. When I was doing workplace education, I was removed from view, for the most part. Nobody was asking, "Are you using the official GED books?"

EAG: It was about the same time of the U.S. national concern about literacy, the country was celebrating the quincentennial. That's when I took a photograph of graffiti spray-painted in red on the side of a building in Santa Fe; the *placa* said " 1492-1992 - 400 years of resistance". That was real; that was authentic; that was a visual made for a Freirean deconstruction. I've used *that* picture in many classes; I still use do. In a wonderful bit of irony, the actual building on which those words of resistance appeared belonged to the local *power* company! How appropriate! Talking about this makes me realize I'm not using as much authentic materials about real lives and authentic situations as I used to. I don't problematize the visuals that I use in class. Sometimes I do have people walk around the classroom to reflect on specific and concrete situations. But, I do this less now because this process takes reflection and, as we have discussed, the system is not set up to allow time for that reflection stage.

DP: Returning to my rite of passage to critical pedagogy... by coincidence, my first Paulo Freire introduction also centered on problem posing. As mentioned earlier, it came to me through conversations with adult educators In Rhode Island who were teaching in community ESL programs, a homeless literacy program, a women's literacy program, state-funded ABE as well as workplace literacy classes. One teacher brought in a workbook created by Elsa Auerbach and Nina Wallerstein's *ESL for Action, Problem Posing at Work* (1987). The book showed how to use codes, develop dialogue, and introduce ideas for taking action. Now we had a model, a starting place. The ESL workbook provided a way to practically put theory to work by using "codes" to develop lessons; it was a useful guide. I then had to work backwards from practice to learn about Paulo Freire's theory. There are so many stories to tell about the experimentation with teaching and the great moments of learning that transpired!

At the time, I was working to develop the Workplace Adult Education Project through the Institute for Labor Studies and Research in Rhode Island. I was teaching in some unionized factories where the majority of the immigrant workforce had been in the country for many years. Many had never taken an ESL class before, so I watched as older workers, in a sense, came back to school. Some wanted their GED diplomas, because that credential now seemed possible. Their union jobs provided good wages and job security, and then just as we were getting down to the business of learning, all of a sudden, job outsourcing to Mexico to the *maquilladora* raised righteous concern. Suddenly, the education and the diploma became more critical because workers saw that they could be headed for unemployment and new, perhaps more skilled, work. Now we faced a real problem with plant closure and job elimination. Those factories slowly, but eventually did close. The RI AFL CIO Dislocated

Workers Program took over the education when the plants closed. I was pleased that one of our "lunch bunch" teachers became the teacher.

I had also started teaching in the community ESL program (Capitol Hill) in Providence. That year, I had to learn to teach ESL in multi-level multicultural, multilingual classes as well as negotiate with management in work settings throughout the state to run GED and ESL classes. I also was teaching GED and ESL at a number of workplaces. Everything was an experiment for me, so trying to use a problem-posing approach made sense some days. Other days, students just wanted to know "How do you say...?" vocabulary, correct English, etc. I remember I bought a camera and started taking pictures and having students take pictures in all the workplaces to create codes. We asked management for tours of the factory. Codes were gathered from realia of written material we could find on bulletin boards, lunchrooms, signs in common areas.

I once asked a class at a factory called *Union Wadding*, "What's "wadding"?" They didn't know the term, in English, that is. That question provided an opportunity for an amazing journey of discovery when we investigated the history of the factory, what wadding was and where it went when it left the factory. By the way, did you know that wadding is the non-fused material used in furnace filters? It is also the glitter-smattered white fabric you lay around the bottom of your Christmas tree.

Opening up discussion was always a challenge since survival for many had meant silence, at work as well as at home and in the community. Problem posing challenged me because I had to be trusted by students but also the management because they always were concerned about the "Ba, Be, Bi, Bo, Bu" method of teaching literacy that Freire so well represents in his example of learning vowel sounds. Time was always a problem in the workplace class: everyone had expectations for what could be accomplished in the 8 weeks of a class. There was often a competition of expectations. We always struggle with time, don't we? When we are trying to establish reflection and action, we need a great of time for that process to unfold.

EAG: How true. There is always the argument that we have a timeframe; we have to write our reports, we have to get started and we do not take the time to really explore and reflect on what we are doing. There is so much emphasis on the product, or time table, or showing numbers!

DP: In our current classes, we face constraints on time with 16 week semesters. Nonetheless, I always hold out the hope that I can provide a safe place for discovery with my students and their knowledge. I can steal time away from the reading of the word to read the world. Students will hopefully take the modeling of listening more openly, or take some risk taking with them into the world. They will then be more ready and able, to pick and choose actions that make sense as they develop voice. They can dare to be brave in school or in the community when it is time to speak and to act. For the final paper, the "question paper", I have students think about their research as discovery, not regurgitation. I encourage the topic exploration to move from the inside out. I have them list five personal problems and free-write on one of them; then they list 5 community problems and free-write on one topic. Recently, as we listed the community problems in Santa Fe, the emphasis fell on the changes occurring in the city with growth and newcomers (both Anglos and immigrant families).The discussion moved into issues of discrimination and brought forth anger. The dialogue skirted around who was to blame. It was an important discussion: one that surfaced attitudes that lay just below the level of comfortable expression. In one class, a young woman blamed lots of

Mexicans for getting welfare. This attitude gave another student the chance to ask, "How many?" The dialogue lead to agreement that we really didn't know, and didn't really know if it was a lot. Here was a possible research topic. Another class brought up the recent City Council meeting on the new Walmart Superstore, a current battleground issue – another research topic.

EAG: That approach really asks the students to name their realities, doesn't it?

DP: Paulo's influence is deeply rooted in us. We have developed as educators who now internalize the value for engaging in "conversation" or dialogue in our classrooms. The dialogue I try to foster is non-judgmental. I don't want to be the "know it all". Whether or not students have ever been invited into conversations typically reserved for "authorities", they need a safe space for engaging in their conversations on their concerns and issues. I want to offer space that encourages the risk-taking of speaking truth to the dominant voice. Students come to college, and that experience takes on different meaning as they take their place in a higher education learning environment. Just being in college is a radical act for many students; noteworthy are the first generation college students. Even though we can't achieve long term contact with students as they complete our classes, we can, for example, offer students tools or approaches that they can use in any context where they face abuse of power in their workplaces, neighborhoods, or homes. So, we teach to dare; and we learn to dare by witnessing the great courage, against amazing odds, that our students engage in by coming to college in the first place!

EAG: "To dare to engage", even that phrase tells about courage! To me that is very powerful.

DP: If we can give students inspiration, some courage, to not give up their struggle, not to quickly say, "There is nothing I can do; I can't fight City Hall," hopefully they will are not fall into apathy and cynicism. I worry when young people express a clear belief that ALL politicians are liars, all of them. I want them to know one decent, honest public servant. The current Bush administration leaves me little hope for finding that honesty at the federal level; but at the local level, there is great hope. Do you find this mistrust of government, authority, dominant power?

EAG: Yes, I think there is a sense that we, all of us, are not being heard, that power is cemented in stone and marble.

DP: That's what I'm saying. Policy and laws that now are in place that would actually put us in the position that we would be breaking the law to participate and dissent or to participate and question; that again is so fascist.

I don't even want to say it -but don't think we are not all thinking that - the climate reflects this oppression. These times are really frightening. We work in colleges and we work in institutions that have held out promise that the university is the place where we can still engage in these conversations.

EAG: Those seem to be somewhat contradictory ideas! What are some of the things that resonate for you in terms of different aspects of Freire's approach (philosophy), practically speaking? We've talked about dialogue; we have talked about inviting all voices into the conversation.

DP: I never run out of opportunities that allow me to view events through the lens of a "What would Freire do?" philosophy. Besides challenging myself every day in a classroom, I may be sitting in a faculty meeting or a college committee where I am nudged by Paulo to speak out to honestly respect student voices and challenge my assumptions as well as my colleagues.

This semester, I started an interview study as a means for discovering how students got to college and how they experience it. While the community college is concerned about the completion rates (graduation), because the funding is tied to success as defined by degree completion, students express success in different ways. We know students come in and out of college over a lifetime; I did that! I came in and out of college over 30 years! But the question is what does "completion" mean? As I was talking to the college researcher, the data person says, "Well, we all know the answers as to why students drop out." And I'm wondering, "We do?" I realized that we don't ask students; we often just use demographic information and statistics to create a picture. This interview study may offer a better picture of students' needs and expectations through description of their lived experience. But, what do we really know, especially in a community like Santa Fe, about how the meaning of higher education translates from promise or myth to reality? For example, is it true that if you get a good education, you'll get a good job? What is a good education anyway? Does the promise of higher education matter for jobs in Santa Fe?

EAG: Well, you have asked good questions; what are the educational outcomes for those who are not middle class? What does succeeding in academia really mean? Who is defining the meaning of completion and perseverance? I am reminded of the story you told me about the young lady student who is working two jobs because she can't support herself on one job due to the low minimum wage and I think the whole socio-cultural analysis is an important piece of the answer. It is important for the college and the students to see that there are forces outside of themselves that have an impact on their lives. They need to know what is going on in the larger world, and be able to analyze how these powerful structures work. We want them to still have hope and the will not to be overwhelmed by the odds.

DP: Perseverance. Yes, I think we have seen that equality emerges in working with students outside traditional academia. Remember in 1991 when we first met and studied together as we were starting our doctoral programs? We bonded in our shared enthusiasm for Freire. When we took Vera John Steiner's *Thought and Language* class, we collaborated on our first research project at the City of Santa Fe with six blue collar workers and an exploration of their ways of knowing. In the spirit of Freire, we developed the piece on having the workers participate as co-researchers; our intent was to practice a Freirean approach that honored the mutuality of learning and teaching that takes place between adult learners. So, after exploring their learning preferences at work and at home; they then interviewed a fellow worker to discover that co-worker's learning likes and dislikes about their educational experiences were. I still love to read the descriptions that those workers from the Streets and Solid Waste Management Departments used to describe how they learned and how they viewed learning at work and at home. Those students were active learners who had been defeated in school, but who succeeded in learning in diverse and dedicated ways as home designers and builders, as musicians, as landscapers, and as small businessmen. As I recall, we also presented on workplace literacy and Freirean culture circles at the New Mexico Adult and Continuing Education Association (NMACE) Conference in 1992 on that research.

EAG: What that research showed me was how many others ways there are of learning that are not part of academia. In our conversation, we re-visited our attraction to Freire's belief in idealism: I re-read Freire's reflection on potential criticism of his position by others; that his view of human liberation was "purely idealistic" because, as he goes on to say that:

> …Some… may even consider discussion of ontological vocation, love, dialogue, hope, humility, and sympathy as so much reactionary "blah." Others will not (or will not wish to) accept my denunciation of a state of oppression which gratifies the oppressors. Accordingly, this admittedly tentative work is for radicals (Freire 1970/1993/1995).

DP: Freire speaks to those of us who question our practice as well as intellectualize teaching. It's a radical act to be continually re-visioning our work. At least, we remain firm as questioning human beings as well as teachers willing to question and demonstrate the questioning life. I guess it is a radical act because we're not accepting the status quo. When I started doing literacy work, I called myself a radical educator. I felt comfortable to use that language. But now, I look around before I use that label to define my work; I look over my shoulder in this life after 9/11. Speaking of labels and language that provoke reactionary responses…

EAG: Yes. One thing we could look at then is how these terms were inflammatory at another time, particularly in Brazil, which was deathly afraid of being taken over by Marxist ideologies and reacted against it. Much of the terminology is still upsetting to some, even today. When I use the term "cultural empowerment" in the classroom in talking about issues, some students react on the basis of "coddling minorities". Just using the terms, Marxist or neo-Marxists, students would get turned off right away – as though they had to protect themselves against these ideas, particularly students in a very rural, conservative area. They seem to fear ideas that would conflict with their own received ideas. I always make it a point to say "neo Marxist" in talking about philosophical approaches that focus on socioeconomic analyses of power, social reproduction theory (Bowles & Gentis, 1976). In fact, it is neo Marxist. For some people, that just turns them off from listening or critically thinking about these ideas.

DP: But you have to laugh. It's ironic. Do those terms still provoke response today? They have virtually disappeared out of the popular lexicon. When you talk to practitioners, do they reference Marxism? Currently, we rarely consider Marxist analysis as a view on education. Does your program introduce Marxist analysis? It seems that the fear of communism in daily life is passé; Marxism, the "M" word is almost dead! Replaced by the new "M" word, - Muslim. Let's really get to what the powers-that-be are trying to frighten us with now. The fear of the "the other" is still an "M" word.

EG: The new "M" word. In a way , it resurfaces in the idea we are being overpowered by alien ideologies and that we have to fight against them. The ideology, because it's different and unfamiliar, makes it hard for some people to see that there's any good in outside ideas. If we examined how these ideas come out of a shared human experience and noted where they merge with all humans' longing for dignity and equality, we would see that there are not such large differences between us. We have demonized Muslims as synonymous with "terrorists" in the dangerous way that Communism was demonized. We are in a very similar situation, a neo-isolationist world view; within it, it's very dangerous to even talk about other ideas.

DP: Again, our job, in a radical sense, is to raise the issues of differing views if we are willing and not afraid to bring those views up in the classroom. That is the act of *daring to teach*. Believe me, over the years, we know it would be so much easier to go the other way, just teach traditionally and support the status quo. Stay neutral; don't provoke controversy.

EG: Absolutely.

DP: We are a little battle weary at times since we have experienced some of the knocks that come from putting ourselves on the line. But if we don't model through our own actions for students, then, they can't see the reality. How do they come to know the possibility for their own liberation if we don't model it in our own liberation?

EG: Some students today doubt the whole idea of engagement in some kind of action will change anything. There's a lack of hope and an attitude that it's futile to try to change anything.

DP: That's the power issue, Elizabeth, right there. Is it that there is less power or that people feel there is less power? Is it a fact that people have less power because of what has come to be created in this country through law and policy? For example, if you can't organize a union here because the NLRB is run by administration appointed officials who rule in favor of businesses over workers who try to unionize, even though those workers have the right to unionize. That's not about feeling powerless; that *is* less power. That illustration is about power being taken from us. Everyday legislation is put in place that robs us of our rights. We don't know about it; the media doesn't cover these law changes. One has to be vigilant in discovering new legislation. It's not most folks' usual choice for spending free time. This past summer the NLRB ruled that employers could ban off-duty fraternizing with co-workers. Now employers can say whether you can talk freely with your co-workers OUTSIDE of work. This isn't just about "talking union"; this is about weakening constitutional rights of free association and individual privacy.

EG: On a smaller scale, the dissolution of our protections by law continues. I'm talking about being able to put up announcements or flyers on a campus bulletin board. Last year (2004) Some freedom of speech issues surfaced on campus right before the presidential campaign. The issue was about what you could post in the hallways, on your doors, and in your offices, and what you could wear on your person (political buttons, etc.) came up. For us, one of the issues was wearing a peace button and whether you could wear it on your person anywhere on campus. The legal interpretation was that hallways are considered public space as opposed to private space in a state-funded institution. The clarification on the campus was that one could (within your office) display anything that you wanted to have but you couldn't hand out propaganda in favor of one party from it. You had to present several views. So the question was resolved on some level, but having just encountered another situation recently with staff person making a judgment as to what was proper or improper to put on college bulletin boards, based on his own opinions and biases rather than university policy. I find this disconcerting. It may seem like a small incident, but the implications are huge.

I agree with you that these incidents have to do with that power. I think you've posed a good question. Are we in fact less powerful? The way that totalitarianism wins is to make people feel that they are powerless. I see that we are not essentially less powerful, but it takes more to move forward; it takes more to have your voice expressed because the power is in place, and one has to overcome inertia. If people are suppressed and silenced, we lose our voice.

We look for and find some like-minded people who are also thrilled to be able to hear somebody else feels the same way. I think that's important, these linkages. This goes back to what Freire said about forming a "coalitional identity", joining together with others. It also relates again to the whole question of idealism. If you're a Freirean then, you are, *per se*, an idealist.

DP: Like your "Friends of Democracy" group that emerged in Portales, in a cradle of the Republican Party. You found other people who wanted to take an active role in, to put it grandly, remaking the world. I think the work at the local level continues to offer the greatest hope to see democracy working. Every victory on an important social justice issue shores up our idealism; I always say that "Once you have won on an issue, you will be changed forever." You can never go back to hopelessness. I tell students that all the time. Some nod their heads in agreement; others look with skepticism.

EG: Paulo was smart enough to predict early on in *Pedagogy of the Oppressed* (1970/1993/1995) that there would be objections to his ideas. But when we saw him in person in 1996, he had not deviated from his commitment in any way, shape or form. He had deepened some of his previous positions but he hadn't changed them. That, to me, is one of the very compelling things about being authentic. That's the model for me. If there's one thing that attracts me to transformative pedagogy, it's not the theorizing, it's not the research, nor constructing a theory that is solid and helpful, - it's the authenticity; being congruent. It's doing and being - in concert with others and yourself.

I remember when I first read *Pedagogy of the Oppressed,* I also first heard the phrase, "Walk your talk." That sums it all up for me; we continue to talk about being congruent. Either your actions have to be congruent with your thinking, or you are a fake. At the time, I thought maybe my actions aren't really all that congruent. It makes you realize that you do a lot of modification and rationalization; you need to get back to really thinking clearly – which takes reflection and time.

What happens simply is that the purity with which we approach our teaching becomes diluted by other demands and time constraints, and conflicting concerns, and often we don't go back to do that. I think if we're talking about practitioners and talking to ourselves as practitioners, we have to keep reminding ourselves that we need the reflection time, we need thinking time; we need to make the time to go back and look at what we're doing.

Freire and the people he worked with in the campaign for literacy in Brazil in other places around the world were very clear about proceeding with action only after they had sat down and reflected. Even the strategizing demanded reflection and so, in a way, it was very similar to what some religious groups do,, for example, go on a retreat You would go away, you would talk to each other, you would look at all of your plans; you would think and really meditate on what you were doing, and that's a crucial step. Freire emphasized that action without reflection was hollow and action without the reflection was wasted energy.. .I think that's one of Freire's convictions that tends to get ignored.

DP: This raises an interesting idea as to whether or not we engage with other practitioners in this reflection. Does that happen anymore? When I did literacy work, it happened all the time because we were a disenfranchised group in our own right. We were poorly paid, piecing our lives together. We were hard put to get recognition, and we had our own oppressive conditions that we worked under. We found ourselves standing side-by-side with our students in concern for bread-and-butter issues.

EG: We need to be creating spaces and places to reflect upon our actions with others. It's that simple.

DP: Lead by my department chair, we work at creating dialogue in our Developmental Studies teacher meetings. We have a number of full time teachers, but often hire part timers to teach since 85% of incoming students test into developmental English or math. Sometimes we hire graduates from St. Johns College where they study the "Great Books" curriculum. One of these teachers, when he looked at the compilation of readings that we had created and published for our Developmental Writing courses, asked, "Are you trying to teach compassion?" Implied by the question was his concern for our charge to teach reading and writing. At first, I was put out by the question because it seemed like a criticism. Afterwards, some of us who had created the books were talking, and we affirmed our decision by answering, "Yes, we are!"

As you know, we find that teachers bring in a variety of agendas into literacy work, no matter what level. There are some very different attitudes about teaching grammar, for example. I do appreciate that my boss, the department chair, believes that we need to talk about our teaching practice. We also need to talk about grading, and what gets graded. There is some resistance from teachers. Teachers want autonomy in the classroom, and that's fine, but what's wrong with talking about practice? What can we learn about what goes on in our classrooms? How else can we know what others are doing? So we can be the teacher/learner.

EG: So these are some of the obstacles. One of the things is this reflection piece does not happen automatically. You have to make time and structure it, whatever that means.

DP: Even as we're reflecting, we need to give time and space to conversation in the classroom and in the faculty meeting– that's the dialogic. Have you thought about this? Isn't it interesting, at the college level, that the assumption is that faculty go off and do their own thing? What do you talk about in faculty meetings? Do you talk about teaching?

EG: That's an interesting question. Teaching practice is virtually never on the agenda. That's what I've been thinking about. We have had a few faculty meetings lately when several people were absent, so we didn't cover the agenda as usual. The result was that we did more talking about our classes and teaching. We all agreed that we should do this more often. Imagine – let's put reflecting about teaching on the agenda!

DP: Yes. Of course, I think we desire it.

EG: This is what we need to be doing. Part of our meeting time should be designated as conversation time.

DP: That's a good example of the place for praxis in higher education. By giving voice to our experience in education, for example, sharing our assumptions about teaching and learning as novice teachers and reflecting on our development over time, we can deepen our understanding and perhaps, make a difference in classrooms as well as the world. Reflecting on how and why we became teachers is a good starting place for the dialogue. Since we didn't come out of teacher education programs, what do you think has been an important lesson about teaching for you?

EAG: I honestly don't know if one learns teaching from the outside. I think that some people just teach intuitively. I really feel that's what happened to me. When I was in college, my father told me that I should take some education classes so that I'd always have a job. That was pretty conventional wisdom. So, I went to one education course with a friend of mine; it was the worse and most boring class I had ever attended, so I said, "I'm never going to do this again," I went back to anthropology. I also had a negative stereotype of public schools then, too; which I think at that time was realistic .What I saw was that education promoted a one-size-fits-all curriculum, lock-step progression, being on the same page on the same day, and knowing that ,behind their closed doors, every teacher in the classroom was king or queen. So teaching was the last thing in the world I wanted to do. It seemed too confining.

What happened to me, however, was that people in Brazil were always asking me to teach English and I said, "Well I don't know how to teach English but I'll try." We were working within a context of community development in a climate of social change, so my teaching grew out of that. I found I loved it, and then, of course, I taught ESL for such a long time. When I returned from Brazil, I had decided to take ESL courses and really learn about how to teach English.

DP: That's the connection for me – it was working in the ESL classroom that really taught me about teaching. Now those experiences carry forward with everything I do in the classroom today. I continually consider all the ways of knowing and learning that one group of students brings into class, and I work to provide multiple ways for students to gain access to the curriculum, even giving the curriculum over to directions not planned for the day. I had to find my way to teach reading and writing. I felt as though I was constantly trying new things and saying, "I don't know how to get this skill across; let's try this angle."

I was watching students and paying attention to learning, and trying to learn from each situation. I didn't have a clue, so I had to constantly search. It seemed like a miracle to me that somebody could learn to read and write. I always held awe for the enterprise of literacy, wondering, How does it happen? What does this student need to learn? How can we create the conditions for learning? What can students tell us about their knowing ?

EG: There's a shift today from saying that we teach people to read and write to saying that we facilitate or try to create conditions in which they learn to read and write themselves. Isn't that the essence of this whole Freirean attitude that we're talking about? That the power is there in them? The word education comes from the Latin, *educare, to* lead forth, to lead out of, to bring forth. To draw forth creates the conditions for something dynamic to happen. You can't force somebody to read. You cannot teach somebody to read.

DP: That's why, as I said, literacy work seemed so elusive that I could not figure it out from any model that I assumed worked, that is, what I had seen modeled in my own education as the teacher depositing the knowledge, or bestowing knowledge as a gift.

EAG: I think one of the other things about our experience in adult education is that when teachers start with Adult Ed, they learn that people want something – it's very direct. They want something they can do. It's not a lot of theory. How am I going to teach them English that they can use? In California, I was part of all kinds of survival English programs and taught with Asians, Cambodians and Vietnamese, who were learning how to become custodial workers, for example.

What you do and maybe it's almost a presumption in Adult Ed which had not been a presumption in other areas of education—public education—is contextualized learning. So I was teaching these men how to say "leaf blower" and "Measure one cup of detergent " and "Make sure to lock the cabinet." I was teaching within a context, within a framework. The learning was focused on concrete results, and I think that's one of the benefits of having learned to teach by teaching. I think it's a benefit, I still do, even though I'm in the Teacher Education program I still hold that it's a benefit to have not had that kind of training to start with. Now, at least in our schools, we have embraced the ideas of social interactionism and constructivist thought to some degree, so *that barriers* have been broken in today's educational system. The whole idea of integrated curriculum is very popular and being enacted so we can bring different disciplines together. Of course, we also contend with obsessive testing in the name of accountability due to the *No Child Left Behind Act (2002)* (NCLB) and we see a step backward into scripted , "teacher-proof" programs and the devaluing of teacher expertise. It is one step forward and one step backward.

DP: My first thought was that the teaching promoted through the NCLB Act militates against constructivist learning and truly emphasizes "banking" education. What were you thinking?

EAG: Yes, once again, we are depositing knowledge rather than letting the learners co-construct knowledge. In the light of these mandates, many of the gains in the educational reform movement in the U.S. since the 1980s are being subverted. Administrative bodies from the district to the federal government are reasserting the "power-over approach" I hear this again and again from veteran teachers who feel demeaned and ignored in the present climate when they are told they are not "highly-skilled" enough; their positive influence, knowledge, and expertise is not recognized. Reliance on bean counters (numbers) and meticulous supervision is one outgrowth of this erroneous approach in education. Paulo would be appalled!

DP: And we would join in his dismay. Instead of students asking the questions and creating the conditions for learning, students instead get bombarded by the curriculum of teaching to the test. I experienced transformation with the test curriculum while tutoring Adela, a custodian at the City of Santa Fe. She set a goal to pass the GED tests. Every time I asked her to take a GED practice test, she would start to sweat. I know I was tired of the multiple choice GED test and book format, too. Finally one day we agreed that we had to just get rid of the books. Now what? What are we going to do? We talked for a while and Adela said, "Let's read together. Just read." Adela loved Sandra Cisneros' work; she and Cisneros are both Tejanas. We had read stories in *Women Hollering Creek*. After we decided to close the GED book, Adela surprised me when she came to class with *The House on Mango Street*. She had bought the book over the weekend. Bringing that book to our tutoring session was so liberating for me! I knew it was wrong to continue with the "drill and kill" approach to test preparation. But, I had trouble reading the situation. Adela wanted to use the GED books at first, but her body was telling her to "beware."

EG: I remember that story because you told me that Adela bought herself the book.

DP: At first, she wanted those GED books, all of them, because it was her model for schooling. Neither she nor I could express our frustration with the numbing read and test approach for a long time. We were respecting our choices, but not saying what was on our minds. We learned together that sometimes we just have to put the school books away.

EG: I think part of your great story with Adela is that you discovered you both taught and learned from each other. Part of teaching is helping another make the discovery that indeed they have it within themselves to do it, read, learn, and go forward So, maybe that discovery is one of the important "a-ha!" kinds of moments.

But you yourself had been involved with labor relations, and workplace literacy and all of that; you came to teaching with a much clearer idea of power, fighting for rights, and united action, and that kind of thing. This was not the background that I had at all so what transformed me was being in Brazil at that time of conflicting ideologies, turmoil, and movements for social justice. That's what opened it up for me. I think you had more of a basis of contesting power structures.

DP: I do believe that improving language skills brings power forth. Support from labor unions gave our workplace program of classes a position of power in the businesses where they took place. Belonging to the union also provided some solidarity between the old and new workforces. Sometimes the business was ambivalent about keeping the classes going, but then the union would push management. Workers would write letters to promote continuation.

I once taught ESL with young Lao workers. We met in the cafeteria of a Kashmir wool factory in Woonsocket RI. The older workers were mostly French Canadian descent. The management would only allow the classes to take place during the lunch break because management insisted that they couldn't stop production. It was awkward to run the class in the lunchroom because workers needed a break, and they wanted to talk and eat. The older workers promoted support for the class and asked management to give over a conference room for the class. They also offered to cover overlap time, so the students who attended classes could leave their machines to get to and from class. I saw that solidarity occur in the hospital ESL classes too. Support for the classes and shift coverage came from other workers who wanted their co-workers to have the chance to attend class.

I mentioned earlier the immigrant workers at Union Wadding who finally got their hands on their union contract. The learning in the workplace, a site for very structured institutionalized power, continues to intrigue me. I taught in workplaces through the "flavor of the month" cooperative labor management schemes of 1980s and 1990s that promulgated the myth that management and workers were not at odds and that we were "all in it together," only to discover it was all a bunch of "blah" with CEO and top brass wages and benefits increasing and rank and file wages depressing and benefits disappearing. I work in an institution of higher learning that assures faculty and staff that we don't need a union because we are part of a "shared governance" model. It seems to work this way mostly: They lead; we follow. Who holds the power?

EG: You came into education by a different route. Not just through the teaching but the sense of identifying with people who have power but don't know it or real situations of oppression where power literally been taken out of the hands of those who had it.

DP: With the re-structuring of the Adult Education Act and the combining of services through the Workforce Investment Act (WIA) adult learners have lost a great deal of power over their learning. Maybe it's good; maybe it's a time to re-vision the purpose of literacy work.

EAG: My most recent example of a literacy encounter illustrates the need for a little reflective practice. A literacy council had received a request from some dairy workers to have ESL classes. I enthusiastically suggested "We'll go to the dairies. Let's see if we can fight for classroom space, a dedicated space in some area of the operations so the classes could be out in the field, literally." The idea was actively suppressed; and their reaction was "Well, that's not the way we're going to do it. Only one person has asked for this. No, we're not going to do it that way and they will have to come here to us."This literacy council provided a handful of county residents with direct literacy tutoring. In an area with serious illiteracy, perhaps theirs is not the right approach.

It was very clear that this was not the direction in which they intended to go. What's the connection? Listening to needs, questioning one's own practices, and respecting the people who are illiterate and disenfranchised is still a struggle, even among well- intentioned literacy volunteers.

DP: Literacy work changed my life. Everyday I am fortunate to see learning occur in students from the inside out because I continue to do literacy work. And I think that I give students a little bit of my idealism: I pass along the idealism that Paulo gave to me.

EAG: May I tell you the postscript of my story about Freire and Brazil? At the Pedagogy of the Oppressed conference in Omaha, in 1996, Paulo was the honored guest. He spoke to us on a variety of occasions and topics. However, he was very frail, and his "handlers" were doing their utmost to protect him from his many admirers. At a certain point, I was finally able to get close enough to tell Paulo [in Portuguese] that I had heard him speak in Sao Paulo in 1964 and that he had been a great inspiration to me ever since. I said I wanted to give him "um abraço bem brasileira," a very Brazilian hug. So I did. Paulo took my hand and put his other hand over mine and said very sincerely, "Muito obrigado," thank you. He looked at me with such love and tenderness that I felt a moment of total affirmation. He was totally present in that moment. His compelling force of his character was apparent, a force that involved both affirmation and a silent urging to go forward, to persevere. I felt that charisma; I was shaky, teary, and weak-kneed for the rest of the day, so powerful was that encounter for me. At the same time, I felt extremely happy about the chance to acknowledge in person his influence in my life to him. Sadly, the following year, in 1997, Paulo Freire passed away.

DP: I took a picture of the moment when you exchanged that embrace. I cherish the memory as well.

REFERENCES

Bowles, S. & Gintis, H. (1976). *Schooling in Capitalist America*. NY: Basic Books.

Horton, M. & Freire, P. (1990). *We Make the Road by Walking*. Philadelphia: Temple University Press.

Freire, P. (1969/1973/1994). *Education for Critical Consciousness*. New York: Continuum.

Freire, P. (1992/1994). *Pedagogy of Hope*. New York: Continuum.

Freire, P. (1970/1993/1995). *Pedagogy of the Oppressed*. New York: Continuum.

Freire, P. (1998). *Teachers as Cultural Workers: Letters to Those Who Dare Teach*. Boulder, CO: Westview Press.

Freire, P, & Macedo, D. (1987). *Literacy Reading the Word and the World*. New York: Bergin and Garvey.

Galligan, E. A. (1996). *Pedagogy of the Oppressed Conference Notes*.

Galligan, E. A. (1991) . *Curriculum Construction: P. Freire and Associates, Building Contractors*. Unpublished manuscript.

King, Jr. M.L. (1967). "The World House." *Where Do We Go from Here: Chaos or Community?* New York: Harper & Row.

Shor, I. & Freire, P. (1987). *A Pedagogy for Liberation*. South Hadley, MA: Bergin   and Garvey.

Stuckey, J. Elspeth. (1991). *The Violence of Literacy*. Portsmouth, NH: Boynton/Cook.

Wallerstein, N. (1953/1983). *Language and Culture in Conflict*. Reading, MA: Addison-Wesley

ACKNOWLEDGMENT

Thanks to educators who guided and informed our practice: Sally Gabb, Judy Titzel, Janet Isserlis, Michael Paul, Rick Brooks, Dawn Anderson, Judy Hofer, Karl Polm-Faudré, Lisa Martinez.

In: Pioneers in Education: Essays in Honor of Paulo Freire   ISBN: 978-1-60021-479-0
Editors: M.Shaughnessy, E.Galligan et al., pp 67-83   ©2008 Nova Science Publishers, Inc.

Chapter 4

A VISION OF PAULO FREIRE'S PHILOSOPHY : UNDERSTANDING HIS ESSENTIAL DYNAMISM OF LEARNING AND TEACHING

Belle Wallace
Great Britain

ABSTRACT

This chapter reflects on a career through a personal narrative of how I, as an educator, together with my students, have tried to walk in the steps of Paolo Freire. My journey has been an international one, but this particular reflection highlights the development of a Project called TASC: Thinking Actively in a Social Context. The Project was developed in KwaZulu/Natal, literally meaning 'the place of the Zulus', an enforced 'homeland' under apartheid rule in South Africa. The case study highlights the resilience and determination of a group of students who were determined to overcome the denial and repression of opportunities for Black students. It is a story of love, joy and success – a pedagogy of hope.

We are sentient, dynamic beings capable of change: but we can be trapped not only in the learned sense of what we are not, but also in a powerful negative mirror image of ourselves that we perceive emanating from others. Yet, we can be released through enabling interactions with those special mentors who offer constant and strong scaffolding that we are, indeed, of great worth and significance as individuals with potential.

Belle Wallace (2006)

INTRODUCTION

I have reflected for some time about the influence that Paulo Freire has had on my professional and personal life, and decided to share with you as honestly and as clearly as I can how his philosophy has impacted on the decisions and actions I have taken over the last 40 years as a school teacher, university lecturer, researcher and national and international education consultant. This personal narrative, I hope, will be outspokenly direct and real to life as I reflect and try to follow in Freire's footsteps of being open and grounded in the process of ongoing metacognition linking action and reflection (Freire, 1998a, 1998b).

When my career first began in education, I was not aware of Freire's writing and teaching, I was concerned with the ethics of striving to provide equality of opportunity for all learners to find relevant meaning and satisfaction through their learning experiences. I was intuitively aware of the need for learners to feel motivated and enthused by the topics they were investigating; and aware of the quality of the relationships I was trying to build in order to create the rapport and trust I felt learners needed in order to risk the sharing of their ideas and questions. This seemed to me to be the basic requisites for communication and understanding.

How can young people learn if they do not feel emotionally and cognitively engaged, and if they are not highly valued and praised?

As a naïve, inexperienced, and enthusiastic young educator, my first encounter with the writing and teaching of Paulo Freire crystallized for me what was, until then, only half formulated in my mind, and clarified what I was trying to achieve, broadly:

- The development of learners' ownership of their learning through the negotiation of relevant problems to be solved in relation to real life understanding;
- The development of dialogue and interaction in the learning/teaching dynamic with reciprocity and equality of teachers and learners as jointly negotiating and constructing meaning;
- The development of learners' self-confidence and independence in decision-making and actions leading to their self-actualisation;
- The mutual respect derived from active listening and talking
  (Freire, 1998a; Freire, 1998b; Fraser, 1997; McLaren, 1993, 1998; Apple & King, 1977; Ramos, 1974).

Although my personal life path has led me to work in many countries for short periods of time, I spent an intensive and extensive period in KwaZulu/Natal (South Africa), and my narrative will trace this particular journey. In writing about South Africa, however, I have both philosophical and emotional reservations in referring to any country as either a 'third' or 'developing' world, or a 'first' or 'developed' world: so I will use the terms SA and KwaZulu, (later called KwaZulu/Natal). In addition, I acknowledge that this is a personal narrative, shared with you from my own perspectives and system of values. I hope, however, that I can provide a rich case-study based on real life experiences milled and refined both cognitively and emotionally through many processes of analysis and reflection, as an individual engaged in quiet contemplation and also as an interactive member of the communities I have worked within partnership, joy and love. Walking in Paolo Freire's shoes, and seeing with his understanding, I have tried:

- to share in the humanity and reality of the community as an equal member of the group, sometimes a mentor, always a learner, but never, I hope, the benevolent imposer of 'liberation' on the 'oppressed';
- to allow the students the ownership of the creation of their own concepts of freedom, autonomy and possible life journeys;
- to develop students' awareness of their own powers of reflective participation in their affairs
  (Freire, 1998a, 1998b; Ramos, 1974).

It is necessary, at this stage, to share with you just a little of my early background so that you can understand the lens through which I learned to view the world as a child and young adult. This early world view has obviously impacted on my adult perception of how I view education principles and practice: endeavouring to influence both by emphasising the indivisible nature of emotion and cognition; the interdependence and reciprocity of teaching and learning; the essential need for relevance and real life experiential learning, and the vital importance of motivation and understanding.

I grew up in an impoverished district in South Wales (UK) in a large family familiar with hunger and poverty, always short of money for even basic necessities: and I won a free scholarship to the town's grammar school[1] at eleven years of age. Thrust into a 'middle-class' professional, articulate milieu, I was one of a minority of learners submerged in 'the culture of silence'; I had no voice in the social milieu of the daughters of doctors, teachers, lawyers and the like. I had neither personal identity nor social significance within their conversations and life-styles.

My education fell neatly and very aptly within the framework of the Freire's 'banking' concept, it was a series of acts of:

'depositing, in which the students are the depositories and the teacher is the depositor. Instead of communicating, the teacher issues communiqués and makes deposits which the students patiently receive, memorise and repeat' (Freire, 1998b, p72).

I was a disengaged observer of happenings and incidents that had no relation to my own life; I was not a participant in an interactive learning-teaching process, I was an object to be processed in the ritualistic practice of listening and memorising towards levels of 'academic' achievement. I was denied access to any form of enquiring, questioning, or real life experiential learning, and was 'disabled' from learning rather than enabled to learn (McLaren, (1993).

---

[1] The scholarship to a grammar school was the result of an intelligence test administered at the age of 11+ years. This meant that the 'top' 10 to 15 percent of children went to a special school supposedly for academic high fliers.

I survived due to the influence of a singular and wonderful teacher who recognised that I had a talent for writing – with her I received the acknowledgement that I had personal worth, that I was an emotional and thinking being, alive and searching for meaning, albeit to often ill-formulated questions. I experienced the glow of excitement that comes from the reciprocal respect derived from active listening and talking: she was in every sense a mentor, the barrier between teacher and learner invisible; the relationship one of loving respect and understanding. It is to this living learning experience that I attribute the formulation of the direction that my life has broadly followed – to understand and to promote the dynamic processes that bring life, reality and vitality to any learning-teaching interaction (Fraser, (1997), Freire, (1997).

LEARNING AND TEACHING THROUGH LENS OF SA (KWAZULU, LATER CALLED KWAZULU/NATAL)

Background

The impact of SA on my life and educational vision has been paramount in formulating and refining my personal life path, my aims for education and my practice. Finding myself in a totally different cultural context from that of the UK, the impact of KwaZulu/Natal (SA) was raw, stark and overwhelming: brilliantly vibrant and colourful, socially, emotionally and politically complex and convoluted; a mixture of resilience and submission; a kaleidoscope of despair and hope; and profoundly challenging in its need for change. This personal life change was almost accidental in that it was not really planned, but evolved in response to an overwhelming sense of the need to work with the nation of Zulu people who were excluded within their own country and forcibly segregated in an impoverished, infertile mountainous area euphemistically called their 'homeland'. So an intended stay of one year's Sabbatical leave became fifteen years of personal commitment from 1984 to 1998: these fifteen years witnessing the crumbling of the apartheid regime. The beginning of this period was characterised by an intense civil war in KwaZulu/Natal, the contest involving members within the system of government of the traditional Zulu king and tribal chiefs; the rising African National Congress (ANC) and the South African National Government; culminating in the release of Nelson Mandela in 1990. The latter part of this time was characterised by a turmoil of instability and change brought about by the new fledgling government, the Government of National Unity, as it endeavoured to establish a new social system: the struggle fraught with considerable contention for political and financial power, and a populace desperate for rapid change and anticipated benefit.

The following perspectives need to be seen in the light of the volatile situation briefly summarised in the preceding paragraph.

CAUSES OF UNDERACHIEVEMENT IN KWAZULU STUDENTS

The 'Banking' System of Education

KwaZulu then consisted of (and is largely still) mainly rural settlements of subsistence farming and low socio-economic urban settlements located outside the main 'White' towns. In 1984, the school enrolment was estimated at 1.5 million with only 67% of that population attending school. Another estimation was that 53% of the entire population was under the age of fifteen. The high levels of school dropout, 'failed' students being retained to repeat the same year several times, and failure in the Senior School Certificate at 17+ years indicated severe 'underachievement' amongst Black students. Only 1% of the initial year group gained a level of matriculation which could possibly allow them entry to university: even for these students there was no financial support. Those students who did manage to gain a place at a university were grossly 'under-prepared' and 'failed' their first year of tertiary study (Dostal and Vergani, 1984; Vos 1986).[2]

The concept of SA education lay firmly within Freire's 'banking' paradigm. Rote learning and repetition characterised overcrowded, ill-equipped, mainly tin-roofed or mud-roofed classrooms that were stiflingly hot in summer and shiveringly cold in winter. Many teachers were grossly under-prepared both with regard to pedagogy and subject knowledge; moreover, because the traditional Zulu culture promoted a deep and compliant respect by the young for the elders, it was considered culturally inappropriate for students to question their teachers, or even to make direct eye contact. In addition, the group culture strongly encouraged group identity and it was considered inappropriate to draw attention to oneself as an individual.

The school syllabus had fixed and immutable content firmly rooted in a Western paradigm that had little reality for Zulu learners – comprehension topics such as 'defrosting a refrigerator', the geography of Japan, the history of the castles of Europe, the microscopic structure of a hydra, had no relevance or reality for learners living in simple brick or mud huts without electricity and running water, who did not possess refrigerators, had never been outside their community, and who had little or no concept of an island, a mediaeval castle, micro-cellular structure. Regular tests (control tests) were compulsory every few weeks with learners being required to answer questions soliciting facts reproduced in the exact words of the teacher who read from the prescribed text book. Students seldom had a textbook of their own.

Even at university, the curriculum was Western oriented and there was little attempt to analyse the causes of the gross underachievement of the few Black scholars who gained entry. The few 'bridging' courses that were beginning to be developed sought to 'bridge the gaps' in students' knowledge from the university perspective, the argument being that if universities changed course content then 'standards' would fall.

---

[2] I use the terms around the notions of 'underachievement' and 'failure' in quotes because they were used on the basis of judgements formed on a narrow definition of school and examination success.

The Deprivation of Language for Learning

Freire's thinking on the power of literacy to enable or to deny access to learning and life opportunities is well known as one of his most fundamental premises. [3]

In KwaZulu, the language of learning and teaching was English, while the home language of the students was Zulu. The majority of students lived in homes where their parents were working away from home in the White towns, and they were cared for by older Aunts and Grandmothers who had received no formal schooling and whose English was sparse and colloquial. A great number of students were themselves caregivers for their younger brothers and sisters, and after school, had the responsibilities of fetching water and wood and cooking the evening meal.

Although positive self-concept is an essential component of learner motivation and self-empowerment, the fundamental processes of learning interactions depend on how learners receive, understand and communicate through language – both verbal and non-verbal. Although there is growing acceptance of pupils' differentiated personal profiles of strengths across the full range of human abilities (Wallace & Maker, 2004), essentially language is the dominant mode of communication between people. Not only is language central to both informal and formal learning, it is essential to the processes of thinking. We rationalise and make sense of the world through language which establishes our cognitive map of processes and meanings. But our language and cognitive development is inextricably bound up with our emotional development: from the earliest exchanges of language, our sense of self, our feelings of worth, our emerging identities are reinforced.

Our 'first' language is non-verbal and we never lose the intuitive awareness of understanding expressions and body language – that sense of feeling in communication with others. But we need verbal language to give symbolic structure to thought, and it is in developing appropriate structures and expressions, that we become truly human (Freire 1998a, 1998b, Schlesinger, 1993). Although debate continues as to whether thought precedes language or language precedes thought, it is obvious that the two processes are closely intertwined. Lev Vygotsky (1978), argues that the quality and quantity of children's language development depends heavily on interaction with adults and more capable peers. When language is developed through interactive dialogue in the active process of problem-solving, then the more capable learner leads the less capable learner through the stages of the uncertainty of not knowing and not understanding, to the full realization of knowing and the crystallization of meaning and understanding. The adult learner reaches out to identify the level of understanding of the child, and constructs and builds understanding within the child's 'zone of proximal development'. We can see immediately what this means for the teaching-learning interaction: through active, relevant problem-solving, mediated by appropriate language, the child understands and gains mastery and is ready for further learning.

Zulu learners *possessed command of language rich in imagery and expression,* but it was mainly language developed in the informal setting of home life and activities in the rural locations and urban townships. Obviously, Zulu learners also possessed a *language of emotion alongside the rich experiential knowing through mediation*; but the content of school learning seldom, if ever, embraced the realities of either the learners' practical learning

---

[3] On a personal note, my facility with language was the gateway to breaking down the cognitive, emotional and social barriers which characterised most of my school learning experiences.

experiences and values or their feelings. In addition, as stated above, school learning was firmly located within the framework of 'banking' and not within the framework of mediation for understanding.

When the school language for learning (L2) is different from the home language (L1), learners are faced with the huge cognitive and emotional challenge of negotiating meaning and understanding between the two modes of expression. Learners with well-developed home language, with appropriate mediation, can build bridges and *acquire* the school language of learning because they have a rich internalised language structure, and can draw parallels and make the cognitive and emotional links between the two languages. However, for this interaction to occur, the learners' home language needs to be fully accepted, used positively and celebrated since it is closely linked with the sense of personal identity and sense of self-efficacy. In addition, the content of the curriculum needs to be derived, developed and extended from the reality of what learners already know.

The acceptance and practice of *additive bilingual* language acquisition as the means of learning and making meaning, actively celebrates both home and school language. Learners can switch between the second language (L2) used in school and their home language (L1), negotiating the meaning from one to the other (Wallace, 1996ff). Additive bilingual learning, however, is still dependent on the learning being related to the social context of the learners: their culture, home background, sense of values, etc. The heavy cognitive load of negotiating meaning by straddling two languages is lessened when learners can identify with the content and find relevance within their own lives (ibid). Moreover, the processes of teaching and learning using an additive bilingual approach are necessarily interactive, with learners having the time and opportunity to think, negotiate meaning, and communicate. In addition, the rules and grammatical structures are initially of secondary importance to the understanding of meaning: when the teacher makes the input comprehensible, the rules of the second language (L2) become internalised naturally by the learner and are used automatically (Omaggio, 1986). We can find a parallel to this process when we analyse how children acquire first language expressions, structures and syntax in a richly verbal home that accepts, celebrates and mediates the child's tentative language efforts, while supporting and extending the base of the child's own emerging language.

However, with children who have under-developed home language (L1), the problems of acquiring the school language of learning are exacerbated. The school language can be a second language in two senses: different, more formal modes of the same language (extended L1); or a completely different language (L2). In both cases, children have not learned a rich range of expressions and structures within their home language (L1); and when faced with learning in the extended L1 of school language, or the L2 of school language, they do not have the parallel or compensatory structures to build bridges linking home language and school language. The same principles of mediation and extension of language through negotiation of meaning, apply to the development of both extended L1 language, and L2 language. Teachers need to begin language mediation from the base of the learners' own language: the language of the street, the peer group, and the home language, extending this to incorporate 'new' language for more formal learning. The teacher input has to be comprehensible and relevant to learners (Freire, 1998a, 1998b)

Dromi, (1993) and Krashen, (1981) identify three variables which relate to learners' ability to access the meaning of teacher/pupil exchange:

- When learners' motivation is high, they can take risks with expressing ideas, however tentative that expression may be;
- When learners have high self-confidence and good self-image, they tend to be more open to accepting adaptations to their everyday home language (L1), and to accepting a new language (L2);
- Low levels of personal and classroom anxieties are indispensable for the acquisition of both extended L1 and L2 language.

I maintain that successful teaching and acquisition of language, and the teaching of problem-solving and thinking skills, are inseparably fused together and, consequently, share the same common aims and purposes:

- Both should seek to develop language and cognitive skills through purposeful real-life situations that provide learners with authentic and meaningful contexts for learning;
- Both should view the acquisition of language and learning to think effectively as active processes. It is not sufficient for learners to learn *about* them; they need to *do* something constructive with the acquired skills;
- Both should see language and thinking skills as vehicles for self-expression, personalisation and ownership of the learning processes;
- Both should see the development of language and thinking as skills to be used and transferred across the curriculum;
- Both should develop a curriculum together with a range of appropriate teaching/learning processes that develop learners' positive self-image, internal locus of control, and the belief in life-long learning.
(Wallace, 1993)

THE TASC PROJECT: THINKING ACTIVELY IN A SOCIAL CONTEXT

To begin to address some of the issues embedded in the school learning of Zulu learners which are outlined above, in 1985, I, together with Harvey Adams, established the Curriculum Development Unit attached to the Faculty of Education, University of Natal, South Africa. We began a Project which was to last for 14 years. The overall aims were to research the needs of the disadvantaged Zulu population in the then apartheid homeland of KwaZulu; to develop teachers' and learners' L1 and L2 language skills; to develop a range of appropriate thinking skills to promote self-esteem, independence and empowerment; and to design curricula which were relevant to, and contextualised in, Zulu culture. We worked within a repeating spiral framework of collaborative, reflective action research, using a constructivist approach involving pupils, teachers, educational psychologists and parents or caregivers.

Vitally and essentially, we did not work from a deficit framework of the skills the learners apparently 'lacked', but from a framework of skills the learners already had: namely strong powers of memory due to their rich oral culture, well developed group listening and leadership skills; democratic ways of working through discussion and sharing of ideas; ease of, and enjoyment in, co-operative learning; a tremendous motivation to learn as a means of self-development; and a deep and incisive awareness of the political, economic, social, and emotional dimensions within a country wracked by division and inequality.

The Project began with an initial group of 28 mid-secondary school students identified by their teachers as amongst the 'most able': this rough and rather crude assessment being based on the fact that these students were achieving relative success in the school when compared with other students. From a purely pragmatic standpoint, we also needed to begin by working with students who had a reasonable command of English, since our command of Zulu was very elementary and we wanted to work in an additive bilingual way, mediating purpose and meaning. We wanted to work in Freire's mode of interactive teaching and learning, with learners and teachers as equal partners; although in practical reality we were learning extensively from the students. As we gained confidence and greater fluency in Zulu, the Project was extended to involve groups of students perceived as 'mixed-ability' in both primary and secondary schools.

The following detailed case study will focus on the intensive work carried out with the first pilot group of 28 mid-secondary students, although the Project rapidly widened its target group as we gained understanding and greater confidence. The Project came to be known as 'TASC: Thinking Actively in a Social Context': its name evolving from a series of workshops where the students and their teachers identified the needs and problems they faced in both home and school. It is important to stress at this point that the learners very perceptively expressed their need to work in ways already discussed earlier in this chapter: they cemented through their personal experience and insight, the interpretation and application of the theories of learning and teaching outlined above. The development of thought and practice were symbiotic – the one refining the other through reflective discussion. The students also identified their need to be able to think and learn in ways that made the Western curriculum manageable, but they could not yet identify or formulate these particular thinking and learning skills. They strongly articulated their need for a more relevant curriculum, but expressed their immediate, practical need to manage their current studies. Generalizing from these vivid and often emotional discussions, and clarified by the current theory and research, the following tenets of TASC emerged:

- Thinking: Although all learners can, and do think, there is a vast range of 'formal' thinking tools and strategies that learners need to develop, so that the capacity of every learner increases. All learners can cope with complexity if they understand the task and can communicate effectively. The power and confidence to engage in effective thinking stems from the individual's belief in self-efficacy and self-regulation. Although language is a major tool for thinking, people can think using the full range of human abilities, for example, through dance, art, music, architecture, etc.

- Actively: Learners need ownership of their learning; they need to play active roles in decision-making about how and what they learn; and they need to be involved in discussion of both immediate and long-term goals.

- Social: Co-operative learning is powerful in its mediatory function; learners need to learn with and from each other. But there is also a need for learners to know how to work independently; and additionally, there is a need for learners to realise that they are globally responsible and enviro-dependent.

- Context: Learners need to start learning in a context that is practical, related to real-life and concrete. The context needs to be relevant and meaningful so that they can relate to it and bring their own knowledge into the learning situation. As they develop mastery, they move into deeper, more abstract contexts, but these contexts are still related to their own world and level of understanding. [4]

Theoretical Underpinning of TASC

The theoretical underpinning of TASC evolved directly from the philosophy of Paolo Freire as outlined in the earlier section of this chapter, but we adjusted our pragmatic application of Freire's ideas to meet the needs of the learners within their particular and immediate contexts. In addition, other theorists played both supportive and formative roles. The work of Vygotsky supported and extended that of Freire: namely that the importance of social and cultural transmission and construction of knowledge as the fundamental vehicle of education, runs parallel with the vital role of mediation for understanding and mastery. Through co-operative, interactive learning, pupils negotiate language and meaning, internalising concepts and gaining conscious control over their thoughts and actions. As they develop these understandings, they form language and thinking tools for further learning: the role of the teacher is to scaffold the task until learners become independent. Modelling thinking behaviour and thinking language is another key strand in TASC: the senior learner demonstrates, verbalises, and facilitates the active learning situation. A further element underpinning TASC is the essential requirement to develop self-esteem, self-efficacy, and self-regulated learners through relevant context, constant success even in small stages, and positive assessment that feeds forward to further learning
(Eggen, & Kauchak, 1997; 1996; Bandura, 1982).

When we consider the range of thinking skills and strategies encompassed within TASC, then the work of Robert Sternberg (1985, 1997, 2001) has had a dominant influence. Sternberg proposes that 'intelligence' consists of three inter-related aspects:

- The contextual sub-theory in which intelligence is viewed as mental activity directed towards the purposeful adaptation to, selection of, and shaping of real world environments relevant to life. There are clear indications in this for the recognition of cross-cultural differences in cognition.
- The experiential sub-theory which proposes that intelligent performance on any task requires: the ability to deal with novel tasks; and the ability to automatize the processing of information.
- The componential sub-theory that specifies the strategy for information processing, i.e.

---

[4] Since the early development of the TASC Project, the 'Western' curriculum is currently going through major revision to produce a curriculum more relevant to learners in a multi-racial, multi-cultural context.

- the executive (meta) processes that are used to plan, monitor and
- evaluate strategies used in problem-solving;
- the performance components used to carry out the task; and
- the knowledge acquisition components that are used to learn how to
- solve problems in the first place.

All three components outlined above, are interactive and need to be trained in parallel.

Many theorists stress the importance of metacognition, which Freire refers to as reflection, but the particular influence of the seminal work of Campione et al; Borkowski, and Sternberg is particularly evident in the development of the TASC Framework (Campione et al 1984; Borkowski, 1985; & Sternberg, 1985). Metacognition is viewed as a component of intelligent behaviour used throughout life; as a process of generalising effective thinking strategies; and, as a key link between intelligence, self-knowledge and self-regulation. Through the process of metacognition, learners reflect upon their learning, crystallizing and automatising thinking skills and processes. Problem-solving is the key to effective learning and involves reflective processes of creative, analytical and practical action and thought.

Teaching and Learning Principles of TASC

The teaching and learning principles of TASC evolved as we engaged in various learning tasks with the students: learners and teachers reflecting on the kinds of thinking they needed to use and develop in order to accomplish the learning task effectively. Teachers and students reflected collaboratively on the most effective strategies for teaching and learning; and how they could generalise and use the strategies across the curriculum and, importantly, in life itself. Gradually, the following principles emerged:

- Derive, trial, refine and adopt a generalised working framework of universal problem-solving, through processes of collaborative action research and evaluation, solving problems relevant to learners. Learners and teachers need ownership and understanding of the problem-solving process.
- Negotiate and use relevant language for thinking and problem-solving: naming strategies and skills appropriately to enable reference to and later recall of these strategies in further problem-solving.
- Model relevant thinking strategies then provide experiences for learners so that they use the strategies and perceive themselves as successful problem-solvers.
- Give attention to motivational aspects through praise and positive reinforcement of thinking and problem-solving behaviour. Celebrate the criteria for success, the criteria having been negotiated with the learners.
- Use co-operative, interactive teaching and learning methods with learners working in small groups.
- Encourage self- and group-monitoring, evaluation and reflection on success, ways of improving and opportunities for transferring skills and strategies to other contexts.

Outline of the TASC Problem-Solving Processes of Teaching and Learning

The processes of the TASC problem-solving framework can best be described as a flexible spiral of sub-processes that are simultaneously cognitive, emotional and metacognitive. The stages are sometimes cyclical, sometimes sequential, and sometimes recursively flexible as the situation demands. Learners evolved the nature of the TASC framework through active and practical, hands-on, everyday problem-solving activities which they identified as problematic to themselves. These everyday problems included:

- how they could locate sources of electricity in order to do their school homework at night. This was negotiated with the local community by offering to give Zulu and English lessons to younger students in the church hall in exchange for the use of the church building which had electricity. The parents of the younger children paid a small fee for this. Previously, the students had either tried to do their homework by candle-light or clustered under a street light, or had simply not done the work.
- how they could get school books for further study. This was resolved when students organised themselves into choirs and gave concerts at local celebrations in return for small donations. In addition, the students negotiated with the 'White' librarian in the nearby town that the library would be available for them on a Saturday morning. They were surprised at the ease with which this was negotiated once they had gathered the self-confidence to make the approach. Previously they had adopted the attitude of 'learned helplessness', feeling that they could do nothing to solve the problem.
- how they could present their grievances to their teachers about the poorly prepared lunch that was provided free. This was resolved by setting up discussion groups, recording and prioritising the most important grievances and appointing leaders to represent them in a meeting with the staff. On a previous occasion, the students had 'rioted' by locking their teachers into the staffroom, 'toy-toying' noisily and very exuberantly outside, and refusing to let the teachers out until their 'demands' were met.

There were many practical problems solved by the students themselves that gradually eroded their common feelings of 'learned helplessness'. During and after each completed action, they reflected on and extrapolated the successful thinking and action strategies they had used, and discussed how they could transfer and regularly use the same strategies both in their lives and also in their formal school learning.

Gradually the TASC Framework for Thinking Actively in a Social Context evolved out of the experiences of the practical problems solved by the students, and encapsulated a wide range of teaching and learning principles for developing thinking and problem-solving skills.[5] The early formative and simplified outline of these principles is given below:

- First **Gather and Organise** what you already know about the subject, topic, problem, situation. Then decide how and where you can find out more information.

---

[5] The TASC Framework of skills and processes is still being refined and extended. See Wallace and Maker 2004 for the most recent developments.

All learners have a store of previous knowledge and learning: they are not all empty pitchers that need filling up. They need to fully recognise this and actively draw on and use prior learning. This stage brings into the working memory a range of ideas and knowledge ready for action.

- Clearly **Identify** what the problem actually is by stating it simply as 'What am I trying to do?' (Goal(s)) and 'What is preventing me from doing it?'(Obstacle(s)). Then decide on the criteria for success and work towards that (Possible Solution(s)). Many learners in situations of disadvantage and frustration are overwhelmed by the emotions of anger and injustice which are all-consuming, debilitating, but which often renders them passive (or aggressive) against seemingly overwhelming circumstances. Taking control over the situation needs thoughtful, planned and sustained action.

- **Generate ideas** – together with others, think of as many possible ways of solving the problem without stopping any flow of thoughts by pre-judging the value of them. Hitch-hike on to other people's ideas, think laterally, allow all ideas without contradiction. All learners are creative, but many are unaware of the creative potential they have – they have been conditioned into receiving ideas and information from the teacher, believing that they need to be spoon-fed with other people's thoughts and ideas.

- **Decide** on the best ideas and outline a possible course(s) of action and plan the stages systematically: outline stages of the task clearly and discuss who is responsible for the carrying out of each stage of planning. Taking responsibility for personal decision-making and consequent action is fundamental to self-actualisation and self-efficacy.

- **Implement** the ideas by putting the decision(s) into action, monitoring progress and adjusting plans as is necessary.

- **Evaluate** progress and successes throughout the project, judged against the agreed goals, obstacles and solutions discussed at the Identify stage. If necessary, backtrack and reformulate ideas and plans previously agreed upon.

- **Communicate** and share ideas throughout the whole project, but also take time to share and celebrate the outcomes and successes. Share successes with the wider community and discuss the stages and processes of overcoming obstacles and achieving goals.

- **Reflect and Learn from Experience** – discuss the success of strategies that were used, evaluate the quality of the group interaction, reflect on how the successful strategies can be transferred to other situations including school. Discuss changes that need to be made in any future project to make the whole action more effective and sustainable.

There was unanimous agreement by students and teachers that the Euro-centred curriculum needed to be completely rewritten to make it Afro-centred: however, students realised that this needed a long process of change. Importantly, teachers and students would need to be involved in any discussions about a new curriculum with the resultant writing of new school texts; and also closely involved in discussions of appropriate pedagogy.[6] Meanwhile, there was an urgent and pragmatic need to embed the problem-solving and thinking skills into the current curriculum so that learners and teachers could not only survive within the Euro-centred curriculum, but use appropriate thinking strategies to surmount the obstacles presented by turgid and lifeless content. Students wanted to break through the barriers of segregation caused by 'failing' the matriculation examination and obtain higher levels of learning so that they could access opportunities that would enable them to become leaders of change.

The 28 students in the first pilot TASC Project all gained the highest matriculation results ever achieved amongst Black students in KwaZulu/Natal in their Senior School Certificate. All students entered universities with bursaries to pay their fees and support their studies. In a follow-up meeting, all 28 students said that the first thing they had done on arriving at university was to set up a TASC club so that they could teach fellow students the problem-solving and thinking strategies they had used to master their studies. Very poignantly, one student said, 'I now believe that I belong in my own country, and that I can lead change.' At that, the group of now young adults burst into the wonderful close harmony of Zulus singing a round of 'Communication! Oh yes, Communication!'. All of these particular 28 pilot students, now adults, are in positions of leadership in education, commerce, business and industry.

CONCLUSION

The 15 years I lived and worked in KwaZulu/Natal taught me a great deal about joy and laughter despite crippling disadvantage; about love, friendship and sharing although there were few resources to share; about resilience and determination to succeed, surmounting all obstacles; about the rich quality of communication and striving towards a common goal.

However, I would not like to end my personal narrative without adding a postscript.

Since returning to England and working as a consultant in schools nationally from 1999, I have witnessed the mechanisation of the teaching and learning processes in schools, and also in other areas of public life, brought about by the insistence of the government on 'measurable' achievement targets and 'universal' standards. I am certainly not against learners and teachers striving to reach goals; but not every learning goal can be quantified and measured, organised statistically and then compared and contrasted in what has come to be labelled 'the shame and blame culture'. Teachers generally are reporting that they are treated as mechanical technicians delivering set content, rather than as educators interacting with learners. They report that increasing numbers of pupils are de-motivated and anti-school.

There is not space here to discuss this in detail, but I refer you particularly to the chapter in this text written by Myriam Torres and Loui Reyes who reflect on the current trends in education in the so-called 'developed' world.

---

[6] See the series of language and thinking texts written within the TASC Framework for pupils from 6 to 18 years of age: *Language in My World* and *Reading in My World.* Juta Educational Publishers, Cape Town, SA.

REFERENCES

Apple, M. W., & King, N. R. (1977). What Do Schools Teach? In A. Molnar & J. A. Zahorik (Eds.), *Curriculum Theory* (pp.108-126). Washington, D. C.: The Association for Supervision and Curriculum Development.

Bandura, A. (1982). Self- efficacy mechanism in human agency. *American Psychologist, 37,* 122-147.

Borkowski, J. E., (1985). Signs of Intelligence: strategy generalisation and metacognition. In Yussen, R. S. (Ed) *The growth of reflective thought in children.* New York: Academic Publications.

Campione J. C., Brown A. L., Ferrara R. A., & Bryant N. R., (1984). The zone of proximal development: Implications for individual differences and learning. In: B. Rogoff & J. Wertsch (Eds.), Children's learning in the "zone of proximal development". *New Directions for Child Development,* no. 23. San Francisco: Jossey-Bass.

Dromi, E. (1993). Language and Cognition: A developmental perspective. In: Dromi, E. (Ed) *Language and Cognition: A developmental Perspective. Volume 5.* Norwood, NJ, USA: Ablex.

Dostal, E. & Vergani, V. (1984). Future Perspectives on South African Education. *Occasional Paper No 4.* Institute for Future Research, University of Stellenbosch.

Eggen, P. & Kauchak, D. (1997). *Education Psychology: Windows on classrooms.* 2nd ed. New Jersey: Merrill.

Fraser, J. W. (1997). Love and History in the Work of Paulo Freire. In P. Freire, J. W. Fraser, D. Macedo, T. McKinnon, & W. T. Stokes (Eds.), *Mentoring the Mentor: A Critical Dialogue with Paulo Freire* (pp. 175-199). New York: Peter Lang Publishing, Inc.

Freire, P. (1998a). *Pedagogy of Hope.* New York: Continuum.

Freire, P. (1998b). *Pedagogy of the Oppressed.* (New Revised 20th-Anniversay ed.). New York: Continuum Publishing Co.

Freire,P. (1997). A Response. In P. Freire, J. W. Fraser, D. Macedo, T. McKinnon, & W. T. Stokes (Eds.), *Mentoring the Mentor: A Critical Dialogue with Paulo Freire* (pp. 175-199). New York: Peter Lang Publishing, Inc.

Krashen, S. D. (1981). *Second language acquisition and second language learning.* New York: Pergamon Press.

McLaren, P. (1998). *Life in Schools: An Introduction to Critical Pedagogy in the Foundations of Education.* Longman.

McLaren, P. (1993). *Schooling as a Ritual Performance.* Routledge.

Omaggio, A. C. (1986). *Teaching language in context: Proficiency oriented instruction.* Boston: Heinle & Heinle.

Ramos, M.B. (1974). *Paulo Freire's Pedagogy of the Oppressed.* New York: Seabury.

Schlesinger, I. M. (1993). If de Saussure was right, could Whorf have been wrong? In Dromi, E. (Ed) (1993). *Language and Cognition: A developmental Perspective, Volume 5.* Norwood, NJ, USA: Ablex.

Sternberg, R. J. (1985). *Beyond IQ: A Triarchic Theory of Human Intelligence.* NY: Cambridge University Press.

Sternberg, R. J. (1997). *Successful Intelligence.* New York: Plume.

Sternberg, R. J., Nokes, K., Geissler, P. W., Prince, R., Okatcha, F., Bundy, D. A. & Grigorenko, E. L. (2001). The relationship between academic and practical intelligence: A case study in Kenya. *Intelligence, 29,* 401-418.

Wallace, B. & Maker, C. J., (et al) (2004). *Teaching Problem-Solving and Thinking Skills: An Inclusive Approach.* London: David Fulton Publishers.

Wallace, B., (et al) (1996ff). *Language in My World.* Cape Town, South Africa: Juta Educational Publishers.

Wallace, B. & Adams, H. B. (1993). *Thinking Actively in a Social Context: TASC.* Oxford, UK: AB Academic Publishers.

Vos, A. J. (1986). Aspects of Education in KwaZulu. In *Paedomenia, Vol 13, No 2.* Journal of the Faculty of Education, University of Zululand.

Vygotsky, L. (1978). In Cole, M., John-Steiner, V., Scribner, S. & Souberman, E. (Eds) *Mind in Society.* Cambridge (MA) USA: Harvard University Press.

ABOUT THE AUTHOR

Biographical Details: Belle Wallace

- Belle Wallace initially worked in an advisory capacity (UK) with the brief for developing Curriculum Enrichment and Extension for pupils across all phases of education; she was Co-Director of the Curriculum Development Unit (University of Natal, SA) with the double brief for developing Assessment Strategies and Curriculum Enrichment and Extension for very able, disadvantaged learners, and training Curriculum Planners; she designed and was senior author of a whole school series of 48 language and thinking skills texts to redress cognitive underdevelopment in pupils from 6 to 17+ years; she edited *'Worldwide Perspectives on Gifted Disadvantaged'* in 1993 (Oxford, UK: AB Academic Publishers), and the second volume *Diversity in Gifted Education: International perspectives on global issues* (London,UK: Routledge) is published in 2006; she now works as a national and international consultant on Problem-solving and Thinking Skills Curricula.

- Belle has been a delegate to the World Council and has also served on the Executive Committee of the World Council for Gifted and Talented Children; she has been editor of *Gifted Education International.* (AB Academic Publishers) since 1981; and is currently President of NACE, UK (National Association for Able Children in Education).

- Her main interests are: the identification and nurturing of potential in *all* children through an enriching curriculum, and the provision of extension activities for those pupils who demonstrate the need; the development of problem-solving and thinking skills across the curriculum within a framework of whole school development; and the development of multiple abilities.

- Her publications are many: most recently, she has published a series of 5 Problem-solving and Thinking Skills books extending topics taken from the National Curriculum Framework, UK (published by NACE/Fulton).

- Recently, Belle has been a made a Fellow of the Royal Society of Arts, in recognition of her service to education.

In: Pioneers in Education: Essays in Honor of Paulo Freire   ISBN: 978-1-60021-479-0
Editors: M.Shaughnessy, E.Galligan et al., pp 85-99   ©2008 Nova Science Publishers, Inc.

Chapter 5

THE EDUCATIONAL PRAXIS OF PAULO FREIRE: TRANSLATIONS & INTERVENTIONS

Aly Juma, Octavio Augusto Pescador,
Carlos Torres and Rich Van Heertum
Paulo Freire Institute, UCLA, USA

INTRODUCTION

Paulo Reglus Neves Freire was born in Recife, Brazil, on September 19, 1921 and died of heart failure in São Paulo on May 2, 1997. In the intervening 76 years, he endowed us with a legacy of writings and action that inspired generations of critical educators to explore the role of education in struggling against oppression and injustice. He was a pedagogue who expanded our perceptions of the world, nourished our will, enlightened our awareness of the causes and consequences of human suffering and illuminated the need to develop an ethical and utopian pedagogy for social change. His death left us with memories of his gestures and passionate voice, his white bearded face resembling a prophet and his marvelous Socratic books.

Paulo taught us that domination, aggression and violence are an intrinsic part of human and social life. He argued that few human encounters are exempt from oppression of one kind or another. Whether it be by virtue of race, class or gender, people tend to be victims and/or perpetrators of oppression. He stressed that racism, sexism or class exploitation are the most salient forms of dominance and oppression, but also recognized that oppression exists along the lines of religious beliefs, political affiliation, national origin, age, size and physical or intellectual handicap.

In struggling against oppression, Freire capitalized on the work of psychotherapists Freud, Jung, Adler, Fanon and Fromm together with the philosophical insights of Hegel, Marx, Marcuse and others to develop his "Pedagogy of the Oppressed." He believed that education could improve the human condition, counteracting the effects of a psychology of oppression and ultimately contributing to what he considered the "ontological vocation of mankind," namely humanization. In the introduction to his widely-acclaimed *Pedagogy of the*

Oppressed, he argued that: "From these pages I hope at least the following will endure: my trust in the people and my faith in men and women and in the creation of a world in which it will be easier to love"(Freire, 1970, p. 19).

Freire was known as a philosopher and theoretician of education who never separated theory from praxis. Throughout his life he worked assiduously to implement his educational philosophy, including his famous experience as adviser to the revolutionary government of Guinea-Bissau in the mid-seventies, resulting in one of his most popular books, *Pedagogy in Process: The Letters to Guinea-Bissau*. Later, when the Partido Dos Trabalhadores (Workers' Party) won the Municipal elections in São Paulo in 1988, a natural choice for the Secretary of Education was Freire, a well-known Brazilian socialist pedagogue who was one of the originators of popular education in Latin America and an inspirational figure in the spread of the Theology of Liberation. His appointment as Secretary of Education of the City of São Paulo in January 1989 created a unique opportunity for him to implement his radical ideas within his home country. Freire took charge of 654 schools with 700,000 students, from K1-8. He also engaged in adult education and literacy training in São Paulo, one of the megalopolis of Latin America. The reverberations of his policy work during those three years are still felt in São Paulo, through innovations in curriculum, teacher training, school governance and literacy training that intimately linked social movements with the state and empowered children and communities.

Paulo became one of the most recognized and revered pedagogues associated with progressive causes, the educational New Left and Critical Pedagogy during his lifetime. Today his words and spirit have spread across the globe inspiring educators, activists, community leaders and students to struggle for a better tomorrow.. Given the wide range of his philosophical and educational contributions, the impact of his work cannot be restricted to literacy training or adult education. Problem-posing education and the methodology for thematic research, two of the main theoretical and methodological innovations resulting from his work, have been implemented not only in social studies and curriculum studies within adult, primary, secondary and higher education, but in a diverse array of subjects including mathematics and physics, educational planning, feminist studies, romance languages and educational psychology.

In his writings, Paulo offers us his metalanguage, his poetics and his epistemology of curiosity. Like Antonio Gramsci (1999) in his *Quaderni del Carcere*, he offers a series of extremely insightful yet fragmented reflections that require deep, deliberate and serious study. He actively engages progressive and radical postmodernism, while maintaining the need to uphold the truth. He argues not against grand narratives but against totalizing certainties. He speaks passionately for school autonomy and against neoliberalism. He argues for an education of truth, utopia, creative imagination and tolerance. And he helps us think and act politically and pedagogically, in a dialectic of unity in diversity intimately linked to the authenticity of his life, thought and work.

In this paper, we explore Freire's inspiration outside traditional contexts – looking at the ways his ideas have been translated in a series of innovative ways. We start by exploring his epistemological approach of critical hermeneutics and how that could inform a more social justice oriented approach to educational research. We then engage two translations that have not been well-studied: early childhood education and community-based activism. We conclude by highlighting one of his most abiding legacies, particularly in the current political milieu of cynicism and nihilism, which is his inexorable hope in a better tomorrow that sprouts from the will and action of subjects in history struggling against oppression.

FREIRE IN THE "LAB"

Objectivity is a foundational goal of Western science. Advocates argue that scientists must seek to extricate bias and prejudice from their work and study the world as it is, rather than as it should be. This entails attempts to establish methods and methodologies that are value neutral, looking at the world from the outside in with clear, non-refracted lenses. With the charge comes the responsibility to minimize the influence of subjectivity on research and to eradicate any normative or ethical consideration.

Many seek to challenge this position, arguing that science has simultaneously used objectivity as a cloak to hide deep ideological biases that inflect their work. Purportedly objective scientific research has been used to label individuals and whole groups as innately inferior, to ground unequal treatment in the realms of law, politics, economics and education and as the theoretical backbone for many of the most insidious projects in history including slavery, eugenics, colonialism and the Holocaust. It has also been used to exclude many voices from science itself, under the guise of European white male access to a higher rationality. Much contemporary research continues to "empirically ground" claims of innate difference along the lines of gender, race and ethnicity that then inform public debate and policy.

A question today is the extent to which objectivity can be maintained as a goal amidst the crisis of Western empiricism germinating from post-structuralism, postcolonialism, feminism and the like. Many no longer believe in the validity or even desirability of objectivity as a goal. Subjectivity has become the focal point of social theory and has spread outward to challenge the hegemony of traditional epistemological approaches. At the same time, positivism continues to dominate the social scientific research community, causing a profound chasm between "hard" and "soft" science.

In seeking to find a middle ground between the extremes of positivism and absolute relativism, Freire offers useful insights and tools. He starts by rejecting the oxymoron of objective, apolitical knowledge, recognizing that teaching and research were by their very nature political acts that necessarily involve taking a position: "It seems fundamental to me to clarify in the beginning that a neutral, uncommitted and apolitical educational practice does not exist" (Freire, 1998, p. 39). The positivism that was coming to dominate educational research in the 1980s and early 1990s was thus of great concern to Freire and his followers, particularly its reliance on a "value free" methodology. The scientism of this orientation not only hid ideological biases and power dynamics that oriented the work, but also allowed researchers to ignore the implications of their work or offer truly innovative solutions to the problems described.

Even forgoing the obvious biases and ideologies that underwrite all language, if one refuses to take a position, it seems fair to claim they are actively supporting the maintenance of the current order and status quo. For isn't adherence to conventional wisdom synonymous with passive retreat? Freire (1997) believed that attempts at objectivity in teaching ignored the ethical responsibility of educators to mold not only the economic potential of children but their moral foundation as well. In schools, by moving from the indoctrination of "banking education" to the transformative potential of problem-posing education, he envisioned a system where revolutionary spirit could be created and fostered into a resolve for change.[1] He was essentially arguing that objectivity was itself an ideology, powerfully inured to the goals of maintaining unequal power relations and unjust economic and social order. He believed that objectivity was but a cloak that protects us from the deeper theoretical and systemic issues at the heart of inequality and injustice.

Freire did not reject the ability to reach a provisional truth, driven by the generalizable characteristics of individual empirical knowledge. And he does not fall prey to the postmodern penchant to reject normative judgment. His approach is founded on critical hermeneutics, working to offer a way out of the impasse of strict positivism and absolute relativity. He employed a reinterpretation of phenomenological epistemology to argue that we can reach a provisional and generalizable knowledge that can be used constructively in the struggle to define and redefine the world. This new knowledge is tied to everyday life, rather than universalizing principles, where dialogue and experimentation lead people to produce new knowledge based on *collective lived experience* (Torres and Morrow, 2002). He thus argues for a reality founded on dialogue where individuals work in fellowship and solidarity to first envision their surrounding reality and then work collectively to change it. In the process, he builds the foundations for a communal vision of humanity, where reality is constructed and negotiated in collective action, rather than through an individual subject looking out at an objective world.

In the process, research creates a space where individuals become conscious of the social, cultural and political world around them, as well as the power relations that underwrite those realities. It capitalizes on a deep reading of the world, inflected with critical reflection on history and the distance between events and their later interpretation. Feminist Donna Haraway (2004) largely agrees with this approach, arguing that a power-charged social relation of conversation between active agents in history is the best way to overcome the extremes of social constructionist relativity and absolute empiricism. The knowledge created by research will thus have a provisional and collective nature, tied to place and time and to larger issues of culture, language and social structures. Research, in this sense, will be social in form and highlight the centrality of intersubjectivity and the collective, discursive nature of all knowledge and reality. And it will be undertaken and/or intimately involve people immersed in the social situation under study.

Freire clearly argued for the limitation of objectivity as a goal of inquiry, but would not argue that researchers should abandon its spirit completely. Instead, research can move to a position where balance, fairness and reflexivity replace value-free norms. Researchers would then be in a position to recognize their own biases and prejudices and, to the extent practicable, communicate those to the audience. They could be clear about their political objectives and offer a project for social transformation based on creating a more just and equitable world.

---

[1] See Freire (1997). Pedagogy of the Oppressed, Chapter 2, for in-depth discussion of the advantages of problem-posing, dialogical education over the current "banking" method that implants information in a hierarchical system that neglects lived experience, student diversity and true critical thinking skills and the cultivation of critical consciousness.

Starting from the subordinate position offers great resources toward this end, by providing unique perspectives from inside oppressive regimes, rather than attempting to contemplate them solely from the outside. It is clear that oppressed group have specific and unique insights into their reality that can help enrich empirical research. This is true of women, African Americans, Latinas, the working class and all other groups that have suffered subordination or marginalization in one form or another. Freire believed that research should germinate from these groups in their struggle to define their world and work to transform it. Rather than having well-intentioned elites create research that simply catalogs the problem, or that blames the groups for their own plight, he advocated knowledge building that can enlighten and empower people to be active subjects in history. To accomplish this in a practical sense, researchers should start their research from the voices, experiences, objective social positions and discourses of the group under study and find ways to minimize their own subjective influence on the research. They could then study larger structural phenomena and institutions, and offer practical alternatives to address inequality and injustice.

To create a new science that is more inclusive, ecumenical and balanced, it is essential that as many voices as possible are heard. At the same time, balance and fairness are goals that should continue to stand at the forefront of all research. Researchers can have a political end in mind, but must not allow this to cloud their judgment or make them blind to disconfirming evidence. Freire offers us inroads toward the realization of this science. It involves tying together theory and practice, communicating positionality, emphasizing results over methods and linking research to material circumstances and relevant policy. More than anything it involves a movement from the cataloging of what is to the struggle to define what can be.

Researchers and practitioners have already undertaken a number of studies of Freire's work that follow this model to varying degrees. These studies have focused on elementary through higher education, in addition to studies on adult education in diverse settings.

Ira Shor, for example, offers methods for implementing an empowering education that translates traditional approaches to critical and democratic ones, from elementary school all the way through college (Shor, 1992). And Boaventura de Sousa Santos (2006) looks specifically at the university and the ways that Freirian pedagogical strategies can offer democratic and emancipatory reform. In the next section, we offer some preliminary thoughts on the possibility of interjecting Freire's pedagogy into early childhood education, followed by his translation into community empowerment and activism.

FREIRE IN THE CLASSROOM

It might seem at first hard to imagine dialogical, problem-solving methods translating well into a preschool or kindergarten classroom. How can we capitalize on the life experiences of children who have experienced so little? Can substantive dialogue really take place among the very young? And doesn't the teacher need to establish relatively stringent rules to maintain control in the classroom? While these are all valid questions that need answers, we believe Freire philosophy and pedagogy can be instrumental in improving learning in these classrooms. By placing his work and the work of his followers in dialogue with human development literature, we thus attempt to explore ways that his practices and techniques can be reinvented for children in the early formative years. This involves transcending discourses on developmental stages, placing greater trust in the resources and abilities these children bring to the classroom and working to redefine the goals of education in a more diverse, multicultural world.

The field of early childhood education has been heavily influenced by human development theory and developmental psychology, resulting in a focus on the practices that can facilitate individual growth and learning within the context of Piaget's (1972) stages of development and experiential expectations. Teaching and learning strategies within this framework are founded on age and skill appropriate curriculum that addresses the specific needs and capacities of children at various levels of development. Absent from this theoretical foundation are critical sociological exploration of issues related to agency, power, policy and the state as they intersect with the multitude of historic, religious, ethnic, cultural, gendered and socio-political orientations.

What results in schools is often a tension between 'conservative' movements in educational practice at the level of the institution; multiculturalism, pluralism and dialogue at the level of organizational culture; and ritualistic and celebratory notions of culture in liberal/progressive education. Early education generally aligns with developmentally appropriate practices, at the level of 'state' legitimacy – promoting individual growth and experience, together with consumerism and competition based on 'National and International' standards.

The tenants of competition and conformity and those of social justice and moral development thus often come into conflict. In many cases it becomes a battle between those that want to open the mind and assist in the movement toward critical consciousness and those who practice a false paternalism that simply reproduces society.

At the inferential level of the state, or more precisely, at the level of accrediting bodies of educational institutions, standards are limited in scope to facilities, administration, curriculum and pedagogy. They do not engage questions of content and contextual outcomes that work toward creating a more just and equitable society by intervening to ensure that tolerance, pluralism and peace and social justice education are integrated. Social justice is given lip service by accreditation and this mentality tends to trickle down to schools. At the same time, the accreditation process dislocates the hegemony of the state by creating intermediary bureaucracies that legitimize schools.

Together with developmental psychology, constructivism has become a popular pedagogical approach utilized across grade levels. Its incorporation into the very root of classroom instruction is generally viewed as a positive move among progressives. However, constructivism is more than a set of teaching techniques; it is a coherent pattern of expectations that underlie new relationships between students, teachers and the world of ideas (Windschitl, 1999). As such, constructivism challenged us to transform the comfortable and familiar, though often unstated, norms, beliefs and practices of the classroom culture.

Whereas constructivism has the aim of individual understanding emanating from collective or group activities, Freirian (1997) pedagogy emphasizes collective learning as a means of challenging oppression in all its various manifestations. In the classroom, it involves using culture circles to name, reflect on and act on the forms of oppression toward the goal of liberation. This works to foster ennobling mutual learning that creates culture, knowledge and social movements that extend beyond the classroom to the level of community and ultimately to the structure of institutionalized knowledge. This knowledge, which is traditionally embedded in banking notions of fact regurgitation and standardized tests, can unearth deeper understanding of structural and institutional power and mechanisms to alter it. In this way, Freirian pedagogy transcends constructivism in its broader goals and expectations.

It is essential to ensure that philosophical orientations such as constructivism and Freirian pedagogy do not appear in the classroom as a set of isolated instructional methods grafted onto otherwise traditional techniques though; for it is a culture - a set of beliefs, norms and practices – that constitutes the fabric of school life. This culture, like all other cultures, affects the way learners interact with peers, relate to the teacher and experience the subject matter. They must all be interconnected to reinforce one another.

Portraying the constructivist classroom as a culture is important because many challenges for teachers emerge when new rituals take root or when familiar norms of behavior are transformed into new patterns of teacher/student interaction (Bolotin, Forthcoming) In reality, they are more likely to be guided not by instructional theories but by the familiar images of what is "proper and possible" in classroom settings (Zeichner and Tabachnick, 1981). The discrete practices of constructivist classrooms – which include lecture, discussion, cooperative learning, problem-based learning, inquiry-based learning, multifaceted assessment or performance assessments, hands-on experiences and scaffolding to name a few – all have the goal of collaboration in learning. This challenges deeply embedded traditional notions of the classroom setting and offers great challenges to instructors.

One of the struggles with a constructivist-oriented approach to learning is that is still assumes that teachers reign supreme in the classroom, with their knowledge of subject matter and various approaches to the understanding of that subject matter fluid or within their immediate comprehension and comprehensibility. They are expected to simultaneously guide student learning from multi-faceted approaches that capitalize on students' experiential base and interests. These teachers thus need to be grounded in theory and practice and need to have had a number of years teaching with a very broad and diverse student populations to effectively navigate the more diverse cultural mélange that defines contemporary urban classrooms. Otherwise, their attempts at engaging student curiosity and employing strategies to build on their previous lived experience can actually work to maintain asymmetries along class, race and even gendered lines.

A Freirian approach, while appearing to some to absolve the teacher of the responsibility of being the bearer of knowledge, requires a number of critical interventions that can address the central problems of constructivism. The Freirian teacher must simultaneously teach and learn with the students, with the aim of gaining subject mastery while working to engage learners in the production of their own collective knowledge. This process requires simultaneously extrapolating understanding of local material conditions and larger structural and societal inequalities and injustices to employ in the struggle for humanization. In the early years, it requires intimate knowledge of the student populations' culture and social milieu, to evoke ideas and knowledge that may not be as readily available through student-teacher dialogue as among older populations.

If the mark of human capacity is observed in technocratic functionalism, then we as educators have severely missed the mark and cornerstone of a good education, which is the process of humanization. Instead we fall prey to the instrumental rationality at the heart of neoliberalism. This sentiment is well explained in the UNICEF 1995 report which states "In recent decades, there has been progress in the skills of imparting literacy and numeracy, but there has been comparatively little progress in imparting life skills, social skills, & value skills. We can produce experts in information technologies, but we seem unable to improve a capacity for listening, for tolerance, for respecting diversity, for harnessing the potential of individuals to the social good, or for strengthening the ethical foundations without which skills and knowledge bring little benefit".

To address this issue substantively, the school community must support instructional expertise, academic freedom and professional collaboration necessary to sustain a Freirian culture. There is an intense need to continue to reinvent him for the cultural domain of American classrooms to help students deconstruct the disjunction between politics and education so that a common humanity can be attained. Unfortunately the persistence of global inequality and injustice lead to acts of resistance and retaliation that often become aligned with notions of difference and animosity that later become interpreted as acts of deep-rooted hatred. Freirian pedagogy can help us fight through this resistance and reorient it toward positive social transformation that can then struggle against the oppression at the root of the unrest and find channels for solidarity and collective struggle toward the common good.

FREIRE IN THE COMMUNITY

Freire's work has also expanded far beyond the classroom to galvanize activists, community organizers and leaders of social movements across the globe. His message of hope, his pedagogical and philosophical insights and his belief in social transformation that sprouts from the people rather than elites or a radical vanguard party have offered useful tools and inspiration to a wide variety of groups. The UCLA Paulo Freire Institute (PFI) is one such organization, growing out of a conversation between Paulo himself, Maocir Gadotti, from the Paulo Freire Institute in Sao Paulo, and the Director of the PFI, Carlos Alberto Torres. While the Institute focuses much of its effort on research, we have also been working to become a partner in the community assisting in the struggle to transform their reality.

During the last three years, the Institute has been cultivating a possible dream alongside academic and community based organizations in Los Angeles. We have been involved in a transformational educational praxis that has assisted these groups while offering invaluable lessons from those who are verbally, physically and spiritually assailed in the struggle to give their families a better life. We struggle with them because we believe that we too are wetbacks, we too are high school dropouts, we too are servants and we too are *pinches indios*.

Although there are multiple efforts being carried out in Los Angeles inspired by, or using, the pedagogical principles of Paulo Freire, this commentary will focus on three organizations PFI collaborates with including Academia Semillas del Pueblo (a K-8 charter school), the Instituto de Educación Popular del Sur de California (an adult education and job placement organization) and the Consejo de Federaciones Mexicanas de Norte América (the Council of Mexican Hometown Associations).

Our work in popular education circles commenced during the 3rd International Paulo Freire Forum, held at UCLA in September 2001. It coincided with the official acknowledgement of California's Latino educational crisis,[2] the national centralization of

---

[2] According to Oakes, Mendoza. & Silver. (2004), only 41% of Latino students graduate from Los Angeles Unified School District High Schools.

school performance oversight (through No Child Left Behind), the emergence of emancipating K-12 local educational institutions[3] and the organizational consolidation of Mexican immigrant associations.[4] The Institute's academic interests intersected on several levels with the groundwork of popular educators creating educational alternatives and organizing community. We collectively identified opportunities to teach and learn collaboratively. At the same time, the PFI received strong support from the UCLA César E. Chávez Center (Chicana/o Studies Department) in the creation of the first Paulo Freire course within Chicano Studies in an American university. The Paulo Freire course, together with a service learning capstone requirement for Chicana/o studies majors, served as a platform to articulate research, reflection and praxis in the barrios of Los Angeles.

In March of 2002, the PFI participated in a popular education forum in San Marcos, California coordinated by a Southern California grassroots organization promoting the conscientization and mobilization of students, parents, tenants and immigrants in defending their rights.[5] On that occasion, we committed to facilitating an academic venue for popular educators, community activists and scholars to reflect on their experiences and define collective agendas for praxis. This initiative crystallized in the creation of the California Association of Freirian Educators (or CAFE) – which has stimulated the growth of a non-hierarchical reflection-action network linking academia, schools and neighborhoods.

During the first annual CAFÉ conclave held in the May of 2003 at UCLA, we established three lines of action that have guided the praxis of the PFI immigration division. The PFI works to: 1) identify the key elements required for an effective pedagogy for California, 2) dignify the work and experiences of undocumented immigrants and 3) strengthen the mobilization and transnational development capabilities of immigrant organizations. Participants reached a consensus that our children require an education that recognizes the social value and moral stature of their *jornalero* fathers and *domestica* mothers; an education that teaches them not to feel ashamed of their skin color, their language or their traditions; an education that deems them capable of learning and holding professional occupations and an education that prepares them to master the law and use it as a tool of empowerment. California children essentially require educational institutions and teachers that treat them as humans capable of love and deserving of respect.

A host of organizations have begun the work of actualizing these dreams, creating a new common sense that prevents the persecution, incarceration and social assault of the people who work on their knees picking crops, removing asbestos, mowing lawns and washing dishes. We will highlight three of the organizations we have worked with along these lines below.

I. Academia Semillas del Pueblo has demonstrated that a new pedagogy for California is feasible and desirable. The students, parents, teachers and administrators at the school have created a world of reciprocal respect and collective growth that has resulted in extraordinary

---

[3] A number of progressive charter schools, popular education centers and early childhood education organizations emerged across Los Angeles in a two-year period.

[4] We have been working with Hometown Associations in collaboration with former Consul General of Mexico José Ángel Pescador Osuna throughout the 1990s.

[5] The convening organization was Mexicanos Unidos en Defensa del Pueblo and there were over 15 groups from Southern California represented at the meeting.

achievement gains for pupils.[6] Their organizational and didactic practices are dynamic, inclusive and regenerative: "Our vision of education emphasizes a student centered school society that cultivates academic excellence, talents, humanist ethics, positive culture and social consciousness … our pedagogy is meant to enrich the human capacity to transform our reality into one that is more just" (Academia Semillas del Pueblo, 2005).

The pedagogical principles of Academia Semillas del Pueblo reflect central tenets of Freirian pedagogy – making education relevant and interesting to students, encouraging their curiosity and opening their minds to their role as subjects in history with the power to change it. They base the curriculum and pedagogy on the language, cultural values and global realities of their immigrant constituency. And they seek to develop students who value curiosity, problem-pose and create knowledge: "Ancestral Mexican schooling ethos embodied social ideals and appreciations intended to develop the child as a complete person. The indigenous heart of our vision is a repossession of an identity denied from our children in standard schools."

The school is thus forming a generation of students and families with a solid sense of dignity. They are individuals who value themselves, who can read the word and their world critically and who are able to respect and love others who are different from them. Their adherence to honor and humility will not allow the regimented, domesticating system to subdue their creativity and integrity.

II. The Instituto de Educación Popular del Sur de California (IDEPSCA) promotes the empowerment of immigrants by providing them with the educational and organizational skills necessary to transform their realities. IDEPSCA's main clients are Latino immigrants with less than six years of schooling, living at or below the poverty line. The organization educates present and future community leaders to create grassroots movements through a series of interventions including: adult Spanish literacy, English as a Second Language, *jornalero* education, community technology-computer literacy, women and youth empowerment and school reform. Even as IDESPCA is an organization operated primarily by volunteers, it serves close to 2,000 community members and has been a highly effective empowering agent in the City of Pasadena and throughout Los Angeles County.

IDEPSCA again uses Freire in establishing pedagogical praxis that enables participants to address the root causes of poverty and their lack of formal education while developing grassroots educational programs. At IDEPSCA, students are not objects in the educational process; they are subjects creating their own knowledge. Learners are acquiring skills to both critically examine their reality and collectively devise strategies to organize their communities and find solutions to their problems. As program representatives explain, "The people's transformational political action has an educational dimension without which its history, the meaning of its struggles and its teachings, that is, its culture, would be lost. This is Popular Education" (IDEPSCA, 2005).

The organization has been an effective agent of social change in Southern California. The *compañeras'* work has helped those who wear the mark of need in reclaiming their rights and dignity. A cohort of emerging transformational community leaders has taught us that the surplus generated by undocumented labor today is analogous to that generated by slave labor yesterday. In this work, the insights and inspiration of Freire are paramount.

---

[6] The increase of Academia Semillas del Pueblo API scores from 2003 to 2004 was three times that of the state and more than double that of LAUSD.

III. The Council of Mexican Federations in North America (*Consejo*) encompasses the most prominent Mexican Hometown Associations in Southern California.[7] The creation of the *Consejo* is the culmination of several decades of organizational efforts by immigrant leaders who have been promoting and financing economic development projects in their places of origin and leading grassroots capacity building programs in the U.S.

California's referenda politics in recent years propelled the mobilization of immigrant leaders in domestic politics. The battles against the citizen initiatives to deprive undocumented children of schooling and health services and to eliminate affirmative action and bilingual education consolidated the transnational political agenda of Mexican immigrant organizations. Hometown Associations have become agents of this process, defending the rights of immigrant communities and promoting the socioeconomic development and political empowerment of their constituents on both sides of the border.[8]

The *Consejo* has partnered with the Mexican American Legal Defense and Education Fund (MALDEF) and the PFI to develop the administrative and leadership skills of Hometown Associations. We have initiated an immigrant empowerment program that will engage our communities in a critical reading of the word and the world.[9] The first cohort of transnational critical leaders graduated in the summer of 2005 and are now advancing a public policy agenda to create a more humane, tolerant and equitable world for all. As Sara Zapata Mijares explained, "we are working to create laws that fulfill the needs of immigrants and their families" (Federacion de Clubes Yucatecos, 2005).

Immigrant mobilization to defend and claim their rights constitutes one of the strongest social forces in the U.S today. Transformational educators and progressive groups—in communion with "aliens"—are finding in these groups firm support to promote a broader social justice agenda. Our voices are being heard even as our praxis has yet to be fully harvested. Together we are combating our concrete fears of humiliation, exploitation, incarceration and deportation. We are transforming our weaknesses into strengths as we continue to face anti-immigrant forces all around us. Our strategy contemplates both technical training in the arts and economic sustainability together with consciousness raising tactics that promote class, ethnic and cultural solidarity. In this work, Freire's spirit has emboldened us to struggle onward, providing invaluable tools in organizing our efforts and inspiring the hope necessary for action.

In closing, we look at the centrality of Freire in maintaining hope in the current political milieu of cynicism and detachment where the channels of change appear to be damned off.

---

[7] The states represented in the Consejo are: Baja California, Colima, Durango, Guanajuato, Jalisco, Michoacán, Nayarit, Oaxaca, Puebla, Sinaloa, Sonora, Veracruz y Yucatán and Zacatecas.

[8] For example, Hometown Association leaders have been coordinating activities to promote naturalization and voter registration/participation. Their leadership was instrumental in the creation of the absentee voting prerogative for Mexican citizens abroad.

[9] It has been women immigrants who have taken the lead in developing and operating community education programs. For example, Sara Zapata Mijares, Founding President of the Yucatán Federation U.S.A. promoted the creation of (and currently directs) the leadership program cosponsored by MALDEF and the Consejo. Ymelda Yañez, Education and Culture Secretary of the Zacatecas Federation of California, coordinated a student exchange between the University of Zacatecas and the PFI.

FREIRE AND HOPE IN A CYNICAL AGE

Utopia offers the opportunity to contemplate another way of organizing society, with alternative needs, and desires and mechanisms to dream of a happier, more just world. It offers a diagnosis of what is wrong with the current social, political and economic world, an image of our deepest desires and the hope needed to galvanize the masses to act (Jameson, 2004). Utopias can build bridges, shatter or transcend artificial boundaries and offer a provisional guide on where we are going. It can provide an escape from the everyday, the pragmatic and the Realpolitik. Freire always stressed their importance in progressive politics, reminding us that we always fight against something and FOR something else. But where are our utopias today?

Today, we seemed trapped in the throes of a cynical and nihilistic age, where the political imagination has collapsed under the force of too many battles lost. We are trapped in the throes of an epoch where people believe the only sensible plan is to react, to reform and to retrench. As Russell Jacoby (2005) argues, utopia has been conflated with totalitarianism and communism, neglecting a broader view of possibility that flower outward rather than wilting inward. Or as Cornell West (2004) argues, we have moved to a state of deep nihilism in the forms of evangelicalism, paternalism and sentimentalism that demonstrate "a cowardly lack of willingness to engage in truth telling, even at the cost of social ills."

Today, there is only work and escape into love, family, friends and the narcoticizing spectacle of entertainment and technology. There is only incremental reform, or struggle and resistance without a clear end in mind. Today there are no goals but the nebulous "just and equitable society." Gone are the thoughts of a life of leisure, romantic dreams of love and freedom, or of small communities of self-sufficiency. Gone also are dreams of a properly functioning democracy and real freedom, where people come together to discuss and solve problems that affect their lives. Today optimism and hope are supplanted by cynicism and disengagement. There is no possibility or dreaming, only reality and its discontents.

Cynicism thus appears ubiquitous today, from youth unwilling to vote or engage in politics, to baby boomers that have turned their backs on 60s idealism, to melancholy leftist academics and activists, to "red state" citizens that increasingly vote on rhetorical "values," a false sense of security or intolerance. Polls have grounded these claims showing a declining trust in the federal government, from 72 percent in 1964 to less than 25 percent by the late 1990s.[10] And the annual UCLA poll of incoming college freshman has shown declining interest in politics across the country since its inception in 1966. Further proof exists in data on voting patterns and political disengagement, the conformist meme of youth that is starting to emerge and the general tenor of academic and political discourse. This cynicism is taught and reinforced at the individual, social and institutional level – all mediated through language. These forces interact to maintain current power relations and oppression, closing off the channels of creativity and avenues for real change.

Freire's pedagogical approach and philosophical insights have clearly worked to combat these trends, emboldening generations of progressive educators and activists across the globe. His project for radical change that germinates from the bottom up rather than top down offers an alternative to the failed utopian projects of the 20th century and a vision of change that is

---

[10] Data from a Gallup Poll on Trust in Government, September 13-25, 2004, from Boggs (1999).

truly democratic in spirit. In this short essay, we have outlined some of the ways that Freire has and can be employed at the local and global level in the pursuit of a more just, humane and equitable world. In closing we would like to highlight one of his most important contributions to projects for radical social transformation – his strident dedication to hope and love as necessary facets of a pedagogy that could overcome the injustices and inequalities of the past and present and the cynicism and nihilism that haunt any progressive alternatives to the fatalistic policies of neoliberalism and neo-conservatism.

Freire's pedagogy starts with the key insight that we must move beyond facilitating recognition of oppression to foster in students a belief in their position as subjects in history with the power to change it. In his final book, *Pedagogy of Freedom* (1998a), Freire argued that hope was essential if people were to overcome the cynical and ahistorical fatalism at the heart of neoliberal ideology. Teachers need to do more than awaken students to the surrounding world; they need to simultaneously give them the faith and strength to work to transform the world. For Freire always rejected fatalism as shortsighted, failing to acknowledge our "unfinishedness" in the world. To him the future is never preordained, unless we accept it as such.

He argued that the "global tendency to accept the crucial implications of the New World Order as natural and inevitable" (Freire, 1998a, p. 23) simply revealed the power of hegemony to spread, through education, the media and civil society, the precepts of the dominant class, transforming them from modes of repression to commonsensical norms. But like Sartre and Beauvoir before him, Freire (1998b) believed that while we are conditioned, we are not determined and are thus free to revolt against that conditioning:

> Our being in the world is much more than just "being." [It is] a "presence" that can reflect upon itself, that knows itself as presence, that can intervene, can transform, can speak of what it does, but that can also take stock of, compare, evaluate, give value to, decide, break with and dream. (p. 25-6)

By taking this position, he eviscerates the deterministic and fatalistic heart of neoliberalism, which relies on a solipsistic vision of reality founded on extreme individualism, instrumental rationality, trust in markets over governments and people and a lack of political imagination. Freire always believed that history was problematic but not determined. As he argued in his final book, "For me, history is a time of possibilities, not predeterminations . . . History is a possibility that we create throughout time, in order to liberate and therefore save ourselves." (Freire, 1998a, p. 38).

Our ability to hope is what separates us from the rest of the animal kingdom and what makes possible the utopian vision of a better future where we work collectively to confront and overcome our "limited situations." Hope is really the leitmotif of Freire's work and a key ingredient in rebuilding a progressive movement that can break through its own fatalistic cynicism to galvanize the populace anew to struggle for collective emancipation. His specter thus stands at the forefront of any progressive movement for social change that is truly progressive in nature and that germinates from the voices of the masses rather than the power elites.

REFERENCES

Academia Semillas del Pueblo. (2005). History. Retrieved December 11, 2005, from the World Wide Web: www.dignidad.org/english/history.html

Boggs, C. (1999). *The end of politics: corporate power and the decline of the public sphere.* New York: The Guilford Press.

Bolotin, J. P. (Forthcoming). Understanding curriculum as culture. In: Bolotin-J. P., Bravman, S., Windschitl, M., Mikel, E. & Green, N., eds., *Cultures of curriculum.* Mahwah, N.J.: Erlbaum.

Federacion de Clubes Yucatecos. (2005). Federacion de Clubes Yucatecos. Retrieved December 11, 2005, from the World Wide Web: www.yucatecos.org

Freire, P. (1978). *Pedagogy in process: The letters to guinea-bissau.* New York: Continuum.

Freire, P. (1998a). *Pedagogy of freedom.* Lanham, MD: Rowman & Littlefield Publishers.

Freire, P. (1998b). *Politics and education.* Los Angeles: UCLA Latin American Center Publications.

Freire, P. (1970). *Pedagogy of the oppressed.* New York: The Continuum International Publishing Group, Inc.

Gramsci, A. (1970). *Selections from the prison notebooks.* New York: International Publishers.

Instituto de Educación Popular del Sur de California. (2005). Instituto de Educación Popular del Sur de California. Retrieved December 11, 2005, from the World Wide Web: www.idepsca.org

Jacoby, R. (1999). *The end of utopia: Politics and culture in an age of apathy.* New York: Basic Books.

Jacoby, R. (2005). *Picture imperfect: Utopian thought for an anti-atopian age.* New York: Columbia University Press.

Jameson, F. (2004). The politics of utopia. *New Left Review*, 25.

Oakes, J., Mendoza, J. & Silver, D. (2004). California opportunity indicator: informing and monitoring california's progress toward equitable college access, UC/Accord Policy Brief.

Piaget, J. (1972). *The psychology of the child.* New York: Basic Books.

Santos de Sousa, B. (2006). The university in the 21st century: Toward a democratic and emancipatory university reform. In: Rhoads, R. A. and Torres, C. A. (Eds.) *The university, state and market: The political economy of globalization in the americas.* (pp. 60-100). Stanford: Stanford University Press.

Shor, I. (1992). *Empowering education: Critical teaching for social change.* Chicago: University of Chicago Press.

Rhoads, R. & Torres, C. A. (2006). *The university, state and market: The political economy of globalization in the americas.* Stanford, CA: Stanford University Press.

Torres, C. A. & Morrow, R. (2002). *Reading freire and habermas: Critical pedagogy and transformative social change.* New York: Teachers College Press.

West, C. (2004). *Democracy matters: Winning the fight against imperialism.* New York: Penguin Books.

West, C. (1999). *The cornel west reader.* New York: Basic Civitas Books.

Windschitl, P. (1999). The challenges of sustaining a constructivist classroom culture. *Phi Delta Kappan*, June, 1999.

Zeichner, K. & Tabachnick, R. (1981). Are the effects of university teacher education washed out by school experience? *Journal of Teacher Education, 32:3*, 7-11.

In: Pioneers in Education: Essays in Honor of Paulo Freire   ISBN: 978-1-60021-479-0
Editors: M.Shaughnessy, E.Galligan et al., pp 101-116 ©2008 Nova Science Publishers, Inc.

Chapter 6

PAULO FREIRE : THE ROUSSEAU OF THE TWENTIETH CENTURY

Asoke Bhattacharya

THIS ESSENTIAL IDEAS OF LITERACY AND LIBERATION AS SEEN FROM AN INDIAN AND THIRD WORLD PERSPECTIVE

Paulo Freire has been called the Rousseau of the twentieth century for his concept of education as the practice of freedom. His work on the educational methods and practices of the oppressed brought about a qualitative change in the philosophy and practice of adult education. As a philosopher, he connected literacy with liberation and as a practitioner, he brought about revolutionary innovations in the techniques of imparting literacy to the adult illiterate. In his unique method, an illiterate person could gain literacy within a period of thirty hours.

Paulo Freire contributed to adult education its philosophical foundation. Adult education, especially literacy, used to be equated with alphabetization. If through acquiring literacy, a person could put his/her signature on papers, identify street names and bus numbers and do such other works, it would be considered an achievement. In India, most of the literate people view adult education in such a narrow domain. Freire discarded all these notions. He linked literacy with human civilization and culture and people's mental and physical liberation.

From his concept of literacy as the gateway to liberation, Freire clarified the concept of authentic education. Like the Einsteinian concept of space-time, Freire innovated the idea of teacher-student and student-teacher. This revolutionary metamorphosis of the concepts of teaching and learning resulted in reciprocal sharing of knowledge between the coordinator and participants of the 'culture circles' where all take part in discussions with a view to changing their existential reality, and achieving insight into the society in which they live.

The evolution of Freirean epistemology can be traced to the conditions of living of the majority of the people in Northeast Brazil. Many of Freire's ideas have their root in the history of Brazil from the period of colonization and thereafter. The condition of living of the majority of the population was extremely precarious. They were insulated and humiliated,

tortured and oppressed. Freire's endeavour was to help them in their struggle for liberation :
not only from physical oppression, but also from mental subjugation.

In this article, we shall briefly address the condition of Brazil as it unfolded over the
centuries. We shall then dwell on Freire's major concepts of literacy. Finally, we shall
investigate how relevant his concepts are for the countries of the Third World and especially
India.

The Historical Background

It is around the 1530's that the economic and social organisation of the Brazilian society
began to take a definite shape. Over the previous one hundred years, the Portuguese had been
in contact with other nations of the world in the continents of Asia and Africa. This
knowledge of other peoples and cultures were instrumental in the attitudinal transformation of
the Portuguese. However, in Brazil, by force of circumstances, they settled down to an
agricultural existence and patriarchy was firmly established (Freyre, 1970). The practice of
slavery imported from the home country-became the principal mode of production. Sugarcane
cultivation first started in the eastern sea-board in the areas of São Vicente and Pernambuco.
A slave-holding aristocracy developed in the sugar cane producing zone. The same pattern
prevailed in the mining region and later in the coffee plantations.

The society which was based upon a very unequal relationship between the white master
race and the indigenous or black slaves, giving rise to a social and physical malady, the latter
due largely to the outbreak of syphilis. Slavery, the most degrading term of social and
economic relationship and the sexual union of the master and the slave brought about a
species of sadism on the part of the white master race and masochism on the part of the Indian
or African. Even after abolition of slavery (1888), this sadism and masochism continued to
haunt the Brazilian society. The scars are still visible in contemporary Brazil (Freyre, 1970).

During the early period of the Portuguese rule, the indigenous male child, who had just
developed the milk teeth, used to be taken away from the mother's lap by the padre. This
child grew up to be the axis of the missionary activity. It was this child who reared by the
missionary would develop into the missionary's 'ideal' being. In course of time, this lad
would be the accomplice of the invader in drawing the 'bones' from the native culture. Then,
shorn of their native characteristics, the indigenous people would be assimilated to the pattern
of catholic morality.

The Indian lad was both the master and the disciple. The padre, while conversing in Latin
with the boy, was learning Tupi, the language of the indigenous people. Thus, the padre
gained an insight into the indigenous social custom and culture. The boy as the 'connective
kid' between two cultures was also the 'teacher' of his own parents and elders (Freyre,
1970).

Every Brazilian carries within the self a shadow of the indigenous or the African race. In
the music, speech, delight of the senses, gait, and cradle songs-- the Brazilian carries the mark
of that influence of the female slave or nanny who rocked, sucked and fed; the influence of
the old woman who told the Brazilian child the tale of 'bicho', the ghost; the mulatto girl who
relieved the white Brazilian boy of his 'bicho de pe", a type of flea that burrows beneath skin
or feet; the black or mulatto girl who initiated the white adolescent boy into physical love
(Freyre, 1970).

Through the old black woman who served as nurses on nannies, African stories of animals fraternizing with humans, talking like them, marrying and feasting with them, came to be added to the collection of Portuguese tales. The language of the young, thus grew softer through contact of the child with the black wet-nurse. Certain words which were hard or sharp-sounding in Portuguese became much softer in the Brazilian tongue (Freyre, 1970).

In the schools of the colonial times, there prevailed certain practices. These were characterised by excesses, turbulence and perversions of the young. There took place criminal abuse of childish weakness. Teachers took real delight in humiliating the child, in doing bodily violence. The teacher was the all- powerful master. Looking down from his chair, he delivered punishments with the terrible air of the plantation owner. The one who did not apply himself as he should, was asked to stand with arms spread apart; the one caught laughing aloud was humiliated by having a dunce cap stuck on his head to make him the laughing stock of all and sundry; another would be forced to crawl on his knees over grains of corn. There were also the ferrule and the rod, the latter often with a thorn or a pin stuck at the end of it (Freyre, 1968).

The rural patriarchy began to lose its grandeur with the arrival of Dom João VI in Rio in 1808 the discovery of gold mines in Minas Gerais was already hurling death- blows to these patriarchs. Brazil, from then on, ceased to be a land of brazilwood and sugarcane.

In Pernambuco, the lines were drawn between the backwoods aristocracy and the bourgeoisie of the mansions of Recife. Realignment of forces- the bourgeoisie in collusion with the king against the plantation owners who allied themselves with the clerics – was evident in the Peddlers' War (1710) which ended in the victory of the urban interests. The Spanish and Dutch domination of Pernambuco during 1580-1654 further accentuated the bourgeois development (Freyre, 1968).

As the strength of the bourgeoisie increased, so also the unity of the lower classes. There developed an ethnic brotherhood and militant defense of the rights of the workers. In Palmares, the runaway slaves organized their own independent state in 1631. Only the combined efforts of the troops of several captaincies could destroy this state within the state after seventy six years (Freyre, 1968).

Music flourished in the city mansions. In 1850, anyone passing the streets of Rio would have heard pianos played by the young ladies (Freyre, 1968). The relatively easy going life in the sugar plantation, already affected by the discovery of gold, declined further with the initiation of coffee-plantations. In the cities, mansions owned by planters degenerated into barns. Rats, bats and ghosts took over the neglected homes.

As urbanization increased, the poor people began to huddle themselves in tenements. It appeared first in Dutch Recife. In Rio and Olinda, the poor lived in shacks built on the fool of the hills. The wealthy, Jesuits and friars took possession of the hills to build their mansions, churches and convents. To the lower classes were left the stinking mud holes, mangrove swamps and marshes. Shanties sprang up in the low foul part of the city. As the swamps and marshes were filled up, the rich came down from the hills and occupied these places too(Freyre, 1968).

During the first three centuries of relative isolation emerged the typical Brazilian- the master and the slave. There also emerged the intermediate species – the mulatto. He was budding out into a university graduate, priest, doctor, etc. He had his academic or military diploma. These were his certificate for whiteness. A weak middle class was emerging (Freyre, 1968).

The division of the society was reflected in the following verse: (Freyre, 1968, p.409)

The white man eats in the parlour
The Indian in the hall,
The mulatto in the kitchen,
The negro in the privy.

On November 15, 1889, in a peaceful revolution, the emperor was dethroned. However, Republicanism did not undo the past. The new rulers pledged to continue the policy of the empire. Their slogan was 'order and progress'.

 The generation born during this period would recollect that their schools had no playground. The use of Palmotoria (beating with palm leaves) was widespread. The students received punishment for the slightest 'offence'. Most of the whites-both males and females- were convinced of white supremacy (Freyre, 1970).

Piano was more widespread in the bourgeois homes during the Republic. The passage from concert hall to private homes took place as the grand piano became a status symbol. It was the manifestation of taste and prestige.

In 1869, Brazil had one primary school for 54 free-born children. Within five years, the ratio increased to 1:314. In 1889, the year of the Republic, it went up further to 1:40.(Freyre, 1970)

There were approximately 3000 manufacturing establishments in the country with Pernambuco having 12,000 industrial workers. The principal industry was textile. Minas Gerais had considerable number of entrepreneurs engaged in mining. Other industries included beverages, cigar, cigarette, mosaic tile, soap, matches, ceramics, canned food and wagons.

Between 1891 and 1904, Carlos Alberto de Meneses had developed considerable social action based on Catholic principles and Christian feelings. As General Manager of an industry in Pernambuco, he had made his company include various principles of social Christianity in its statutes. He instituted a program of social service for workers at the Goiana mill and Camargibe factory. It was due to his initiative that the first Catholic cooperative in Brazil was established. He later reorganized the social program for Camargibe factory into a large workers' cooperative in 1900. It had a mixed management of workers and executives. He was instrumental in the formation of the Federation of Christian Workers which held its first Congress in 1902. Pernambuco was highly predisposed to initiatives of this kind. During colonial times, Fourierism was propagated here. It was followed by Christian Socialism (Freyre, 1970) .

Brazilian economy underwent profound changes during the quarter of a century prior to 1960. Essentially a feudal country specializing in some tropical commodities, Brazil changed itself to a semi-industrialized economy. There took place a large concentration of urban population. Thirty five million people out of a total 80 million lived in urban centres. With Gross Internal Product standing at 30 billion U.S. dollars, Brazil ranked eleventh among the world economies.

The social tensions that characterised Brazil by the middle of 1960s were due to intensification of economic and industrial progress in a predominantly semi-feudal country. Only three decades prior to 1960s, the ruling class of Brazil was almost entirely composed of great landowners. The practice of slavery which lasted for four centuries gave way to a system in which labour relations were marked by a profound social differentiation between the employer and the employee. The representative system, initiated during the monarchical regime continued under the Republic (Furtado, 1965). After 1930, the old semi-feudal agrarian structure which served as a prop for the political system, began to break up. With the decline of agricultural export and related activities and development of an urban industrial sector, new basis for political power emerged. The industrial entrepreneurs and workers' organisations, started participation in political movements. However, the effectiveness of these interventions was somewhat reduced by the rigidity of the old institutional framework. The federal system, providing for an exclusively large representation to the congress of the less developed regions, contributed to the difficulties of the transitional process. On the other hand, incorporation of the working class into full political activity was made difficult by the law that gave voting rights only to the literate community (Furtado, 1965).

The population in the Northeast stood at 25 million in the 1960s. Two third of them worked on the land. These people had no political organizations and had no idea how to demand better living conditions. Cut-off from all human, social and political relationships, they worked in the sugar plantations from morning till night. This isolation began to change in the 1950s. The great industrialization process generated an increase in income. National consumption of sugar rose from 30 million tons in 1953/54 to 46 million tons in 1962/63. This necessitated an extension of acreage for cultivation of sugarcane and a resultant reduction in food crops agriculture (Furtado, 1965).

As a result of this process, a section of peasants called morador who were engaged previously in cultivation of food crops became wage-earners. Deprived of their land, these people organized themselves. Their movements for higher wages soon met with violent resistance of the mill owners. However, the peasants-turned-workers devised innovative ways and means to organize themselves and confront the threats of the propertied classes. They transmitted their messages through symbols, communicated through ballads; they created martyrs in a land where death in any case was the essential outcome. The peasant leagues achieved in a few years what would have taken decades in normal circumstances. What happened in the Sertão region also took place in the intermediate zones of Mata and Catanga. The Northeast, as a whole, experienced this surge in people's movements. People demanded their inalienable rights be granted in democracy. They took part in the process of transition. Illiteracy debarred them to act as citizens. Panlo Freire's philosophy and practice of literacy emanated directly from this socio-political scenario. The concept of 'conscientizacao' gave these people their voice. His method of literacy gave these people their right to choose their own representatives in a democracy (Furtado, 1965) .

Education as the Practice of Freedom

Freire's concepts on education emanate from the realities of the then semi-colonial, semi-feudal Brazil. Therefore, these ideas are more appropriate to the needs of the people of the developing world. Freirean epistemology is primarily based on the process of literacization of the adults living in these parts of the world. Like Karl Marx who saw in the working class of the newly developing capitalist societies the prime-mover of social progress, Freire discovered in the adult illiterate of the third world an untapped revolutionary potential which he felt, could be properly harnessed to usher in a new dawn in the developing countries.

No one before Freire developed the philosophical basis for the educational practice of illiterate adults. Freire not only filled in this gap; he propounded a theory of knowledge based on practice which revolutionized the whole concept of adult education. Thus he obliterated the dichotomy between theory and practice. Given the divergence of the reality of the developing world, characterised by their different courses in history, this epistemology could be region-specific or country-specific. But the unique contribution of Freire lies in the fact that in most of the developing world, Freirean theory and practice can be successfully adapted to local needs and peculiarities.

Essential elements of the Freirean concepts on the education of adults are available in his book 'Education as the Practice of Freedom'. Written just after the military coup in Brazil (1964) the military targeted him for his philosophy of adult education- we find his recent experiences unadulterated by too much of theorizing. He writes,

"Experiences as the Coordinator of the Adult Education Project of the Movement for Popular Culture in Recife led to the maturing of my early educational convictions. Through this project, we launched a new institution of popular culture, a "culture circle" since among us a school was a traditionally passive concept. Instead of a teacher, we had a coordinator; instead of lectures, dialogues; instead of pupils, group participants; instead of alienating syllabi, compact programs that were 'broken down" and "codified" into learning units".

The reader will observe that one can sense that here the programme is dealt for people who are not to be "taught" but discussed with. The participants are not 'students' but individuals who have a lot of wisdom and who deserve a dignified approach. The "teacher" is absent and so the top-down approach.

"In the culture circles, we attempted through group debate either to clarify situations or to seek action arising from that clarification. The topics of these debates were offered us by the groups themselves. Nationalism, profit remittances abroad, the political evolution of Brazil, development, illiteracy, the vote for illiterates, democracy were some of the themes which were repeated from group to group. These subjects and others were schematized as far as possible and presented to groups with visual aids, in the form of dialogue" (Freire, 1998, pp. 42-43).

It is from this premise that Freire developed his methods for literacy. After six months of experience with the culture circles, "we asked ourselves if it would not be possible to do something in the field of adult literacy which would give us similar results......" (Freire, 1998,p. 42). It is from the organisation of culture circles that the idea of adult literacy evolved. Literacy was a further instrument in the hands of those who discussed their own plight and that of the society in the culture circles. Literacy was not the end, but the means towards clarification of human life.

Freire writes, "From the beginning, we rejected the hypothesis of a purely mechanistic literacy program and considered the problem of teaching adults how to read in relation to awakening of their consciousness. We wished to design a project in which we would attempt to move from naiveté to a critical attitude at the same time we taught reading. We wanted a literacy program which would be an introduction to the democratization of culture, a program with men as its subjects rather them as patient recipients a program which itself would be an act of creation, capable of releasing other creative acts, one in which students would develop the impatience and vivacity which characterize search and invention."(Freire, 1998, p.43)

Freirean method was based on dialogue which is a horizontal relationship between persons (p. 45) and not vertical relationship….. (p 46). "Whoever enters into dialogue does so with someone about something; and that something ought to constitute the new content of our proposed education. We felt that even before teaching the illiterate to read, we could help him overcome his magic or naïve understanding and to develop an increasingly typical understanding" (Freire, 1998, p. 46.)

"It is remarkable to see with what enthusiasm these illiterate engage in debate and with what curiosity they respond to questions implicit in the codifications. In the word of Odilon Ribeiro Coutinho, these 'detemporalised men begin to integrate themselves in time.' (Freire, 1998, p.47).

Discussing work and culture, Freire writes, "The participants go on to discuss culture as a systematic acquisition of human experience, and to discover that in a lettered culture this acquisition is not limited to oral transmission, as is the case in unlettered cultures which lack graphic signs. They conclude by debating the democratisation of culture which opens the perspective of acquiring literacy."(Freire, 1998 p.48)

Elaborating 'generative word', Freire says, "I have the school of the world" said an illiterate……….which led Professor Jomard de Brito to ask in an essay 'what can one presume to "teach" an adult who affirms "I have the school of the world"(Freire, 1998, p.50)..

Here, in this book, we find some valuable insights regarding the practical and epistemological characteristics of education for illiterate adults. The first that Freire prescribes is 'researching the vocabulary of the group with which one is working'. Very often, the language they speak and read does not have anything in common. Freire wanted to ground literacy to the reality as experienced by the adult learner. This mechanism provides adult literacy with a solid foundation. The knowledge gained by the adult does not belong to an unknown world. The participants of the Culture Circle can relate the topics of discussion to their own existential reality. The to and fro movement from the text to the context and vice-versa, as Freire explained in many of his articles on this theme, develop the critical thinking of the adult learners. The language of discourse finds pride of place in the text and eventually embellishes the language itself. The language of the common folk usually extremely rich in its metaphor and ornamentation rejuvenates enormously the so-called elitist language and help survive occasional degradation. Like a tree which is rooted in the soil, the language which is sustained by the common people regenerates itself. Thus in Freirean concept, adult literacy if conducted properly can rejuvenate the language.

Freire's second prescription is regarding selection of the generative words. These words have to be carefully chosen from the reality of the learner so that these serve not only as the gateway to literacy but also to conscientization or development of critical consciousness. The following criteria should govern their selection: a) Phonemic richness b) Phonetic difficulty (the words chosen should correspond to the phonetic difficulties of the language, placed in a sequence moving gradually from words of less to those of greater difficulties); c) programmatic tone, which implies a greater engagement of a work in a given social, cultural and political reality.

Thirdly, creation of what Freire calls 'codifications'- the representation of typical existential situations of the groups with which one is working.

Fourthly, the elaboration of agenda which should serve as mere aids to the coordinators and never as rigid schedules to be obeyed.

Pedagogy of the Oppressed

The philosophy and practice of adult education that Freire presented in "Education as the Practice of Freedom" was further elaborated and scientifically represented in "Pedagogy of the Oppressed". This classic work brought forth the whole gamut of Freirean philosophy of adult education. Previously adult education was synonymous to alphabetization and skill development. 'Pedagogy of the Oppressed' rejected all such notions as flimsy and unacceptable. Instead, he lifted the notion to an epistemological plane. He synthesised elements of linguistics, psychology, politics and philosophy and placed the adult illiterates who constitute the majority of the people of the developing world on the centre-stage.

The first postulate that he presented was characterization of the realty of the third world. His essential theme was 'oppression'. Echoing Frantz Fanon, the ideologue of the Algerian war of liberation, Freire said, "While the problem of humanization has always, from an axiological point of view, been humankind's central problem, it now takes on the character of an inescapable concern. Concern for humanization leads at once to the recognition of dehumanization, not only as an ontological possibility but as an historical reality" (Freire, 1996, p.25) . But while both humanization and dehumanization are real alternatives, only the first is the people's vocation. This vocation is constantly negated, yet it is affirmed by that very negation" (Freire, 1996, p. 25).

From the quotations cited above, it is apparent that Freire universalizes the Brazilian reality into that of the entire developing world. From this premise he concludes "… the great humanistic and historical task of the oppressed: to liberate themselves and their oppressors as well. The oppressors, who oppress, exploit and rape by virtue of this power, cannot find in their power the strength to liberate either the oppressed or themselves. Only power that springs from the weakness of the oppressed will be sufficiently strong to free both" (Freire, 1996, p. 26).

Thus, the adult illiterate is not merely a person who is to be made literate. She /he is in fact, destined not only to liberate herself/ himself, but the entire society. Like Karl Marx who bestowed upon the working class the task of freeing itself and the society from class exploitation, Freire calls upon the adult illiterate to liberate the society of oppression. The adult illiterate, according to Freire, has to be 'conscienticized' to take upon themselves this historic task. But the oppressed, because of the continuous nature of the process of oppression suffers from 'Fear of Freedom' syndrome. This sometimes leads some members of the oppressed class to opt for the role of the oppressor or desire oppression since freedom from oppression is a phenomenon unknown to them. One of the basic elements of the relationship between the oppressed and the oppressor is 'prescription'. Every 'prescription' represents the imposition of one individual's choice upon another, transforming the consciousness of the person prescribed to into one that conforms with the prescriber's consciousness. Thus the behaviour of the oppressed is a prescriber's behaviour, following as it does the guidelines of the oppressor (Freire, 1996 pp 28-29).

"Self depreciation is another characteristic of the oppressed, which derives from their internalization of the opinion the oppressors holds of them", says Freire. "So often do they hear that they are good for nothing, know nothing and are incapable of learning anything- that they are sick, lazy and unproductive- that in the end they become convinced of their own unfitness"(Freire, 1996, p.45).

Almost never do they realize that, they too, "know things" they have learned in their relations with the world and with other women and men. Given the circumstances which have produced their reality, it is natural that they distrust themselves, comments Freire (Freire, 1996, p.45) .

How naturally Freire connects a social phenomenon, often observed by members of the upper classes in the developing world with the educational practice of the illiterate adults! Freire says, "Not infrequently, peasants in educational projects begin to discuss generative theme in a lively manner, then stop suddenly and say to the educator, "Excuse us, we ought to keep quiet and let you talk. You are the one who knows, we don't know anything." They often insist that there is no difference between them and the animals; when they do admit a difference, it favours the animals. "They are freer than we are."(Freire, 1996, p. 45).

Terming the conventional teacher-student relationship as 'narrative' and the concept as 'banking concept', Freire defines the banking concept as 'an act of depositing.' Here the teacher, instead of communicating issues communiqués and makes deposits which the students patiently receive, memorize and repeat (Freire, 1996, p 53). In the banking concept of education, knowledge is a gift bestowed by those who consider themselves knowledgeable upon those whom they consider to know nothing (Freier, 1996, p53). Freire observes that 'the banking concept of education regards men as adaptable, manageable beings. The more the students work at storing the deposits entrusted to them, the less they develop the critical consciousness which would result from their intervention in the world as transformers of the world. The, more completely they accept the passive role imposed on them, the more they tend simply to adapt to the world as it is and to the fragmented view of reality deposited in them."(Freire, 1996, p54)

Freirean concept can be comprehended adequately if one goes back to etymology. Teacher is the master, not only of knowledge, but of property in general. Present day student can be traced to learners in the guild, servants in the household, and slave in the slave-society. How naturally we relate master with the servant and the slave. This servile relationship lying hidden in the etymology also influences the psyche. Otherwise how could the notion of the conventional teacher be an object of fear, awe, and respect- all of which are not based on teacher's knowledge but power?

Freire goes to the root of this power relationship and seeks to negate this notion of oppression and found it connected to human relationships.

Freire seeks to reverse this top-down approach implicit in conventional teacher-student relationship. He identifies communication as the remedy. He says "Yet only through communication can human life hold meaning. The teacher's thinking is authenticated only by the authenticity of the students' thinking. The teacher cannot think for her students, nor can she impose her thoughts on them. Authentic thinking, thinking that is concerned about reality, does not take place in ivory tower isolation, but only in communication. If it is true that thought has meaning only when generated by action upon the world, the subordination of students to teachers becomes impossible."(Freire, 1996, p.58).

Proclaiming that education is liberation in the real sense of the term, Freire says," Those truly committed to liberation must reject the banking concept in its entirety, adopting instead a concept of women and men as conscious beings..... they must abandon the educational goal of deposit –making and replace it with the posing of the problems of human beings in their relations with the world. "Problem-posing" education, responding to the essence of consciousness .... rejects communiqués and embodies communication."(Freire, 1996, p. 60).

Problem-posing education, which breaks with the vertical patterns characteristic of banking education, can fulfill its function as the practice of freedom, states Freire. And here he brings forth his notion of 'dialogue'. He says, "Through dialogue, the teacher of the students and the students of the teacher cease to exist and a new term emerges: teacher-student with student-teachers. The teacher is no longer merely the –one-who- teachers, but one who is himself taught in dialogue with the students, who in turn while being taught also teach. They become jointly responsible for a process in which all grow. In this process, arguments based on "authority" are no longer valid; in order to function, authority must be on the side of freedom, not against it. Here no one teaches another, nor is one self-taught. People teach each other, mediated by the world, by the cognizable objects which in banking education are "owned by the teacher."(Freire, 1996, p.61).

Thus, quite smoothly Freire formulates his thesis of co-reading of the word and the world. He writes "As we attempt to analyze dialogue as a human phenomenon, we discover something which is the essence of dialogue itself: the word. But the word is more than just an instrument which makes dialogue possible; accordingly, we must seek its constitutive elements. Within the word we find two dimensions, reflection and action, in such radical interaction that if one is sacrificed-even in part- the other immediately suffers. There is no true word that is not at the same time praxis. Thus to speak a true word is to transform the world."(Freire, 1996, p. 68).

Freire further elaborates, "Human existence cannot be silent, nor can it be nourished by false words, with which men and women transform the world. To exist, humanly, is to name the world, to change it. Once named, the world in its turn reappears to the namers as a problem and requires of them a new naming. Human beings are not built in silence, but in word, in work, in action-reflection."(Freire, 1996, p. 69).

This locus permits him to arrive at his classic observation on dialogue as "the encounter between men, mediated by the world, in order to name the world. Hence, dialogue cannot occur between those who want to name the world and those who do not wish this naming-between those who deny others the right to speak their word and those whose right to speak has been denied them. Those who have been denied their primordial right to speak their word must first reclaim this right and prevent the continuation of this dehumanizing aggression."(Freire, 1996, p. 69).

Characterizing dialogue as non-existing in the absence of a profound love for the people, Freire went on to emphasize that dialogue should be founded upon love, humility, faith, hope and critical thinking. "Only dialogue, which requires critical thinking, is also capable of generating critical thinking. Without dialogue, there is no communication and without communication, there can be no true education".(Freire, 1996, 73-74)

Thus, Freire, as if by the sleight of hand, put adult education in the general framework of education and utters some axiomatic truth about all education. Here lies the beauty of Freirean analysis.

Two important theorizations, having wide ramifications in societal context are expounded in his article 'Cultural Action for Freedom.' The first deals with the relationship of the former colonized nations with the colonizing powers. Here we find Freire effectively incorporating the cultural context along with the economic and political aspects of Andre Gunder Frank's thesis on underdevelopment of Latin America. Freire writes, "From a non-dualistic view-point, thought and language, constituting a whole, always refer to the reality of the thinking subject. Authentic thought-language is generated in the dialectical relationship between the subject and his concrete historical and cultural reality. In the case of the alienated cultural process characteristic of dependent or subject societies, thought-language itself is alienated, whence the fact that these societies do not manifest an authentic thought of their own during the periods of their most acute alienation. Reality as it is thought does not correspond to the reality being lived objectively, but rather to the reality in which that alienated man imagines himself to be. This thought is not an effective instrument either in objective reality, to which alienated man does not relate as thinking subject, or in the imagined and longed for reality. Dissociated from the action implied by authentic thought, this mode of thought is lost in ineffective, false words. Irresistibly attracted by the life style of the director society, alienated man is a nostalgic man, never truly committed to his world. To appear to be, rather than to be, is one of his alienated wishes. His thinking, and the way he expresses the word are generally a reflection of the thought and expression of the director society."(Freire, 1975, pp. 13-14).

From this perception of the society as a whole, Freire addresses the plight of the individual. He writes, "A two fold pattern emerges. On the one hand, the culturally alienated society as a whole is dependent on the society which oppresses it and whose economic and cultural interest it serves. At the same time, within the alienated society itself, a regime of oppression is imposed upon the masses by the power elites which in certain cases are the same as the external elites and in others are the external transformed by a kind of metastasis into domestic power groups."(Freire, 1975, 13-14) From this context, he seamlessly connects one of his most important hypotheses – the culture of silence. He writes, "In either case there is a fundamental dimension to these societies resulting from the colonial phase: their culture was established and maintained as a 'culture of silence'. Here again, the two fold pattern is apparent. Externally, the alienated society as a whole, as the mere object of the director society, is not heard by the latter. On the contrary, the metropolis prescribes its word, thereby effectively silencing it. Meanwhile, within the alienated society-itself, the masses are subjected to the same kind of silence by the power elites."(Freire, 1975 p. 16).

He elaborates the hypothesis later in the book. He writes, "Let us return to the relationship between the metropolitan society and the dependent society as the source of their respective ways of being, thinking and expression. Both the metropolitan society and dependent society, totalities in themselves, are part of a greater whole, the economic, historical, cultural and political context in which their mutual relationships evolve. Though the context in which these societies relate to each other is the same, the quality of relationship is obviously different in each case, being determined by the role which each plays in the total context of their interrelation. The action of the metropolitan society upon the dependent society has a directive character, whereas the object society's action, whether it be response or initiative, has a dependent character."(Freire, 1975, pp. 58-59).

"The relationships between the dominator and dominated reflect the greater social context, even when formally personal. Such relationships imply the introjections by the dominated of the cultural myths of the dominator. Similarly, the dependent society introjects the values and life style of the metropolitan society, since the structure of the latter shapes that of the former. This results in the duality of the dependent society, its ambiguity, its being and not being itself, and the ambivalence characteristic of its long experience of dependency, both attracted by and rejecting metropolitan society."(Freire, 1975,p. 59). And he concludes the discussion by saying that, "The dependent society is by definition a silent society. Its voice is not an authentic voice, but merely an echo of the voice of the metropolis –in every way, the metropolis speaks, the dependent society listens."(Freire, 1975, p. 59).

With the collapse of the Brazilian democracy in 1964, Paulo Freire, as we know, went into exile, first to Bolivia and then to Chile. He, thereafter, stayed for sometime in Mexico and interacted with famous personalities like Erich Fromm, Ivan Illich etc. Finally, after a brief stay in Harvard, Freire settled in Geneva where he worked at the World Council of Churches.

Pedagogy in Process

As Freire settled in Geneva, he longed for further constructive work. Opportunities came when a Brazilian professor named Jose Maria Nunes Pereira wrote to Freire about his discussion with Mario Cabral, the Minister of Education and Luis Cabral, the President of the newly independent state of Guinea Bissau. Thus, with time, Freire got involved with the literacy and post-literacy activities in Guinea Bissau, Cape Verde and Sao Tome (1975-77). Correspondence with Luis and Mario Cabral were published in a collection named "Pedagogy in Process: The letters to Guinea Bissau". Freire wrote a detailed introduction where he dwelt on the various phases of his work there. In his foreword, Jonathan Kozol termed this booklet as "............. Unquestionably his most accessible.......also his most powerful and human." (Kozol, 1978 , p.4)

At the very outset, Freire stressed that, "only as militants could we become true collaborators, even in a very small way- never as neutral specialists or as members of a foreign technical assistance mission."(Kozol, 1978 p. 8) "We analysed carefully the relation", wrote Freire, "between literacy education, post-literacy and production within the total plan of the society. We looked at the relation between literacy education and general education. We sought a critical comprehension of the role that literacy education for adults might play in a society like that of Guinea, where people's lives had all been touched directly or indirectly by the war of liberation...... The political consciousness of the people had been born of the struggle itself. While 90 percent of the people were illiterate, in the literal sense of the term, they were politically highly literate-just the opposite of certain communities which possess a sophisticated kind of literacy but are generally illiterate about political matters.(Kozol, 1978, p. 10)"

Recalling his earlier conviction, formed in Brazil, that educators need to reorient themselves, Freire wrote, "In transforming the educational system inherited from the colonizers , one of the necessary tasks is the training of new groups of teachers and retraining of old ones. Among these teachers... ....there will always be those who perceive themselves to be 'captured' by the old ideology and who will consciously continue to embrace it; they will fall into the practice of undermining either in a hidden or an open way, the new practice. From such persons one cannot hope for any positive action toward the reconstruction of the society. But there will be others who, also perceiving themselves to be captive to the old ideology, will nonetheless attempt to free themselves from it through the new practice to which they will adhere. It is possible to work with these persons. They are the ones who "commit class suicide"(Kozol, 1978, p. 15).[57]

One should recall the educational scenario in Guinea under the Portuguese. From 1471 till 1961, only 14 Guineans finished higher education courses and 11 the technical level.[58]

In ten years under the revolutionary system, more people graduated than in five centuries of Portuguese domination. In the academic year 1971-72, there were 164 schools in the liberated zone where 258 teachers taught 14,531 students.

Freire's task was to experiment with his literacy methods among the people who had just liberated themselves from Portuguese colonial rule. On the one hand it was necessary to give due importance to the armed struggle that was highly relevant during Freire's involvement; on the other hand, the learners were engaged in the production process. Therefore, the schools were directly linked with people's day to day life and struggle. Freire tried to combine these two necessities in his overall scheme of imparting literacy. Freire says," It is imperative to reformulate the programs of geography, history and the Portuguese language, changing all the reading texts that were so heavily impregnated with the colonialist ideology. It was absolutely imperative that Guinean students should study their own geography and not that of Portugal, the inlets of the sea and not the Rio Tejo. It was urgent that they study their history, the history of the resistance of their people to the invader and the struggle for their liberation....... It was necessary that the Guinean students be called to participate in the efforts toward national reconstruction........It was also important to begin, perhaps timidly first, to bring about the first steps towards a closeness between the middle-school students of Bissan and productive work (Kozol, 1978, p. 20).

All these objectives Paulo Freire and his team constituted of activists and experts from IDAC and World Council of Churches tried to put into practice. A glimpse of such efforts can be found in his article and interviewed entitled "The people speak their word: Literacy and Action" and "Literacy in Guinea Bissau Revisited" published in the collection "Literacy: Reading the word and the world".

Paulo Freire says, "………the materials developed for both the literacy and post literacy phases should be challenging and not patronizing " (Freire & Macedo, 1987, p.69) . To show how this was done in São Tomé and in Principe, parts of the exercise book he excerpted in this article. Freire continues, The first stage of "Practice to learn" is comprised of two codifications (photographs): the first, a photo of one of the beautiful coves of São Tomé, with a group of young people swimming; the second, a photo of a rural area, with a group of youths working. Next to the picture of the youths swimming is written: "It is by swimming that one learns to swim". Next to the picture of the youths working is written: It is by working that one learns to work." And at the bottom of the page: "By practicing , we learn to practice better." (Freire & Macedo 1987, p.169).

Various issues like learning by practice, nature of culture, critical thinking etc were explained through the work book. The literacy phase primers provide ample materials to the adults to master literacy and develop knowledge about his/her society and culture.

The materials in the post-literacy stage are quite illuminating. Considering the fact that the previous phase gave the learners materials for thinking on various aspects of life and struggle, the text-materials in the post-literacy phase enable the learners to think more abstractly. Passages on 'The act of studying', 'National Reconstruction', 'Work and Transformation of the world' 'The struggle for Liberation', 'The New Society', 'Manual and Intellectual work' take the learner to the level of responsible discussant on issues concerning the society and the world. They, thus, can act as matured thinking subjects. It is quite apparent that what Freire achieved in Brazil in the 1950's and 60's was further improved through his own development and participation of his colleagues. It is my considered opinion that all primer- writers in the field of adult literacy should go through the primers developed by Friere and his colleagues in Africa before venturing into this area.

The Freirean philosophy stresses that through an illiterate adult lacks the knowledge of the alphabets, he/he is otherwise highly knowledgeable in worldly matters and therefore his / her learning of alphabets should be very different from the process of alphabetization of the child. The validity of this theory has been eloquently explained in the primers developed by Freire in Africa.

Relevance of Paulo Freire for India

Theory and practice of Paulo Freire for their application in other countries of the Third World, and especially for India, can now be briefly investigated. Movements for imparting literacy to illiterate Indians date back to the era of Bengal Renaissance of the mid-nineteenth century. It is generally believed that, Keshub Chandra Sen, the stalwart of the Hindu Reformsit movement called Brahmosamaj, started night schools for working class adults way back in the 1870s (Shastri and Lahiri, 1985, p.54). However, it was only just before and after the First World War that the movement received momentum. Night schools sprang up in the provinces of Bombay, Bengal and Madras. In the princely state in Baroda, libraries were established. A few educational institutions introduced extra-mural lectures for the local community. The Cooperative Movement, which was spreading in India at that time, got linked up with adult education, especially literacy (Bhattacharya,n.d. pp. 2-3).

The nationalist leaders championed the cause of adult literacy as they struggled for gaining political independence. Both Rabindranath Tagore and Mahatma Gandhi experimented with adult education in general and literacy in particular. Many of Gandhi's associates and followers including his wife Kasturba established Schools in the villages for teaching adults (Ghandi, n.d.). Even before India gained independence (1947), the state governments, run by Indian National Congress, decided that adult education would be the responsibility of the governments (Mukhopadhyays, n.d., pp.116-130).

However, in spite of such enlightened thinking, literacy scenario in India remained bleak. The percentage of literate population was 16.10 in 1941 (Bhattacharya,2005, pp194). After Independence, the governments at the Centre and the states laid more emphasis on adult education. But adult education was never considered a priority. Therefore, excepting for the south Indian state of Kerala, literacy remained a problem for India as a whole. As the population increased, the absolute numbers of people remaining illiterate stood at an alarmingly high number. By the beginning of 1980's, the Indians constituted half of the world's illiterate population.

It was only during the 1980s that the state governments and the government at the Centre, took up the cause of adult education seriously. Previously there were controversies as to what methods would be adopted to impart literacy to adults. Usually primers of children were used for the adults too. This created serious psychological problems among the illiterates.

Freirean methods began to be adopted from 1980s onward. Bengal Social Service League, an organisaiton started by an associate of Tagore in 1915, began to produce primers in Bengali using the Freirean methods (Shyam, 1997, p.37). The same methods were universally applied for other Indian languages also. Apparently, techniques of Freire being extremely convenient for adaptation, the percentage of literacy rose quite significantly in

1980s and 1990s (Sarkar, 2003,p.57) . But since the government was more interested in Freirean technique rather than in his philosophy of liberation and conscienticized, adult neoliterates continued to exist as an underclass.

To reverse the scenario, what is necessary is to adopt a synthetic approach. The socio-economic reality of India today is very different from that of Brazil of 1950s and 1960s. Political democracy is an accepted fact of life in India through the concept has not been meaningfully translated in the day to day practical life of the poor and marginalized population who constitute more than fifty percent. Grundtuing's concept of democracy and enlightenment are very relevant in this context. As we know, Freire was aware of the Grundtuigian Folk High School movement of Scandinavia.(Horton and Freiere, 1990, p. 21) Thoughts of Tagore and Gandhi, emanating from the Indian soil are also highly instructive in this respect.

We have argued elsewhere how we can synthesise the essential elements contained in the thoughts of Freire, Tagore, Gandhi and Grundtuing (Bhattacharya, 2005, p. 10). Only a synthetic approach is what we Indians need at this crucial juncture.

REFERENCES

Asoke Bhattacharya, (2005) 'Tagore, Gandhi and Freire : Synthesizing their educational thoughts with that of Grundtvig; Viewed from a Third World Perspective' in *Journal of World Education, [Ed. Ore Korsgaard] Vol. 35, No. 2*, Copertrayen.

Asoke Bhattacharya, *'NFS Grundtvig :* Educationist Extraordinary' in *Grundtvig Studier 2005*, [Ed. J.H. Schjorring et tal] Aarhux University Press, Aarhus, 2005, p.194.

Asoke Bhattacharya, *Empowering the Neo literates*, Raktakarabi, Calcutta, pp.2-3.

Freire, Paulo (1996*) Pedagogy of the Oppressed*, Penguin Books, Middlesex , 1996.

Freire, Paulo (1998) 'Education as the Practice of Freedom' in *Education for Education for Critical Consciousness*, continuum, New York.

Freire, Paulo (1975) *Cultural Action for Freedom*, Penguin Books Middlesex.

Freire,Paulo. and Doraldo Macedo, (1987) *Literacy : Reading the Word and the World*, Bergin & Garvey Publishers, Inc., Massachusetts.

Freyre, Gilberto (1970) *Order and Progress*, Alfred A. Knopf, New York

Freyre, Gilberto (1968) *The Mansions and the Shanties*, Alfred A. Knopf, New York.

Freyre, Gilberto (1970) *The Masters and the Slaves*, Alfred A. Knopf, New York.

Furtado, Celso (1965) *Diagnosis of the Brazilian Crisis*, University of California Press, Berkeley and Los Angeles.

Horton, Myles and Paulo Freire (1990) *We made the Road by walking*, Temple University Press, Philadelphia.

Kozol, Jonothan (1978) Introduction in Paulo Freire, *Pedagogy in Process: The Letters to Guinea* , The feabury Press, New York, 1978, p.4.

Mohandas Karamchand Gandhi, Selected works, Vol. , *Gandhi Centenary Society*, Calcutta, p. (Bengali).

Pabitra Sarkar, 'India's Literacy Scenario : Achievements and Failure,' in *Education and Development* [Ed. Mitra, rt tal] , Jadavpur University, Calcutta, 2003, p.57.

Prabhat Kumar Mukhopadhyays, *Tagore's life and work, Vol. 4.* Visvabharati, Calcutta, pp.116-130.

Ruchira Shyam, 'Short History of Bengal Social Service League' in *Rememburing Satyen Moitra*, BSSL, Calcutta, 1997, p.37.

Shibram Shastri, *Ramtonoo Lahiri and Contemporary Bengali Society*, Bishwabani Prakashan, Calcutta, 1985, p.54.

In: Pioneers in Education: Essays in Honor of Paulo Freire   ISBN: 978-1-60021-479-0
Editors: M.Shaughnessy, E.Galligan et al., pp 117-131 ©2008 Nova Science Publishers, Inc.

Chapter 7

RESURRECTING DEMOCRACY IN PUBLIC EDUCATION THROUGH FREIRE'S PEDAGOGY OF INDIGNATION AND HOPE

Myriam N. Torres and Loui V. Reyes
New Mexico State University, USA

When everything in education seems lost to accountability and the increasingly unprecedented control of public schools by corporations, reaching full bloom with the NCLB act and its state replications, Freire's proposal for education—philosophy and praxis--gives us a hopeful vision of education as a liberating and transformative project. We consider Paulo Freire's Pedagogy of Indignation and Hope as one of the most influential philosophies of education of the 20th Century, and it continues to be highly relevant for the 21st Century. In this chapter, we argue that Freire's Pedagogy of Indignation and Hope may help us with the reasoning, insights, and strategies to counteract the ideological, political, economic and strategic attack on public and democratic education launched by business and corporations in this country.

In the context of Freire's liberating education, participatory democracy, or what he calls *radical democracy* (Shor & Freire, 1987), means that stakeholders (teachers, parents, students, and community members) participate actively and on an equal footing in the most important decisions that determine the quality and relevance of education provided to the children, youth, and adults members of this society. Those decisions include policy making (overarching goals, principles, and strategies), school government, curricula, pedagogy, and evaluation criteria and approaches.

For Freire (1992, 2003), the dispossessed and marginalized are entitled to high quality education in which they participate on an equal footing in the identification and articulation of their own problems, and in the study and critical understanding of them through dialogue and democratic debate.

Why do we want to target radical democracy in Freire's philosophy of education, and in general, of life? Radical democracy is one of the core values of his philosophy. It is the essential ingredient for teaching, learning, knowing, research, community work, institutional and societal affairs, if they are to be oriented to assist *all* people to reach their potential as human beings and not simply as productive pieces of society. In this sense, radical democracy for Freire (1992, 2005) is a *means* for attaining humanization. But radical democracy is also an *end* in itself, because humanization for him implies the betterment of the world, a world where society will be radically democratic, less ugly and cruel, that is, more humane. In addition, democracy, as a highly regarded common value, might permit the "unity in diversity" (Freire, 1998b) in which there remain reconcilable differences. That is, visualizing democracy as a value in itself can be a strategy for moving people to act to defend it, specifically to defend democracy in schools.

Using democratic values for promoting 'unity in diversity' is extremely important today given the fragmentation of progressive democratic movements, what Freire (1998) refers to as "Lefts", and "The Right". The political right (conservatism) is united around one shared deep core value: market principles. Differences between conservatives and neoconservatives are forgotten when the market agenda is on the table. This agenda is also shared by Neoliberals. So now we have what Michael Apple (2004) calls the "New Alliance" of conservatives of all hues, and neoliberals, sharing the principles of the market as the sole force dictating the rules of society and directing the fate of human beings at global and domestic levels. The bottom line of their agenda is profit before anything, including people. Everything and everybody has a price and is commodifiable; it can be bought and sold. Thus, 'the end justifies the means'. Meanwhile, as Freire (1998) points out, democrats, progressives, leftists, and postmodernists are engaged in a "raging sectarianism" with a subsequent lack of strength, solidarity, and effectiveness. We consider that the type of democracy proposed by Freire provide the necessary common ground for "unity in diversity".

The latest U.S. federal education policy—No Child Left Behind (NCLB)-- is just the tip of the iceberg concerning the invasion of schools and education in general system by the market ideology of corporate agenda. Following Freire's teachings, we need to be able to "read the world" before we are able to work toward its transformation. Currently, the 'reading of the world' requires us to understand critically how education has been highjacked by corporations. Emery & Ohanian's (2004) extraordinarily well documented book has helped us to learn the concrete organization, actions, and purposes, with which business and corporations, for at least the last three decades, have invaded each pillar, corner and node of the school system. Their agenda is comprehensive, well organized and funded, and above all, relentless. It includes influencing and even determining standards, testing, textbooks and educational materials, pedagogy, professional development, teacher education, and teacher accreditation through corporate endowed foundations, school boards, teachers unions, researchers ,educators, parent organizations, and a systems of rewards and punishment, etc.

The values brought to the education systems are the values of "market fundamentalism" as Giroux (2004) argues. In the name of accountability, these business corporations have imposed market criteria and values—competence, effectiveness, efficacy, cost-benefit dictum--with the acquiescence and support from the government through the NCLB legislation. The alignment of educational institutions with these values is not only demanded, but monitored by external highly costly 'consultants', whose main job is to control what teachers do in classrooms, especially if they follow the prescribed curriculum and schedule. The authors have observed directly, and hear over and over again from teachers working in nearby school districts and from those attending graduate school, how this harassment and violation of teachers' and students' academic freedom is taking place on a daily basis in their classrooms. There is no recognition of the inefficiency of this type of top-down curriculum when motivation, engagement and performance of students are not taken into account in planning and delivering the following lessons.

Giroux (2004) points out the paradoxical situation we face today. On one hand, we have the dark times brought by the globalization of the Neoliberal doctrine of "free" markets with its passport to trespass borders and force privatization of social services including education, to erode sovereignty, to despoil natural resources and the dignity of human life, as well as reducing the meaning of democracy to just 'consumer choice'. On the other hand, this same extreme situation may help resurrect hope. We contend that Freire's Pedagogy of Indignation and Hope may help in the resurrection of a true democracy—a participatory democracy in the educational system.

The above glimpse of the impact of the Neoliberal market ideology of business corporations through the NCLB Act and many other assaults on the US education system helps us to look more acutely at Freire's proposal on liberating education. We agree with Glass (2001) when he assures us that today Freire's *Pedagogy of the Oppressed* is as necessary today, as it was when it was written.

However, Freire's latest writings may be more helpful for tackling the new faces of oppression today. Therefore, we argue for a *Pedagogy of Indignation (2005) and Hope (1994)* to start resurrecting democracy in schools and in society at large. This pedagogy consists by and large of two interrelated projects: *denunciation* and *annunciation*. The *denunciation* process refers to the deep comprehensive and critical understanding of the so called "new world order" and how it impacts our lives and drives the current education reform. In dialectical relationship with the denunciation is the *annunciation* of the possibility of another world, more just, democratic, and humane in which people come before profit and are never used as means to achieve other people's ends.

Denunciation includes the legitimization of feeling angry, not as pathology, but as a demonstration of our sensitivity to the most recent assaults by neoliberal policies and right wing governments on important values of human dignity such as democracy, agency and solidarity (Freire, 2005). Conscientious people, especially educators, are called on to denounce injustices such as children of color and poor children receiving the worst of everything for their education, as the NCLB Act is implemented. This has been well documented in recent publications (Meier and Wood, 2004; Valenzuela, 2005; and Kozol, 2005), to mention some prominent authors.

Fatalism is a recurrent theme in Freire's latest writings (2005, 2003, 1998a, 1998b, 1998c, 1996, 1994, and others), at a time when Neoliberalism and Postmodern Pragmatism were sitting prominently on stage in the socio-political and educational scenarios. Fatalism for Freire is an immobilizing ideology that kills people's dreams for a better world—less ugly, more just--by promoting an understanding of the future as inexorably driven by market mechanisms and globalization. George (1999) notes how Margaret Thatcher—the 'iron lady'— the promoter of the Neoliberal revolution in Great Britain in the late 70s and early 80s, used an acronym TINA, which stands for *There Is No Alternative* to market mechanisms. Freire strongly rejects this determinism and calls for conscientious people to stand up before those who declare that "we can do nothing to change the march of socio-historical and cultural reality because that is how the world is anyway." (Freire, 1998a, p. 27).

Freire is very concerned with what is happening in the world, starting with his own country (Brazil) under what he calls the "immobilizing backwardness of conservatism"

(Freire, 2005, p. 32). Actually, what we see happening today in the US and worldwide is an immobilizing threat on the progressive and radical movements by the conservative and the Neoliberal agendas as they move toward taking over the public services and social provisions of welfare states (George, 1999). US business and /or corporations executing those agendas are attacking on two fronts: privatization of social services, and lobbying for deregulation to relieve them from obligations to the public and to protect the environment. Thus, while corporations take over social services, included education, the government is abdicating its responsibility to provide services to those who are entitled to receive them. We now know that the NCLB Act is more a strategy for 'bashing' public education than for improving it (Emery and Ohanian, 2004; Valenzuela, 2005). And the power of businesses and corporations is increasing even more as they create organizations, task forces, institutes, and committees aimed at moving their agenda into education, covered with very altruistic language. In the "Business Roundtable" website, Initiative "Education & the Workforce" [1] there is an statement, copied below, which reflects the scope of the Business Roundtable's agenda with respect to "education reform strategy":

"We asked our corporate members to create or join state coalitions of business leaders and others committed to improving schools. These coalitions are central to the success of Business Roundtable's education reform strategy. Due to constant changes in political and business leadership, the organizations provide much-needed continuity and stability over time. Most of the organizations focus on K-12 education, but we are beginning to see an expanded focus on pre-K to 16 that adds early childhood and higher education to the mission".

The agenda for privatization is clear: We are moving from a welfare state to corporate welfare by moving resources from public to private hands under minimal or no accountability to the public. The school voucher is an example of this privatization doctrine--it is a doctrine because it is based on myths. How can a private school better serve the children, especially the most needy, if those schools are not accountable to the very people they serve? Chances are that these children and their parents and communities are going to have even fewer possibilities than in today's public schools to have an influence on important educational decisions for the future of their children. To whom are these parents going to complain if a 'chosen' private school does not accept their child because he/she may need extra help, and the cost is not included in the voucher?

Another strategy for the taking over of public education by corporate business is under the altruistic façade of their own foundations. Barbara Miner (2005) examines three major foundations created by the magnates of the globalized 21st century capitalism-Gates (Microsoft), Walton (Wal-Mart), and the Broad Foundation (Eli Broad and his emporium of retirement services companies, among others). Although these foundations apparently have distinct agendas, their overarching goal is privatization. Certainly, it is good that they are 'giving' money to educational projects, but we have to see the price for students, educators, and parents, and the public at large.

First of all, these foundations are private institutions, whose private boards make decisions that are not accountable to the public. Therefore, there is no guarantee that they are

[1] Website: http://www.businessroundtable.org/taskForces/taskforce/issue.aspx Accessed 11-24-05.

going to serve public education. What is quite clear is that there is often a great service they are doing for themselves. We all know the dubious practices of Microsoft and Wal-Mart, and the foundational and altruistic social purposes attached to foundations can help them improve their public image, while at the same time they are receiving large tax deductions.

But one may say that at least educational institutions receive some money from those foundations in times of government budget cuts. Yes, but it is like putting on a band aid when you are sentenced to death. The corporate 'generosity' through their foundations serve their purposes of privatization because it excuses the government's abdication of its responsibility to provide a free quality education for all people. In addition, these foundations have the power to fund the initiatives they consider 'necessary' and sound for their agendas, and not the public agenda. So today, with the continuous cuts in government budgets for education, the only new initiatives are those funded by those corporations at their discretions, not the initiatives most needed, given the "the restoration of apartheid schooling in America" (Kozol, 2005, book subtitle).

The trend of handing the public schools by the US government over to private businesses and corporate agendas involves not only the imminent danger of losing one of the latest remaining public institutions, but also the alarming ways in which schooling has become dehumanizing for students and their parents, conscientious teachers and administrators. Accountability has been reduced mainly to raising scores on standardized tests, which forces "teaching to the tests" and discards anything that will not appear on the test. Test-scores driven schooling justifies any practice, even the most dehumanizing and careless practices. Teachers and children are treated as machines whose basic mission in school is to raise test scores. Preparating for the test, drilling and more drilling, suppressing physical education, arts, and recess, with no chance for meaning and joy in teaching and learning, are becoming common practice. Very often, this is not what teachers and even administrators want to do, but they have been threatened with losing their jobs or seeing the whole school get 'reconstituted' if the children do not raise the test scores according to the established Advancement or Annual Yearly Progress (AYP).

Kozol (2005), Valenzuela (2005), Kohn (2004), Wood (2004) present studies that give testimony to the dehumanization and disconnection of the curricula and purposes of schooling with the real needs of the public/communities the schools are serving. Donaldo Macedo, in the foreword to Freire's *Pedagogy of Indignation* (2005), points out the problems exacerbated from the NCLB implementation, which are plaguing our public schools today. These problems include blaming the victims for the assault on public education, precluding critical thinking, adopting a mechanical methodology, and enacting a linguoracism against, for example, Spanish speaking children and their families and communities. In a couple of nearby school districts, all books in Spanish were collected from the libraries of the schools and put in the district warehouse to make them inaccessible because children need to learn English.

Blaming the victims for the shortcoming and unfairness of the NCLB mandate because they are not raising their scores to meet the specified standard; paves the road to justify a takeover by the state government that may go to probation, correction, reconstitution states, and finally handover to a private company. Edward Rust (1999), a business leader and promoter of Business Roundtables in each state, chair of several organizations and committees aimed at promoting their business agenda in education reform, admitted their commitment to punish public schools that do not measure up to expected standards. He declared: "Schools don't change because they see the light, they change because they feel the heat". Therefore, "States should establish accountability systems with clear consequences for schools, principals and teachers who persistently fail over time to meet standards. Consequences may include replacing personnel, restoring or closing schools, and providing options for students to enroll elsewhere". This declaration seems very much the blueprint for the NCLB. Actually, this is what is happening in the public schools across the nation, especially the schools whose student population is 'majority minority'.

This section started with Freire's plea to *denounce* the injustices that are disserving the most vulnerable members of our society, and to understand how fatalism kills people's dreams and their desire to get involved in the struggle for a better world and future. Of course, we may feel very pessimistic concerning what we are able to do given the circumstances. Freire (2005) gives specific advice for dealing with fatalism regarding both Neoliberal and postmodern pragmatism. First of all, we need to challenge its immobilizing and inexorable character. Freire (1998b) argues for breaking the myth that the future is inexorable, that there is no alternative (Thatcher's TINA) to the Neoliberal doctrine of the market. He maintains that the future is problematic, but not inexorable. When we are able to see that *yes*, there are alternatives to a market driven society, that people's agency can be restored and agency and hope are taken back by participating in popular mobilization, political decisions and interventions, and a hopeful and lucid leadership (Freire, 2005).

PEDAGOGY OF HOPE

The previous paragraphs are full of *denunciations* about what is wrong in the world and in the US about the attack on people's common good and social services including of course, public education. *Denunciations* are part of our process of understanding critically these issues and our own conscientization of our duties as educators committed to work precisely with those most marginalized by the current social and educational system. But along with *denunciations* we have to *announce* hope and the dream for a better world. Freire (2005) expresses this *denunciation-annunciation* dialectics rather eloquently: "I have the right to be angry and to express that anger, to hold it as my motivation to fight; just as I have the right to love and to express my love for the world, to hold it as my motivation to fight..." (p.58-59).

Freire maintains that *hope* is inherent to human nature, and therefore a necessary component of education. He grounds his belief in a humanist praxis. "It is not possible to live fully as a human being without hope" (Freire, 2005). He hopes that the world will change to become more "livable, sustainable, and humane" (Freire, 2003). That world is what he refers to as his "dream" or vision of a "not yet world". He also calls that world a "utopia" or a "viable vision of a better world". This dream world is less ugly, less cruel, less unjust and, necessarily, people--not profit-- oriented (Freire, 2005, 1998b, 1994: Shor and Freire, 1987). Nevertheless, Freire warns us that this dream world may not be achieved in our lifetime; but we must work hard for this dream and as educators pass the torch for future generations to continue (Freire, 2003).

The possibility of another world is also the dilemma of six consecutive World Social Forums (WSF), which meets at the same time as the World Economic Forum of the WTO, that another world is not only possible, but is on the way. These WSFs give testimony that the world that Freire envisioned is viable despite the fatalism of the present times; however, we need a strong conviction of its possibility and we need to be able to *take risks* (Freire, 2005) and engage in the struggle for hope (Freire, 1998b). Taking risks by involving in struggles should be based on a lucid perception and understanding of those possible changes in the world and the power of the various forces and ideologies that have put us in such oppressive conditions (Freire, 2005). Hence, *solidarity* (Freire in Rossatto, 2005) and dialogue (Freire, 1992) are *sine qua non* conditions for the success of those struggles for liberation.

Contrary to the fatalist and immobilizing ideologies predicated by the newly allied neoliberals and conservatives, for whom the "free market" is the solution to all human problems and the only good road to progress, and who belief globalization is inevitable, Freire (2005) *announces* with certainty the capability of humans for transforming the world, to comprehend and name their realities, to counteract fatalism, and to work toward liberation from those fatalist oppressing systems. He warns us that engaging in transforming the world is hard today, and becomes harder every day, but it is *possible*. The type of possibility that Freire is talking about is not based on a *blind optimism* but on what Rossatto (2005) calls Freire's *transformative optimism*. It is based on a critical understanding of the situation and the paths to change it. For Freire (1994) changing the world is not possible without a *dream* or *vision* of a better world. "There is no change without dream as there is no dream without hope" (p.91). Dreams are developed through dialogue and in solidarity with others willing to engage in collective actions in these struggles for a better world (Freire, 2005) . It is important to highlight that his proposal is very clear concerning working in *solidarity* with others not only because as he warns us that "Acting alone is the *best* way to commit suicide" (Shor & Freire, 1987, p. 61), but because both the realization of dreams and liberation are not done *for* others, but *with* others, working in solidarity. These struggles should be carried out with enthusiasm, hope, and indignation, but also with respect for others (Freire, 2005)

Intervention in the world from a Freirean perspective implies a set of "up-stream" struggles against the flow of determinism, fatalism, greed, exclusion, and rampant racism (Andreola, 2005). Although these struggles are possible and necessary, we need to ground them on a deep understanding of material and sociohistorical conditions and of the strategies of those with multidimensional power (Freire 2005). In the US, concerning Education Reform, we may be surprised as to how entrenched and invasive the power of business and corporations is. To give an account of these characteristics Emery & Ohanian (2004) entitled a chapter "No matter who's talking of education reform, look for the footprints of the Business Roundtable" (p. 114). These authors provide evidence that supports their claim. However, understanding the characteristics of power should not be the end of the struggle for changing the world. "A change in understanding, which is of basic importance, does not of itself, however, mean a change in the concrete." (Freire, 2005, p.26).

Dialogue, as Freire (1992) understood it, conduces to planning and organizing for collective involvement in concrete *actions*, including reconstructing identities and discursive practices of dialoguers themselves (e.g. educators). We as educators have ever more urgent actions to take, such as demanding autonomy as education professionals, respect for the profession, basic rights at work, and the right to protest social structures that oppress us. Dialogue for Freire (1992) is central for reclaiming our rights and humanness, which in the actual circumstances everywhere schools are pretty much under siege. "Dialogue, as the encounter among men [and women] to 'name' the world, is a fundamental precondition for their true humanization" (p.133). Dialogue is central to Freire's praxis for transforming the world, which he summarizes as: "the dialectics of reflection and action". He warns us not to forget this concept of dialectics and thus fall into reflection alone which degenerates to *verbalism*, and action for action's sake, without a reflective dialogue, which degenerates to *activism*. The struggles for transforming and betterment of the world involve this dialectical and the dialogical dynamics as well.

Engaging in the dialectics of reflection (including reading and re-reading of the world) and transformative action demands also that we discern continuously in the name of whom, and for what, we fight for. That is, we are in these political struggles as 'ethical beings'. We need to ask:

"How can struggle be taken and in the name of what?. To me, it should be undertaken in the name of ethics, obviously not the ethics of markets but rather the universal ethics of human beings,--in the name of the needed transformation of society that should result in overcoming dehumanizing injustice" (Freire, 2005, p. 35).

Freire's view of ethics is humanistic, somewhat essentialist his critics would say, with a focus on justice, common good, human self-realization, dignifying work, decent salaries and social services, participatory democracy, etc.; that is, a society oriented to people not just merely to profits and material things. This contrasts with what Freire calls "market ethics", by which the bottom line is profit before people, hence ends justify means (Freire, 1998b). Roberto Iglesias, in the introduction of Freire's book *El Grito Manso [The Gentle Shout] (2003)* writes a biographic sketch of Freire and highlights some features of his work which reflect his ethics in action. First of all, Freire's work was:

"at the service of the most needy, and from there he constructed, not only a methodology but a revolutionary proposal that has to do with life and how to deal with the changes of the world. . . Always tolerant, he valued traditions, beliefs, popular wisdom. When he needed to criticize, he did it without raising his voice, using no strong words. . . When he knew, he said so, and when he made a mistake, he retracted it. . . In these times of easy ascending status based on money and hopeless cultivated by those in power, the persistent novelty of his coherence shines as never before." (pp. 4-9, my translation).

What is the role of education in the world transformation? Education is necessary but not sufficient to reinvent the future (Freire, 1998b). It is certainly not the primary lever for social change, but may contribute in the ignition of it, and above all in starting the students' process of liberation and conscientization through a pedagogy of indignation and hope. As educators, we should be able to work for those opportunities and to enact democracy as a living experience as well (Freire, 2005; Horton & Freire, 1990). In his dialogued book with Miles Horton, but unlike him, Freire considers it very strategic to work both inside and outside the education system: "The ideal is to fight against the system (schooling) taking the two fronts... we have much space to work *outside* the system. . . but we also can create the space *inside*... I think politically". He considers that we need to work simultaneously inside and outside the schooling system. However, he warns us to avoid becoming ineffective in both places by overextending ourselves (S & F, 39)

Going back to the question posed about the role of education in the change of society, Freire is very cautious in thinking of it as a panacea or a lever for social change. But he did not miss any opportunity to build a pedagogical proposal as a practice of democracy. For him, the democratization of the school is not a simple result of the democratization of society, but an important factor for the transformation of the world.

The democratization of schools should be a priority in the US today, and Freire's proposal can be a light in that tunnel. His ideas on democratic schools include the involvement of students in choosing the curricula content and teaching learning strategies, as well as the examination of the mandated curriculum in terms of whose knowledge and experiences are included or excluded, who chooses the content, etc. In a democratic school, parents, teachers, and other members of the school community are also entitled to participate in the most important decisions for education of the children the school serves, who are the future generation of our society. It does not make sense, nor is it fair, when business and corporate people--not educators or persons with an educator vocation--are using their economic and political power to take over the education system, and to try to "help improve it', by crushing any remaining democracy and public character in public schools.

Deborah Meier (2004) documents how the pillars of local control in schools have been undermined across time in favor of the efficiency model by decreasing the number of school boards while the total population has increased. She indicates that this number went down from around 200,000 in 1930, to 15,000 nowadays. As we know, school boards are 'representatives' of the respective community which elects them democratically. The equation is clear: the fewer the number of school boards, the fewer the chances of meeting the needs and interests of the diverse communities to be represented, responded to, or even acknowledged. This under-representative democracy may easily degenerate into just partisan politics.

Unfortunately, as Emery & Ohanian (2004) document, the Business Roundtables in almost each state are taking this problem of lack of representative democracy which has degenerated into partisan politics in some districts as an excuse to attack school boards who in one way or another, resist their market agendas. The Business Roundtable people are lobbying for downsizing, the decision making power of the school boards or eliminate them altogether because they are only 'playing politics'. Another strategy by the Business Roundtable people has been that of "highjacking" school boards by supporting economically and politically the election of people who are sympathetic to the respective Business Roundtable agenda. Freire's ideas on democratic schooling could help us to build a counter proposal aimed at improving significantly the chances for democratic participation in a diverse, creative, socioculturally responsive education.

Outside the formal schooling system, popular education owes to Freire many insights about the democratic perspective. For him, one of the main tasks of popular education is to enable working class people to develop their own language, not the academic and elitist, but rather a language that allows them to articulate and communicate their interpretations of reality, their dreams, and their life experiences as well. Culture circles are central, although not limited to, Freire's perspective on popular education. In the culture circle dialogue participants learn to "read and write the world and the word: based on their own reality" (Freire & Macedo, 1987).

Actually, this statement epitomizes the goals of education in general and literacy in particular, as proposed by Freire. As participants in the culture circles share, and expand their readings of the world in the light of their own reality, they are enabled to start cultural action or cultural revolution (Freire, 1992, 2000). The development of their language may include examination of the discourse of self-rejection; they may see that they are merely blaming themselves for their failures without examining the failures of the system that oftentimes are the main cause (Freire, 1994).

LIBERATING CRITICAL EDUCATOR

One of Freire's most recent definitions of *liberating education practice* sets the tone for the characterization of the role of the liberating critical educator:

"values the exercise of will, the role of emotions, of feelings, of desires, of limits , the importance of historical awareness, of an ethical human presence in the world, and the understanding of history as possibility and never as determination—is substantively hopeful, for this very reason, produces hope. " (Freire, 2005, p. 24)

This notion of liberating educational practice highlights the wholeness of the person in its historical and ethical dimensions, and his emphasis on hope in opposition to determinism and fatalism.

In this vein, the work of the liberating critical educator, according to Freire, needs to be continually and thoroughly enlightened by her/his dream or vision of a better world. Her/his central job description is to motivate and assist students to articulate the world of which they dream, and to find ways to work in solidarity with others toward it. The tasks of liberating critical educators can be summarized into three major inter-related dimensions: *academic, ethical,* and *political.* In *academic* terms, liberating critical educators need to master content of the area of expertise, and have no excuse for not doing so. Nevertheless, content by itself is far from being sufficient preparation for their job. Critical educators need to question the content: Whose knowledge is valued? Whose knowledge and experiences are excluded and even denigrated? Who benefits by the type of science and scientific activities that are privileged in educational institutions? (Freire, 2005).

Liberating critical educators are there in the classroom to organize the learning environment in order for students to discover their need and arouse their curiosity for knowing (Horton & Freire, 1990) and to experience and articulate participatory democracy at work (Freire, 2005). In brief, for Freire the academic tasks of educators include having solid knowledge and experience in the subject matter while being open to learn *from* students, *with* the students, and *about* students (Shor and Freire, 1987, p.101). At any rate, the educator is the responsible person for devising the learning situations for the student and herself/himself. Thus, teaching and learning is multidirectional: between students and their teacher, and among the students as well.

Freire & Macedo (1996) call into question the problems generated when educators call themselves *facilitators* in the name of a more dialogical and democratic classroom. The problems occur when these *facilitators* abdicate their responsibility as educators and hand the classroom over to students who may see this as a *laissez-faire* situation, a time for pure enjoying or chaos without learning anything. He points out the common confusion between authoritative responsibility and authoritarianism, which results in moving from a "banking education" approach to a *laissez-faire* approach. Freire insists on the *directive* nature of education, in which the liberating critical educator has clear authority, (not authoritarianism) yet acknowledges, values and integrates into the curriculum students' experiences, knowledge, and opinions. "The teacher is unavoidably responsible for initiating the process and directing the study." (Shor and Freire, 1987, p. 157). Freire calls this initiation process the "inductive moment": "The liberating critical educator makes the induction process in a way that develops the students' own initiative in making their inductions," (Shor and Freire, 1987) and taking as their own the process of learning that specific topic. Freire clarifies that 'banking education' is not necessarily the *expository style* that everybody characterized this approach. Actually, what characterizes the "banking education" model is the lack of dialogue in the class, and the lack of democratic participation of students in decisions that determine the quality and relevance of their education (Freire, 1992 & 1994; Shor & Freire, 1987; Freire & Macedo, 1996).

Concerning the *ethical* dimension of liberating critical educators, Freire insists on the absolute importance of giving testimony--by example--of consistency between what we say and what we *do* (Freire, 2003 & 2005) . This includes the respect for others' dreams, ideas, ways of living, cultures, etc.; as well as to live and let others (e.g.students) according to the ideal of democracy. In a dialogue with Ira Shor (Shor & Freire, 1987), Freire analyses the difference between being radically democratic from being domesticator and/or *laissez-faire* educator by pointing to some ethical issues implied:

> "I can't manipulate [students]. On the other hand, I can't leave students by themselves. The opposite of these two possibilities is being radically democratic. That means accepting the directive nature of education... We must say to the students how we think and why. My role is not to be silent. I have to convince students of my dreams but not conquer them for my own plans. Even if students have the right to bad dreams, I have the right to say their dreams are bad" (p.157).

The prior statement helps us to see the fine, but yet very important, line between being a liberating educator and a domesticator/manipulator. This is, by the way, one of the most common criticisms from conservative students, since in their minds anything that sounds radical, socialist, or communist, is indoctrination. However, they never question their own indoctrination to this mindset. It is important to clarify here the quite common tendency of newcomers to Freire's ideas of liberating education, that of feeling and acting as 'liberators' of others less fortunate. For Freire, these 'liberators' readily descend to an "antidialogue" rather than a liberating education. In this vein, nobody liberates others, rather people working in solidarity liberate themselves, since liberation involves individual and social conscientization and collective action.

Another *moral* issue on which Freire insists everywhere in his writings is the right and duty of challenging the *status quo* that preserves inequity, domination and human suffering. Therefore, liberating critical educators have the right, and duty, to change the world in solidarity with others (Shor & Freire, 1987; Freire, 2005). This moral imperative of changing the world leads us to examine the *political* dimension of the critical liberating educator's type of work. Freire argues everywhere that education is not neutral, and therefore, teaching is a political act. It may be useful here to make a distinction between partisan politics which is not exactly what he means by the political character of education. In this respect Freire (1996) contends: "The democracy that is solely political denies itself. In it, the only right that is offered to the masses is that of the vote. Under the perverse circumstances of misery [and injustice] in which masses survive, the vote is insulted and degraded." (p.146). The type of politics in the service of democracy that he is talking about has to do with the impact on the students of our decisions as educators—virtually any decision.

Embracing the political dimension implies that liberating critical educators think through social, political and historical processes and help students to connect their own experiences and realities with those larger processes and contexts.

Often, critical educators believe that in order to be in solidarity with less fortunate people, you need to be, and live like those people, or even live in those communities; if you are a popular educator, you cannot enjoy some comforts. Although the popular educator should avoid messianic authoritarian practices in which the people's own understanding of the world are ignored and are imposed with other people will, solidarity is not just a geographic or class issue, and we need to democratize comforts in life, rather than reject them. This is quite distinctive from the empty *bourgeoisie* way of life (Freire, 2005).

Freire's latest writings (Freire, 2005, 2003, 1998b, 1998c, among others) show his increasing concern with the globalization of the neoliberal doctrine of market driven societies and human affairs. Specifically, he warns educators to be aware of, and work against the tricks of the neoliberal pragmatism in teacher education, which in name of technology and globalization has reduced teacher professional preparation to just training in "methods for teaching", or what Aronowitz (1993) calls "method fetish" (p.8). This type of training creates teachers who are "subordinated intellectuals", not professional educators (Freire, 2005). Actually, in these times, especially under the US NCLB mandate, conscientious educators are under tremendous pressure; they must dare to teach:

> We must dare, in the full sense of the word, to speak of love without the fear of being called ridiculous, mawkish, or unscientific, if not antiscientific. We must dare in order to say scientifically. . . that we study, we learn, we teach, we know with our entire body. We do all these things with feeling, with emotion, with wishes, with fear, with doubts, with passion, and also with critical reasoning... We must dare so as to never dichotomize cognition and emotion. We must dare so we can continue to teach for a long time under conditions that we know well: low salaries, lack of respect, and the ever-present risk of becoming prey to cynicism (Freire, 1998c, p.3).

CRITICISMS OF FREIRE'S PHILOSOPHY OF EDUCATION

Coherent with his philosophy is the openness to critique. Freire solicited and welcomed those criticisms which allowed him to reflect and rethink his ideas and action projects. One example was the flooding of letters from feminists objecting to the sexist language in his book *Pedagogy of the Oppressed*. He learned the lesson and retracted from that mistake, which led him to write an extended prologue which eventually became the book *Pedagogy of Hope*.

The relevance and comprehensiveness of his philosophy and pedagogy have inspired many, and disturbed many others. Among the critics there are feminists, postmodernists / poststructuralists, orthodox Marxists, Neoliberals and conservatives. Many of them point to his theoretical weaknesses, others to the lack of applicability in the 'first world' since Freire's experiences are mostly in the so called 'third' world'. There are those who 'don't feel empowered' because of the persistence of repressive myths of critical pedagogy (Ellsworth , 1989) or because of the failure of critical pedagogy "to address adequately the question of race" (Landson-Billings, 1997, p.127). Others point to some problematic aspects of his philosophy and pedagogy, for example his over-reliance in utopia or 'utopianism' (McLaren, 2000), the teleological overtones of the theory of liberation which may sound inappropriate for postmodernists and poststructuralists (Aronowitz, 1993), and the metaphysical argument of humanization as an ontological vocation (Glass, 2001). At any rate, Freire's Pedagogy of Indignation and Hope is a promising antidote to the massive attack on public education and the growing fatalism and cynicism even among progressive educators.

AS A WAY OF CONCLUSION: LESSON # 1
STARTING FROM THE BEGINNING - BUILDING SOLIDARITY

As indicated so far, Freire's Pedagogy of Indignation and Hope is grounded in a social and existential philosophy of education in particular and human life and society in general. Hence, it is far more than recipes of methods and strategies to create a dialogical classroom, and even farther from being an approach to teaching with the guarantee that standardized tests scores are going to be raised.

Nowadays, when oppressive forces are becoming more and more powerful and globalized, democracy and freedom are reduced to merely voter or consumer choice, and media have become embedded with corporate and government interests, we need to recreate the approaches tried by Freire in various countries and continents, but to enhance them with new technologies of communication such as the Internet for *promoting an organized flow of information*. We know that mass media are necessary for a participatory democracy to work. "There is no substitute for being an independent informed citizen" maintains Janine Jackson from Fairness and Accuracy In Reporting (FAIR: www.fair.org). Although the internet may facilitate communication among many of us, we need to remember that many people have limited or no access at all to the Internet. So, we should continue using local systems of communication to keep people debating and acting upon issues that concern them, in coordination with national and perhaps worldwide groups. We should search for, support and/or create independent, non-profit, public service driven media, as alternative to corporate self-serving media.

This networking should be aimed at building understanding, resistance, and commitment to action, especially concerning recent policies and their implications, to the *utopian* project of a society that practices justice, equity, equality, and peace. We need to be constantly searching and reinventing new strategies of struggle. For example, types of organizations to replace hierarchical organization of movements which historically have been reduced or exterminated by co-opting or eliminating their leaders.

REFERENCES

Andreola, B. A. (2005). Letter to Paulo Freire. In P. Freire. *Pedagogy of Indignation*. Boulder, CO: Paradigm publishers.

Apple, M. (2004). *Ideology and Curriculum* (Third Edition ed.). New York & London: Routledge Falmer.

Aronowitz, S. (1993). Paulo Freire's radical democratic humanism. In P. McLaren & P. Leonard (Eds.), *Paulo Freire: A critical encounter* (pp. 8-23). New York, NY: Routledge.

Business-Roundtable. *State Business Coalitions*, [Web Page]. Available: http://www.businessroundtable.org/taskForces/taskforce/issue.aspx [2005, Nov. 24-05].

Ellsworth, E. (1989). Why doesn't this feel empowering? Working through the repressive myths of critical pedagogy. *Harvard Educational Review, 59*, 297-324.

Emery, K., & Ohanian, S. (2004). *Why is corporate America bashing our public schools?* Portsmouth, NH: Heinemann.

Freire, P. (1992). *Pedagogy of the Oppressed*. New York, NY: Continuum.

Freire, P. (1994). *Pedagogy of Hope*. New York, NY: Continuum.

Freire, P. (1996). *Letters to Cristina: Reflections on my life and work*. New York, NY: Routledge.

Freire, P. (1998a). *Pedagogy of freedom: Ethics, democracy, and civic courage*. Lanham, MD: Rowman and Littlefield Publishers.

Freire, P. (1998b). *Pedagogy of Heart* (D. Macedo & A. Oliveira, Trans.). New York, NY: Continuum.

Freire, P. (1998c). *Teachers as cultural workers: Letters to those who dare teach* (D. Macedo & A. Oliveira, Trans.). Boulder, CO: Westview

Freire, P. (2000). *Cultural action for freedom (Revisited edition)*: Harvard Educational Review.

Freire, P. (2003). *El grito manso [The gentle shout]*. Buenos Aires, Argentina: Siglo XXI Editores.

Freire, P. (2005). *Pedagogy of Indignation*. Boulder, CO: Paradigm Publishers.

Freire, P., & Macedo, D. (1987). *Literacy: Reading the word and the world*. Westport, CT & London: Bergin & Garvey.

Freire, P., & Macedo, D. (1996). A dialogue: Culture, language, and race. In P. Leystina & A. Woodrum & S. A. Sherblom (Eds.), *Breaking Free: The transformative power of critical pedagogy* (Vol. 27, pp. 199-228). Cambridge, MA: Harvard Educational Review.

George, S. (1999, March 24-26). *A Short History of Neoliberalism*. Paper presented at the Conference on Economic Sovereignty in a Globalising World.

Giroux, H. (2004). Neoliberalism and the demise of democracy: Resurrecting hope in dark times. *Dissident Voice. Available at:* www.dissidentvoice.org/Aug04/Giroux0807.htm.

Glass, R. D. (2001). On Paulo Freire's philosophy of praxis and the foundations of liberation education. *Educational Researcher, 30*(2), 15-25.

Horton, M., & Freire, P. (1990). *We make the road by walking: Conversations on education and social change*. Philadelphia, PA: Temple University Press.

Iglesias, R. (2003). Trabajar con la gente; Breve semblanza de Paulo Freire [Work with people: Biographical Sketch of Paulo Freire. Introduction to P. Freire *El grito manso* [The gentle shout] (pp. 3-6). Buenos Aires, Argentina: Siglo XXI Editores.

Kohn, A. (2004). NCLB and the effort to privatize public education. In D. Meier & G. Wood (Eds.), *Many children left behind: How the No Child Left Behind Act is damaging our children and our schools* (pp. 79-97). Boston, MA: Beacon Press.

Kozol, J. (2005). *The shame of the nation: The restoration of apartheid schooling in America.* New York:: Crown Publishers.

Landson-Billings, G. (1997). I know why this doesn't feel empowering: A critical race analysis of critical pedagogy. In P. Freire & J. W. Fraser & D. Macedo & T. McKinnon & W. T. Stokes (Eds.), *Mentoring the mentor: A critical dialogue with Paulo Freire* (Vol. 60, pp. 127-141). New York, NY: Peter Lang.

McLaren, P. (2000). Paulo Freire's pedagogy of possibility. In S. F. Steiner & H. M. Krank & P. McLaren & R. Bathruth (Eds.), *Freirean pedagogy, praxis, and possibilities: Projects for the new millennium* (pp. 1-22). New York, NY: Falmer Press.

Meier, D. (2004). NCLB and democracy. In D. Meier & G. Wood (Eds.), *Many children left behind: How the No Child Left Behind Act is damaging our children and our schools* (pp. 66-78). Boston, MA: Beacon Press.

Meier, D., & Wood, G. (Eds.). (2004). *Many children left behind: How the No Child Left Behind Act is damaging our children and our schools.* Boston, MA: Beacon Press.

Miner, B. (2005). Who's behind the money? *Rethinking Schools, 19*(4), 24-25.

Rossatto, C. A. (2005). *Engaging Paulo Freire's pedagogy of possibility: From blind to transformative optimism.* Lanham. MD: Rowman and Littlefield Publishers.

Rust, E. (1999). *No turning back: A progress report on the Business Roundtable Education Initiative.* Washington, D. C.: Business Roundtable.

Rust, E. (2001). Edward Rust Testimony, *Committee on Education and the Workforce* government.http://edworkforce.house.gov/hearing/107th/edr/account3801/rust.htm. Washington, DC: US

Shor, I., & Freire, P. (1987). *A pedagogy for liberation: Dialogues on transforming education.* South Hadley, MA: Bergin & Garvey Publishers.

Valenzuela, A. (Ed.). (2005). *Leaving children behind: How "Texas-style" accountability fails Latino youth.* New York, NY: SUNY.

Wood, G. (2004). A view from the field: NCLB's effects on classrooms and schools. In D. Meier & G. Wood (Eds.), *Many children left behind: How the No Child Left Behind Act is damaging our children and our schools* (pp. vii-xv). Boston, MA: Beacon Press.
December 1, 2005

In: Pioneers in Education: Essays in Honor of Paulo Freire   ISBN: 978-1-60021-479-0
Editors: M.Shaughnessy, E.Galligan et al., pp 133-143 ©2008 Nova Science Publishers, Inc.

Chapter 8

FREIRE'S LEGACY:
A HOPE FOR THE XXI CENTURY

Lucía Coral Aguirre Muñoz
Instituto de Investigación y Desarrollo Educativo
Universidad Autónoma de Baja California, USA

Paulo Freire has been both an example and a guide for the educational practitioners who have tried, and are still trying, to contribute to a better and more egalitarian way of living. They have been working for many years, at least for two decades marked, alas, by disastrous events, in the direction proposed by Freire's Critical Pedagogy. Thus, instead of praising his work, I rather will apply his thought to this presentation of his Critical Pedagogy. For Freire, indeed, it was important to seize and understand the relationship between our doings and our existential experience, as a part of a social and historical experience.

In this essay, I intended, on the one hand, to establish a concrete context by addressing the circumstances we are living in, and, on the other, to bring forward an analysis of Postmodernism as a theoretical context, as Freire could have suggested it (1996). Why Postmodernism? Postmodern thinking these days is the dominant thinking among intellectuals in western societies, and as such is framing whatever social change which may occur.

In the last part of this essay, I tried to make a synthesis showing that in present day the critical pedagogy is an obvious frame of action for educational practitioners. Insofar, as much has been written about Freire, considering he explains his position much better than anyone else; instead of elaborating a new perspective on what has been said about him in various documents, I have tried to follow his line of thought and to apply his critical pedagogy to practice.

Social Life in the Early XXI Century:
A General Panorama with a Critical Perspective

Here are, as part of a context, a few significant events which occurred during the first years of the 21st century, sketched from a reflexive and critical point of view; events such as war and peace, wealth and poverty (material, intellectual and spiritual), imperialist policies and dominated countries, regressive and progressive forces. This will give the opportunity to estimate what could be the tendencies with a view to look at the consequences they may have on the development of Humanity.

What's Up?

A quick review of the events which happened at the beginning of the 21st century shows a profound change, like a universal historical break, where everything seems to be open to question. This change challenges the mental and the social frameworks of individuals and groups. A new socio-historical reality is taking shape manifesting itself in the fields of geography, ecology, economy, politics and culture (lanni, 2001).

The Cold War has given up its place to permanent and localized conflicts. The consent of war fares finds its justification in fear. Terrorism is putting up an increasing collective paranoia, which in turn promotes the assault of countries that never have had a deed against the invader. Such actions, which meaning is more than perverted, find their justification in the defense, the protection and the promotion of Democracy. There is some sort of an ambiguity in a country's decision to support this kind of armed intervention. Are the people conscious or not of the strategic economic motives? Of the convenience of unduly taken away resources, such as oil? Of getting control over the (entire) world?

Certainly, we are facing a new world; with a different geographic distribution of power, a different map of actors. As a consequence of militarization, the citizens, who are very, very small compared to the totalitarian-like states, feel an overlapping oppression in their everyday life. If this is true in the metropolis, it is also true in the dominated world, where the effects of such oppression are far more devastating. Day by day the conservative forces associated with the dominating powers are strengthening, as the emancipation lure is fading away, in an inverse correlation. What kind of a New Order are we speaking of? Shouldn't we, instead, speak of a take-over? Or a New Global Disorder?

In this world wide process, where the neo-liberal economy is allowed to use arms as an argument, the media play a major role. Propaganda induces the acceptance of actions which could or should be considered as State or War crimes, such as the use of white phosphorus against civilians in Iraq. Omnipresent media are the source of alienation and mass manipulation; they channel opinions not only about political matters or consumption patterns, but also about the entire social and cultural life; giving a fragmented vision of the world and misleading the masses' understanding. The marketing techniques subdue the democratic processes and political programs are treated as commercial goods.

Differences among nations as well as among individuals grow bigger. Wealth is increasingly concentrating itself in the North within small groups, while the exclusion expands itself to more and more people, as well as to states of the South.

Whether the culture of poverty relies on scarce material resources or on the control of the Global Market for resources and goods, such features like poor or deficient health, lack of access to education, everyday hunger, crowded *favelas*, promiscuity and violence, are typical of this culture, nowadays global, in the South as well as in the North. The alienation the oppressed people suffer from because of the media, the international policies, and poverty leaves them without any emancipating project. Poverty, indeed, is not solely a material issue, it is also an intellectual issue marked by the lack of ideas, ideals and willingness. Here, the humanistic approach is lagging behind the fast moving technology, the emergent goddess. Poverty, when considered at a spiritual level is even worse; the symptoms are indifference, apathy, lack of faith in collective processes, intellectual cynicism and rises in personal interests, generally immediate and short terms, above all considerations of common well-being.

To consider each and every aspect of social reality from a "global" point of view may be conceived as a feature of our time. Well! For some authors, however, (Morin, 2003) globalization is not a new phenomenon, it is simply another phase of the westernization of humanity which started with the conquest of America, kept going through violence, destruction, slavery, genocide and an overall exploitation, and resulting ultimately in the economic (and political) subordination of Latin America and later on of Africa to western interests.

In its present stage, further to the transformation of the industrial organization into a post-industrial one, further to the transition from an energy society to an information one, further to the rise at a planetary level of financial and commercial exchanges, further to the division of the world into regions, westernization has taken the shape of the United States' cultural hegemony and military power (Aguirre, 2001; Touraine, 2001). The national states are less and less leading and regulating their own economy and are more and more put away from the order, rights and ruling a civil society usually establishes (Castel, 2001). One may even think there is an agenda to destroy all collective actions (Bourdieu, 2002).

The relentless mass consumption of mostly unnecessary items in Western societies leads to spoiling the soil, the water and the air, to the overexploiting of natural resources, to the reduction of flora and fauna, to the destruction of the human specie *oikos*, in one word and in all, to kill life. However, there is a paradox: human needs are far from being satisfied. According to news published on October 18th, 2005 by the Food and Agriculture Organization of the United Nations (FAO), it seems that 852 million people are still suffering from hunger (AFP, Reuters y DPA, 2005). Africa holds the worst conditions with the highest proportion of undernourished population; however, hunger is also present in Latin America and India, and the rich countries are not exempt from it.

As far as social groups or communities are concerned, the weakest ones are the most vulnerable. Seniors have seen their economic belongings threatened and sometimes bluntly diverted! More often than not, they have to face abandonment, poverty, illness and loneliness, and this may be even worse in industrial societies where former, if not ancestral, community ties have been destroyed. Young people are harassed by drug trafficking, while their education and working opportunities are worsening. Women, now widely incorporated into the economic field of activities, still do not have full access to decision levels, nor equal wages. Minorities, especially the one based on those migrants leaving a dying South on an exodus for a dream future, are not only marginalized, they encounter a hostile North, and they literally are the target of an exacerbated xenophobia, even though their cheap labor plays an important role in those countries' economies.

There is a growing social disinterest to guarantee or simply to offer young people opportunities to develop themselves (Giroux &Giroux, 2004); and, above all, as Galeano (1998) denounces it, children on who traditionally each generation were counting on the outcome of a bright future, are now exploited as a commonplace resource for sexual turpitude, violence exhaust, and cheap labor. One could think the ugliest features associated with the rise of the industrial capitalism are back to life; not enough, children are now exploited as resources by the organ international trading. Is this progress?

An innovation of the Western culture?

For sure, this point of view may be considered as partial and pessimist. But is it unreal? This is what anyone may read daily in the news, even though the events related by the media are so fragmented that they hardly may be perceived in their entirety, losing thus their meaning. These events are the symptoms of a wrongly organized global social system which, fortunately, emphasize its internal contradictions.

Nevertheless, it is time to ask oneself what is the meaning of "collective action", if collective has still any meaning; perhaps what describes best the current human action of today is the sum of individual survival strategies.

Where To?

One of human beings' distinctive characteristic is their ability to be conscious, maybe the most significant one. Consciousness permits them to analyze their own actions and to foresee their consequences, giving them the possibility to change, modify and create. Considering the panorama roughly sketched above, several scenarios emerge. Let's deal first with what seems to be a logical outcome of current trends.

If things go on following paths as those described, one plausible scenario is that contradictions heighten to the point of no return. Since consumption, plus industrialism, plus capitalism is the perfect formula to destroy the environment, it is quite possible to foresee a world where nature would be so damaged, it would become uninhabitable, where individualism would be so exacerbated that community life would be a wishful thinking. Since a degraded world would affect as much the rich and as the poor, so would inequality, and anyone with a privileged situation would be the target of theft, kidnapping and all sorts of violence. All this would occur in a reciprocal chain of fear and terror.

Opposite to that apocalyptic scenario, one may think of an alternative one, aiming at a better world, setting right a planet from an upside down skid, as Eduardo Galeano did conceive it (1998). If it is true that the future is build up at present days, if the human kind is able to reach a truly humanist state, then such a scenario is plausible and possible. If this option is perceived as way-out, as some sort of a utopia, well, why not? Freire told us utopias were necessary to lead human action towards a better and hoped for world. Hasn't he?

What should the characteristics of such a desirable world be?

The World We Want!

Having in mind to begin a discussion with the people encountered daily what such a desirable world could be, a simple survey about what kind of world they would like to live in proved to be a gold mine of ideas and wishes far away from up-to-date reality.

First, and above all, Peace! They imagine a world in peace, where differences can be discussed and conflicts overcome. According to them, it would be necessary to foster consciousness and respect toward the *others*. This might contribute to settle differences about ethnic, religious or sexual orientation, among others things.

It is clear for them that peace cannot be achieved under unequal conditions and ruling. A scenario of justice would require that every human being have an equal right to satisfy their basic needs like food, housing, health and education. Labor is for them a fundamental factor for individual and collective development, but its current organization is far from being satisfactory.

Working opportunities for everybody should be imperative, people should be able to work in occupations they like, and their job should provide an income adequate to cover their basic needs, so no one should have to work overtime and neglect his/her families because of lack.

Attitudes would also have to change. According to one of the interviewed person: "it is not fair to be eyed up and down by those in a higher position, even though this attitude is obviously unconscious". Another aspect emphasized is that because of the work processes intensity and pace, they lose touch with their personal objectives, and the quality of their functioning is lost; ultimately they are worn out and disgusted by their job. What happened with this idea of the beginning of the industrial capitalism that machines would free men from hard tasks? Nowadays, the technological progress is increasing the production pace raising the exploitation of labor. Stress and burnout are the signs of our times.

In the hope for world of the interviewed people, children grow up safely and freely; they behave simply like children, not having to work, but playing with clean toys and games, free from the violent garbage offered by the media, and being educated with opportunities to improve themselves. As to the youngsters, it seems more difficult to describe a better world for them, they are so disoriented, seduced by technological gadgets, the newest cell phone, the last PM3 internet site, they barely socialize. People think news conditions should be created in order to bring them together, to involve them in cultural, artistic and sportive activities.

Physical and psychological violence against women would have to come to an end. Even though working conditions were more satisfactory, women should seek better wages and working schedules. Moreover it would also be necessary "to take seniors out of the remote places of society they are confined to"; as they need to be listened to. Besides food and medicines, their physical and psychological needs should be met. They require special activities and attention; they need to feel useful so that "the obsession about age vanish and the idea of growing old be again an honor".

In the just society, people are dreaming that there is no room for racism, religious tolerance is the rule, and the natural resources of the earth are protected. Education faces no economic or bureaucratic limitations. There is no pressure of any kind on people to study something in particular; students can follow their own personal penchants. That should be a life-long right. "We have to reach that point where there is not a great gap between what we want for our children and what the world is offering us".

Some of the suggested actions were: to liberate medicine's patents , to increase the cost of weapons, to put an end to national economies and to equally distribute the universal income *per capita*, to subordinate scientific and technological development to people's well-being, to rationally produce material goods, to avoid consumption of luxurious items. If the time of globalization has come, why rationality could not be universalized to human actions, to equality, solidarity and fraternity?

To build such a world, it would be urgent to stop the current one-way economic development, to stop man from being a wolf unto man. It would be worthwhile to find the right path to overcome contemporary barbarism, the inner barbarism one from which the rest derive (Mattei, 1999). As one of the interviewed people put it: "our words are poor, but we all must try to get to the same point *".*

If this account seems to be nothing more than a long letter to Santa Claus, funny for a few, pointless for others, it is nevertheless an interesting exercise. It is worth it to realize how far the real social, and now global, organization stands from ordinary people expectations, wishes, and dreams. It is clear that a program of actions ought to stand up from here. Such a large discrepancy between people's claims for a just society and how societies are organized *de facto* may only be a drive to social changes or a precipice to eternal dissolution. So, how could we get where we want to go?

As intellectuals, as educational practitioners, as citizens, we certainly have a responsibility towards our fellow men in promoting, or not, social changes to fill this gap. Taking some distance from deterministic positions opens the door to human action, but then having a dream to share is indispensable. Far from thinking that wishes will come true as if they were "a gift from History", we have to understand, what Freire (1996, p. 97) meant when he said, that we have to build the future. According to Wallerstein (2002) we need to explain the present through a projection in time. To do so, let's go back to Braudel and his long-term panoramas! From the analysis of the current world conditions arises the necessity to emphasize the close links between the intellectual, the moral and the politic. Once the analyses are complete and a moral stand point taken, rational thinking and actions will show us which political efforts are the most effective to build a better world

In harmony with this position, Bourdieu (2002) brings up the necessity to link *scholarship* and *commitment.*[1] He states that the researcher's task is to work towards a "collective invention of inventive collective structures" with which it will be possible to conceive and initiate new social movements; such as new contents, new goals and new international means of action.

POSTMODERNISM: ITS CONSEQUENCES FOR EDUCATION

As a horizon to Postmodernism, here are a few aspects of postmodern thinking such as the uprising of skepticism towards the power of reason, the lost of fundamentals, the dissolution of the meaning of History, the lack of trust in utopias. Along this perspective, the situation of education should be stressed, caught in the middle of two worlds, one which is not totally dead, and one which is not yet completely born.

How Come We Stand Here?

Postmodernism represents the continuation of Modernism and at the same time a break from it (Coutant, 2003). To come close to the distinctive features of Postmodernism it is necessary to remember the characteristics of Modernism from which it sprang. Postmodernism in Western culture starts where the patterns derived from the Modern thinking reach their limits: the primacy of reason, the vision of change in society as a process towards progress, the absolute meaning of conceptions. Emerging from the Renaissance, Modernism modeled itself on the Cartesian straight and clear way of conceiving reality, and enforced the methodical doubt as a mean to elaborate distinctive and valuable ideas. Modern thinking reached its peak in the XIX and XX centuries with the development of Sciences, the generalization of Education, the establishment of parliamentary democratic systems in western countries, plus the hopeless, but still waved illusion that Nature could be controlled and subordinated to human willing.

Even though Modernism did endorse that the philosophical meaning of reality could be based indifferently on God, on Nature, Reason or History, its basic conception was that the reality of things was such as perceived. This vision of the world allowed to enforce a set of ruling principles centered on such features as the power of the human thought, on reason as the perfect logical tool, on the certainty that truth could be reached ; and lastly on the claim for an absolute moral order. This way of thinking however, found its limits within the Western culture itself and history; the XX century was also the century of two world wars and of Hiroshima.

The breaking up of the Modern project gave way to a new way of thinking, the Nihilistic Postmodernism. This one was… No! This movement is characterized by several aspects, the first one worth mentioning is the overall disenchantment towards human reason. After all, Darwin unveiled the animal origin of human beings, Freud and Marx set out the irrational aspects of human conduct and organization, Nietzsche with his Nihilism contributed to undermine human century old fundamentals, his famous "God is dead" as a logo.

The human way of thinking has changed one's color and nowadays a large number of contemporary intellectuals no longer endorse the Kantian-like objective axiology; the secularization of reality, among other factors, has opened the way to relativism (Maritain, 1996). Skepticism towards Humanity's great deeds is now a commonplace, utopias as well as idealistic views are distrusted.

Certainly, 20th century humanity has lived through abominable atrocities, several founded on "modern" ideas; it has experienced a lot of "isms": Fascism, Nazism, Bolshevism, Colonialism, Imperialism…; it has been terrified for more than half a century by the Cold War; and then, unexpectedly, there arose a new hope with the fall of Berlin's wall plus the collapse of the Soviet Union, but it was still a silly dream which vanished within a generation after the United States launched a new crusade against a new Evil called Terrorism. It should come as no surprise if skepticism is now a generalized way of perceiving reality. And what about History? Could its sense survive?

If this outline of some of the 20th century features highlights Western Modern and Postmodern cultures, it does not help to build an emancipator project; on the contrary, it

---

[1] In English in the original document.

endorses the *status quo* by supporting the belief there is nothing that can be done to change whatsoever.

The Critical or Progressive Postmodernism, as conceived by Freire (1996), endorses all of the Modern project's limits but with a different spirit than the nihilistic one. Developed from a partial and banal reasoning, the Critical Postmodernism sets the acceptance of differences, the search for the *other* and the encounter with him through dialog, as the unavoidable conditions to improve the present. Freire (1996) sets out to shake historical anesthesia off, and to overcome existential weariness in order to unfold suitable conditions for a new world. Things being what they are now, it is hard to foresee whatever social change or transition without fighting, and Freire (1996) warned us it will be a fierce one.

If formal education is still trapped within the scheme of Modernism, young people on their part are more and more seduced and overwhelmed by the postmodern views, nihilist or critical depending on what their life trajectory has been made of. Seen from this point of view, it is clear education has an important role to play in developing a critical consciousness within youth. It is up to educators to compensate for the flaws of educational systems all around the world; and to do so, they just have to follow Fromm's statement, which Freire repeatedly referred to (1996), for whom educational practice must be put in force as a historical, socio-cultural and political psychoanalysis. Let us ponder and think just a minute as to what this really means!

THE PEDAGOGY OF HOPE: A WAY OUT

The Pedagogy of hope which Paulo Freire left as an inheritance is up to date, the only tool at disposal to escape from the vicious and mortal circle capitalist thinking that has framed the future of Humanity in over centuries. So Freire's thinking is as important for Western societies as well as for Third World ones. There will be no redeeming deed as a getaway, and we shall disappear or we shall survive, all together. To understand the value Freire gave to hope as an ontological need, one has to go over his thought and consider his contribution to the understanding of present and future times, a step further is to ask oneself if the critical pedagogy is worth not only for the "oppressed" people but also for the "oppressors".

Freire's Contribution to Human Development

Above all, Freire (1997a) has put forward that a future for humanity was not only possible, but feasible. His conviction about humanity was such that he thought it possible to build a Utopia and, aiming at it, to imagine and empower changes in the course of things, this as an alternative to passive obedience to the dominant destructive trends. The key to this kickback arising stands on the contradictions of the Capitalist system, which generates historical opportunities giving way to changes to the World as desired.

To rescue the human capacity to dream, to think of social alternatives, to establish communal bonds again, Freire proposed to build a Utopia, his own hope being as great as the times' needs. To do so, it is necessary to develop a conscious of the critical situation humanity is living in; it is imperative to stretch to what is feasible but hasn't yet been done.

Now, more than ever, hope is an ontological need; it is a matter of survival, not only for the North or the South, for the rich or the poor, but for all the human specie. To become concrete history, this ontological requirement needs to be put in practice (Freire, 1996).

According to Wallerstein (2002), those who hold on to the present system of privilege have wealth, power and the possibility to buy knowledge on their side; those who seek a democratic and egalitarian world are at a disadvantage. Their only hope is to build a broad front based on diversity, so to form a new alliance, some sort of a plural rainbow, aiming at generating a "global" family which requires mutual respect and understanding to survive. It is the intellectuals' job to create the language needed to support such alliance and to interpret its literature.

When taking an inventory of the resources at hand to build the new world, the first options to appear are always the same deadly weapons. But how could violence could be the way to reach peace, democracy and dialog? Other ways and means to achieve this new world could be to intervene in politics through intellectual action or militancy, or to search for new ways to self organize. A third option could be the cultural action plotted to underline the irrationality of the present conditions. Finally, education could also be an efficient, effective alternative.

Nowadays, formal schooling has a limited impact on human formation, but still, even though the school is aimed to reproduce society as is, to foster resistance using the institutional limitations is a step in the right direction. More importantly, we should move towards informal education thru talks, creating, exploring dialogue spaces; and by doing so, to open oneself to other's thoughts. The idea is to not perish in isolation (Freire, 1996).

Cultural production may be a valuable means to oppose to miseducation as generated by mass-manipulation media. Contemporary schooling is striving to make students able to *read the words* but, not to *read the world*, because of the aseptic and meaningless school environment immune to a critical vision which is exactly contrary to what Freire proposed (1996). In this sense, Giroux & Giroux (2004) pointed out that critical pedagogue ought to help their students to learn again that knowledge is related to action, conception to implementation and learning to social change. Against the overall power of the fatalistic and pragmatic reactionary discourse, Freire insisted that consciousness ought to be developed (Freire, 1997a),

The component of critical pedagogy closely related to social and political aspects is the one emphasized here, but the others are as important to Freire, such as: content selection, rigor and discipline in the process of knowing, pedagogic practices, and the teacher-student relationship. They all contribute to Freire's conception of education (1994). His legacy includes an anthropological conception of the *human incompleteness*; since human beings are unfinished by definition their possible and inherent development is open (Freire, 1997 b). He offers a teleological dimension to education, a set of practical knowledge, what to do and how to do it. To conclude, the real legacy of Freire is his critical pedagogy as paradigm, since this pedagogical approach leads from philosophical statements to working techniques, according to the sense Khun (1986) gave to the concept of paradigm.

A word about the oppressors; according to Freire (1996), as individuals as well as class, the oppressed does liberate the oppressor when freeing himself; just because there is no one to oppress. Nevertheless, it is important to consider that because of his privileges, the oppressor finds it difficult to humanize himself. The spread of world problems at the beginning of the 21st century did not and does not exempt the oppressors. An example of this is the damage to the environment, terrorism and overall violence. Although it will not be easy to educate the oppressors, besides developing our own critical consciousness, this double action should be accepted as a challenge.

To conclude, for Freire the alternative lies between an education for *alienated domestication* and an education for *freedom*; that is to say should educational practices strive to confine human beings as objects of History or as subjects of History (Freire, 1982).

Let's hope these lines will foster dialogue.

REFERENCES

Aguirre, L.C. (2001). The Role of Critical Pedagogy in the Globalization Era and the Aftermath of September 11, 2001. Interview with Peter McLaren. *Revista Electrónica de Investigación Educativa, 3* (2). Retrieved May 20, 2004 from: http://redie.uabc.mx/vol3no2/contenido-coral.html

Bourdieu, P. (1998, March). L'essence du neoliberalisme. *Le Monde diplomatique*. Retrieved November 10, 2005, from: www.monde-diplomatique.fr

Bourdieu, P. (2002, February). Pour un savoir engage. *Le Monde diplomatique*, Retrieved November 10, 2005, from: www.monde-dilpomatique.fr

Castel, R. (2001). *Empleo, exclusión y las nuevas cuestiones sociales en desigualdad y globalización*. Buenos Aires: Facultad de Ciencias Sociales, Universidad de Buenos Aires-Manantial.

Colom, A. & Melich, J. C. (1994). *Después de la modernidad. Nuevas filosofías de la educación*. Barcelona: Paidós.

Coutant, P. (2003). *Le contexte postmoderne*. Retrieved November 10, 2005, from: http://1libertaire.free.fr/sommaire.html

Freire, P. (1982). *La educación como práctica de la libertad*. Mexico: Siglo XXI Editores.

Freire, P. (1996). *Pedagogía de la esperanza*. Mexico: Siglo XXI Editores.

Freire, P. (1997a). *Pedagogía de la autonomía*. Mexico: Siglo XXI Editores.

Freire, P. (1997 b). *Cartas a quien pretende enseñar*. Mexico: Siglo XXI Editores.

Galeano, E. (1998). *Patas arriba. La escuela del mundo al revés*. Mexico: Siglo XXI.

Giroux, H. & Giroux, S. (2004). *Take back higher education. Race, youth and the crisis of democracy in the post civil rights era*. New York : Palgrave Macmillan.

Lanni, O. (2001). *Las ciencias sociales y la modernidad-mundo*. Buenos Aires: Facultad de Ciencias Sociales, Universidad de Buenos Aires-Manantial.

AFP, Reuters and DPA. (2005, October 18). Padecen hambre 852 millones de personas en el mundo: FAO. *La Jornada*. Retrieved November 10, 2005, from: http://www.jornada.unam.mx/2005/10/18/036n1mun.php

Khun, T.(1986). *La estructura de las revoluciones científicas*. Mexico: Fondo de Cultura Económica.

Mattei, J. F. (1999). *La barbarie interieure. Essai sur l'immonde moderne*. Paris: P.U.F.

Maritain, J. (1996). *Humanismo integral.*. Buenos Aires: Lohle-Lumen.

Morin, E. (2003). *Educar en la era planetaria*. Barcelona: Gedisa.

Touraine, A. (2001). *El fin de la ola liberal. Desigualdad y globalización*. Buenos Aires: Facultad de Ciencias Sociales, Universidad de Buenos Aires-Manantial.

Wallerstein, I. (2002). *Un mundo incierto*. Buenos Aires: Libros del Zorzal.

In: Pioneers in Education: Essays in Honor of Paulo Freire   ISBN: 978-1-60021-479-0
Editors: M.Shaughnessy, E.Galligan et al., pp 145-149 ©2008 Nova Science Publishers, Inc.

AFTERWORD

Peter McLaren
University of California, Los Angeles, USA

PAULO FREIRE: THE POLITICS OF PEDAGOGY AND THE PEDAGOGY OF POLITICS, A TRIBUTE

For over a century, the U.S. government has intervened both forcibly and covertly to topple the governments of numerous countries, including Nicaragua, Guatemala, the Philippines, Panama, South Vietnam, and Chile. For instance, to cite just one of dozens of examples, when the U.S. overthrew the left-leaning president of Guatemala, Jacobo Arbenz, and imposed a military regime, a 30-year civil war ensued in which hundreds of thousands died. One reason that you find in Latin America some of the most open political rebellions against U.S. policies is because this is a region where the U.S. has frequently intervened and where populations have been brutally victimized as a result.

From the day of my very first visits to Cuba and Mexico in the 1980s, to my current visits with educators in Colombia, Venezuela, Brasil and other Latin American countries, I have taken inspiration for my work from teachers and cultural workers who share a profound respect for the teachings of Paulo Freire. I was honored to spend time with Paulo, both in Brasil and the United States, and continue to be influenced by his work and example.

Since arriving in the United States from my native Canada in 1985, I have spoken out—and continue to speak out—against acts of imperialist aggression by the United States government. I have done so in numerous books, articles, and speeches over the past thirty years (as a Marxist humanist, I have also been a sharp critic of all forms of terrorism, whether associated with Islamic fundamentalism or with the state terrorism of the United States). The broader context for these writings has been my work in critical pedagogy that involves, among other things, publishing critiques of mainstream educational policy and practice and revealing how such policy and practice is underwritten by the politics of neoliberal capitalist globalization. I have also engaged in anti-capitalist, anti-racist and anti-imperialist activism as part of my ongoing struggle for a socialist alternative to capitalism.

Not surprisingly, in the course of my work, I have often been attacked by both right-wing and liberal critics. Lately, a right-wing group has placed me at the top of a list of dangerous professors at UCLA called "the Dirty Thirty" (the group had made offers of a hundred dollars to secretly audiotape leftist professors, or fifty dollars to hand over their lecture notes). Recently, I have been challenging the efforts of right-wing politicians and conservative social critics who are attempting to pass a bill (International Studies in Higher Education Act, H.R. 509, and the Academic Bill of Rights) in various state legislatures throughout the United States that, under the pretext of establishing political neutrality in the classroom, is designed to curtail the rights of professors in universities to speak out against social and political injustice (Fassbinder, 2006). Right-wing critics charge that professors like myself, who follow a Freirean example, 'indoctrinate" students with leftwing propaganda. If passed, the bill will expressly forbid professors from using the classroom supposedly to 'propagandize' their views. In other words, the classroom will become even more of a politically contested site than it is at present, with neoconservatives trying to shut down critical dialogue surrounding initiatives of the Bush administration.

Charges such as these have been addressed by Paulo Freire, specifically in his magisterial book, *Pedagogy of Hope*, and they serve as an excellent resource for teachers, especially those in the United States are being labeled as 'traitors' and 'supporters of terrorism' because they use the classroom as spaces for critical dialogues about U.S. imperialism, the war in Iraq, political Islam, fundamentalist Christianity, the struggle for socialism, and other controversial topics, dialogues that are actually designed to create a well-informed public that can work towards a future world unmarked by terrorism. It is important for teachers to visit or revisit the work of an educator who, although we mark the tenth anniversary of his death, many of us still use as a compass for our pedagogical life, a life that does not end when the door to the classroom is closed for the day, but that we have integrated into our hearts and minds, and adapted to the everyday rhythm of our lives. He was an educator who championed academic freedom all of his life. For Freire, living in a culture of silence was tantamount to accepting injustice and defeat.

Freire observes that educational practice reveals a "helplessness to be 'neutral'". There is, Freire argues, no "educational practice in zero space-time", that is, there is no neutral practice. This is because educators are disposed to be ethical agents engaged in educative practice that is directive, that is political, that indeed has a preference. Freire writes that as an educator, he must "live a life full of consistency between my democratic option and my educational practice, which is likewise democratic." Freire agrees that we find authoritarianism on both the right and the left of the political spectrum. Both groups can be reactionary in an "identical way" if they "judge themselves the proprietors of knowledge, the former, of revolutionary knowledge, the latter, of conservative knowledge." Both forms of authoritarianism are elitist. Freire underscores the fact that we cannot "conscientize" students without at the same time being "conscientized" by them as well. Teaching should never, under any circumstances, be a form of imposition. On the other hand, we cannot shrink from our democratic duty and fear to teach because of manipulation. We always run this risk and must do so willingly, as a necessary act, as a leap across a dialectical divide that is necessary for any act of knowing to occur. This is why critical educators stress the idea of the hidden curriculum as a way of self-examination, of remaining coherent, of remaining tolerant and at the same time of becoming critically disposed in their teaching because, as Freire reminds us, tolerance breeds openness and critical disposition breeds curiosity and humility.

Knowing is a type of dance, a movement, but also a self-conscious one. Criticality is not a line stretching into eternity, but rather it is a circle. In other words, knowing can be the object of our knowing, it can be self-reflective, and it is something in which we can make an intervention. We inherit cognition as a species being but we acquire other skills along the way, and we need to grow integrally and with coherence.

Freire reminds us that teaching cannot be reduced to the one way transmission of the object of knowledge, or a two-way transaction between the teacher and the student, but rather teaching is a form of dialectical transformation of both the teacher and the student, and this occurs when a teacher knows the content of what is to be taught and a student learns how to learn. Teaching occurs when educators re-cognize his or her knowing in the knowing of the students.

Freire argues that teachers must challenge students to move beyond their commonsense beliefs and assumptions regarding their self-in-the-world and their self-with-in-the-world but must do so by respecting the commonsense knowledge that students bring into the classroom. Freire notes: "What is impermissible—I repeat myself, now—is disrespect for the knowledge of common sense. What is impermissible is the attempt to transcend it without starting with it and proceeding by way of it" (p. 83). Yet at the same time we have a duty to challenge the students' feelings of certainty about their own experiential knowlege. Freire asks:

> What kind of educator would I be if I did not feel moved by a powerful impulse to seek, without lying, convincing arguments in defense of the dreams for which I struggle, in defense of the "why" of the hope with which I act as an educator? What is not permissible to be doing is to conceal truths, deny information, impose principles, eviscerate the educands of their freedom, or punish them, no matter by what method, if, for various reasons, they fail to accept my discourse—reject my utopia. (p. 83).

Freire makes it clear that we reject a "focalist" approach to students' experiental knowledge and approach a student's experiential knowledge contextually, inserting our respect for such knowledge "into the larger horizon against which it is generated—the horizon of cultural context, which cannot be understood apart from its class particularities, and this indeed in societies so complex that the characterization of those particularities is less easy to come by" (p. 85). Students' experiences must be understood within the contextual and historical specificities in which such experiences are produced. They must be read dialectically against the larger totality in which they are generated. For Freire, the regional emerges from the local, the national emerges from the regional, the continental emerges from the national, and the worldwide emerges from the continental. He warns: "Just as it is a mistake to get stuck in the local, losing our vision of the whole, so also it is a mistake to waft above the whole, renouncing any reference to the local when the whole has emerged" (p. 87). We are universalists, yes, because we struggle for universal human rights, for economic justice worldwide, but we begin from somewhere, from concrete spaces and places where subjectivites are forged and commodified (and we hope de-commodified) and where critical agency is developed in particular and distinct ways. And when Freire speaks of struggling to build a utopia, he is speaking of a concrete as opposed to an abstract utopia, a utopia grounded in the present, always operating "from the tension between the denunciation of a present becoming more and more intolerable, and the "annunciation," announcement, of a future to be created, built—politically, esthetically, and ethically—by us women and men" (p. 91). Utopias are always in motion, they are never pregiven, they never exist as blueprints which would only ensure the "mechanical repetition of the present" but rather they exist within the movement of history itself, as opportunity and not as determinism. They are never guaranteed.

While it is vitally important that we, as educators, never underestimate knowledge produced from our daily, commonsense experience, (since such a rejection of popular knowledge amounts to a form of nearsightedness that is sectarian, elitist and myopic and that occasions epistemological error), by the same token it is important not to engage in the "mythification of popular knowledge, its superexaltation" (p. 84). And while it is important to dream of a better world—since dreaming is "a necessary political act, it is an integral part of the historico-social manner of being a person...part of human nature, which, within history, is in permanent process of becoming" (pp. 90-91)—we need to remember that "there is no dream without hope".

Progressive teachers in the United States can see their dreams and longings of a world arching towards social and economic justice reflected in the mirror of Freire's pedagogical dream, a dream inspired by a hope born of political struggle and a belief in the ability of the oppressed to transform the world from 'what is' to 'what could be', to re-imagine, re-enchant, and recreate the world rather than adapt to it. The reverse mirror image of such a dream is the dream that drives the 'neutral' pedagogy that neoconservatives are struggling to bring about in the United States. Pressuring professors to be silent about politics in their classrooms by threat of legal action is itself an abridgement of academic freedom, it is the attempt to remove a critical politics from the classroom by means of imposing a narrow, sclerotic and reactionary politics on the education process itself. Academic freedom means freedom from having my curriculum being scrutinized by a political act of adjudication, by the establishment of some crude political scale from 'liberal' to 'conservative' that actually prevents critical knowledge to thrive. It means being accountable, yes, but not from the perspective of adhering to a false notion of neutrality.

Neoconservative educators in the United States defend the false 'freedom to choose' to be poor or rich, to live in a mansion or under a bridge, the freedom to vote or not to vote, the freedom to be a Christian or a barbarian, the freedom to be 'with Bush or against civilization'—but truly free choice is a choice in which I do not merely choose between two or more options given me with a pre-given grid approved by legislative or moral fiat, but the freedom to change the very grid or political calculus in which those choices are lodged. That is what the concept of freedom means in the practice of critical pedagogy, in the struggle for social justice. And that is what makes Freire's work so important, as important today as it ever was, perhaps even more.

We now occupy a moment in history when we can appreciate the legacy of Paulo Freire, especially his landmark opus, *Pedagogy of the Oppressed*. That Freire can still make contact with our time is a testament that he was always far ahead of his own time.

Paulo Freire, Presente!

A version of this article was written for a Brazilian magazine, *Patio*.

REFERENCES

Fassbinder, Samuel Day. (2006). The "Dirty Thirty's" Peter McLaren Reflects on the Crisis of Academic Freedom. http://mrzine.monthlyreview.org/fassbinder060406.html

Freire, Paulo. (1994*). Pedagogy of Hope: Reliving Pedagogy of the Oppressed.* With Notes by Ana Maria Araujo Freire. Translated by Robert R. Barr. New York: Continuum.

INDEX

D

E

exploitation, 3, 4, 50, 85, 95, 108, 135, 137
extra help, 120
eyes, 30, 52

F

fabric, 55, 91
facilitators, 126
failure, 8, 16, 53, 71, 85, 129
fairness, 88, 89
faith, 86, 97, 110, 135
family, 16, 49, 50, 69, 96, 141
FAO, 135, 142
fatalism, 26, 32, 34, 35, 97, 122, 123, 126, 129
fauna, 135
fear, 12, 16, 19, 51, 58, 109, 128, 134, 136, 146
fears, 95
federal government, 63, 96
feedback, 12
feelings, 16, 21, 72, 78, 104, 126, 147
feet, 102
females, 104
feminism, 87
fight or flight response, 25
film, 46
filters, 55
financial support, 71
financing, 95
first generation, 56
First World, 114
flavor, 64
flight, 25, 30, 36
flooding, 128
flora, 135
flora and fauna, 135
fluid, 91
focus groups, 46
folklore, 45
food, 29, 104, 105, 137
formal education, 94, 140
fragmentation, 118
framing, 133
free association, 59
free choice, 148
freedom, 7, 8, 12, 16, 22, 34, 37, 38, 48, 49, 52, 53, 54, 59, 69, 92, 96, 98, 101, 108, 110, 118, 129, 130, 142, 146, 147, 148
friendship, 21, 80
frustration, 19, 29, 30, 63, 79
fulfillment, 7
functionalism, 91
funding, 57

G

gait, 102
Gallup Poll, 96
garbage, 137
gender, 1, 26, 42, 85, 87
general education, 112
generalization, 139
generation, 49, 56, 94, 104, 125, 136, 139
Geneva, 112
genocide, 135
geography, 71, 113, 134
gestures, 85
gift, 14, 38, 62, 109, 138
glass, 27, 42
globalization, 98, 119, 123, 128, 135, 138, 142, 145
goals, 2, 30, 51, 75, 79, 80, 88, 89, 90, 91, 96, 117, 125, 138
God, 4, 22, 139
gold, 28, 103, 137
governance, 47, 64, 86
government, 2, 42, 47, 48, 50, 51, 52, 56, 63, 70, 80, 86, 96, 97, 114, 115, 117, 118, 119, 120, 121, 129, 131, 145
government budget, 121
grading, 61
graduate students, 1, 29
graffiti, 54
grains, 103
grass, 26
grassroots, 45, 46, 93, 94, 95
Great Britain, 67, 119
greed, 123
grounding, 4, 53
group activities, 90
group identity, 71
groups, 2, 3, 4, 25, 26, 27, 29, 36, 39, 46, 51, 52, 60, 75, 77, 78, 87, 89, 92, 93, 95, 106, 107, 111, 112, 129, 134, 135, 146
growth, 41, 55, 81, 90, 93
Guatemala, 145
guidance, 48
guidelines, 108
guilt, 32
Guinea, 22, 42, 86, 112, 113, 115

H

hands, 28, 51, 64, 78, 91, 106, 120
harassment, 118
harm, 26, 49, 80, 138
harmony, 80, 138

New York, 4, 5, 9, 19, 22, 23, 37, 38, 39, 65, 81, 98, 115, 130, 131, 142, 149
newspapers, 51
next generation, 49
Nicaragua, 145
Nietzsche, 139
No Child Left Behind, 63, 93, 118, 131
no voice, 47, 69
North America, 95
novelty, 124
nurses, 103
nursing, 9

O

obedience, 140
objectification, 16
objective reality, 111
objectivity, 87, 88
obligation, 34
obstruction, 42
oil, 134
openness, 128, 146
oppression, 15, 26, 31, 33, 39, 52, 56, 58, 64, 85, 87, 90, 92, 96, 97, 102, 108, 109, 111, 119, 134
optimism, 3, 4, 96, 123, 131
oral transmission, 107
organ, 136
organization, 16, 45, 48, 50, 51, 92, 93, 94, 118, 129, 135, 137, 138, 139
organizational culture, 90
organizations, 45, 92, 93, 95, 105, 118, 120, 121, 129
orientation, 87, 137
outsourcing, 54
oversight, 93
overtime, 137
ownership, 19, 68, 69, 74, 75, 77

P

p53, 109
Panama, 145
paranoia, 26, 134
parents, 71, 74, 78, 93, 102, 117, 120, 121, 125
Paris, 142
participatory democracy, 48, 117, 119, 124, 126, 129
partnership, 69
passive, 2, 14, 18, 20, 79, 87, 106, 109, 140
patents, 138
paternalism, 17, 90, 96
pathology, 15, 119
Patriot Act, 48

pedagogy, 2, 8, 15, 16, 20, 21, 22, 37, 41, 42, 43, 44, 47, 49, 50, 51, 52, 54, 60, 67, 71, 80, 85, 89, 90, 91, 92, 93, 94, 97, 98, 117, 118, 119, 124, 128, 130, 131, 133, 140, 141, 145, 148
peer group, 53, 73
peers, 20, 72, 91
Pentagon, 53
perception, 69, 111, 123
perceptions, 30, 85
performance, 76, 91, 93, 119
permit, 118
perseverance, 57
personal, 4, 11, 21, 36, 48, 55, 67, 68, 69, 70, 71, 72, 73, 75, 79, 80, 135, 137
personal identity, 69, 72
personal life, 68, 70
personal problems, 55
personality traits, 36
persuasion, 13
pessimism, 47
phenomenology, 30
philanthropy, 17
Philippines, 145
philosophers, vii, 10, 11
phosphorus, 134
photographs, 113
physical education, 121
physical health, 36, 37
physics, 86
physiological arousal, 36
planning, 79, 86, 119, 123
plants, 55
Plato, 17
pleasure, 35
pluralism, 90
PM3, 137
poison, 47
police, 1, 35, 51
policy making, 117
political aspects, 110, 141
political power, 105, 125
politics, 4, 10, 34, 52, 53, 87, 92, 95, 96, 98, 108, 125, 127, 134, 141, 145, 148
poor, 42, 50, 52, 103, 115, 119, 135, 136, 138, 141, 148
population, 35, 51, 70, 74, 101, 104, 105, 114, 115, 122, 125, 135
Portugal, 113
positive reinforcement, 77
positivism, 87, 88
postmodernism, 86
poverty, 16, 50, 51, 69, 94, 134, 135
poverty line, 94

T

therapeutic process, 39

thinking, 2, 7, 10, 11, 12, 19, 21, 22, 42, 44, 47, 50, 53, 56, 58, 60, 61, 63, 69, 71, 72, 74, 75, 76, 77, 78, 80, 82, 88, 107, 109, 110, 111, 113, 114, 121, 124, 133, 136, 138, 139, 140

Third World, 101, 102, 114, 116, 140

threat, 35, 52, 120, 148

threats, 105

time constraints, 60

tin, 71

torture, 51, 52

toys, 137

trade, 45

trade union, 45

trading, 136

tradition, 1, 4, 8, 11

traditional practices, 43

training, 49, 62, 82, 86, 95, 112, 128

traits, 36

trajectory, 140

transformation, 19, 21, 52, 63, 88, 92, 97, 102, 118, 124, 125, 135, 147

transgression, 29

transition, 17, 35, 105, 135, 140

translation, 89, 124

transmission, 9, 13, 18, 19, 20, 21, 76, 107, 147

trend, 121

trial, 37, 77

trickle down, 90

triggers, 36

trust, 15, 16, 45, 46, 68, 86, 89, 96, 97, 138

turbulence, 103

tutoring, 63, 64

U

U.S. history, 29, 35, 36

UK, 69, 70, 82

uncertainty, 44, 72

undergraduate, 29

unemployment, 54

UNESCO, 42

UNICEF, 91

unions, 45, 64, 118

United Nations, 135

United States, 2, 4, 5, 25, 28, 29, 34, 35, 39, 45, 47, 54, 135, 139, 145, 146, 148

universities, 71, 80, 146

unmasking, 29

urban centres, 104

urban population, 104

urban settlement, 70

urbanization, 103

USA Patriot Act, 39

V

validity, 87, 114

values, 28, 68, 72, 73, 94, 96, 111, 117, 118, 119, 126, 127

variables, 73

variation, 32

vehicles, 74

vein, 32, 126, 127

Venezuela, 145

venue, 93

veteran teachers, 63

victims, 20, 35, 39, 85, 121

Vietnam, 29, 145

violence, 2, 15, 28, 33, 36, 49, 85, 103, 135, 136, 137, 141, 142

Virginia, 25, 40

vision, 1, 2, 8, 12, 15, 41, 42, 44, 47, 64, 70, 88, 94, 96, 97, 117, 122, 123, 126, 134, 139, 141, 147

vocabulary, 55, 107

voice, 44, 47, 48, 49, 51, 55, 56, 59, 61, 69, 85, 105, 111, 124

voting, 95, 96, 105

Vygotsky, 72, 76, 82

W

wages, 54, 64, 105, 135, 137

Wales, 69

walking, 43, 49, 116, 130

war, 47, 48, 50, 70, 108, 112, 134, 145, 146

war on terror, 50

weakness, 36, 103, 108

wealth, 7, 16, 134, 141

weapons, 138, 141

wear, 48, 59, 94

web, 40

welfare, 56, 120

welfare state, 120

well-being, 14, 135, 138

western countries, 139

windows, 32

winter, 71

women, 15, 18, 36, 42, 44, 51, 54, 86, 89, 94, 95, 109, 110, 123, 137, 147

wood, 72

wool, 64

workers, 45, 46, 53, 54, 57, 59, 62, 64, 103, 104, 105, 130, 145

Workforce Investment Act, 64